Skipper's check list for

GETTING UNDER WAY

	File a float plan for your trip.
	Open all hatches and ventilators, making sure that there is a free flow of air through the boat.
	Turn on the blowers.
	Check the bilges. Pump, if necessary. Open all through-hull seacocks and exhaust cut-off.
	Check fuel and water tanks. Start with full tanks, if possible.
	Check personal flotation device for each passenger.
	Check charts and navigating equipment.
	Check ground tackle.
	Check running lights.
	Plot any courses you anticipate running.
	Start engine, running slowly.
	Check oil pressure.
	Check water temperature.
	Show passengers how to use life jackets. Assign them stations.
	Stow all stores and gear securely so they will not come adrift in a blow.
	Take in fenders and overhaul any trailing lines.

SAMPLE FLOAT PLAN

FILE WITH NEIGHBOR, FRIEND, OR RELATIVE ASHORE.

1. Name of person reporting
and telephone number

2. Description of boat: Type ______________ Color Hull ______________
Trim ________ Ton ________ Registration Number ______________
Length ________ Name ______________ Make ______________
Other: ____

3. Persons Aboard __________ Total __________

NAME	AGE	ADDRESS AND TELEPHONE NO.

4. Engine Type ________ H.P. ________ Normal Fuel ____________Gals.

5. Survival Equipment: (CHECK AS APPROPRIATE) Life Jackets Cushions
Flares Mirror Smoke Signals Flash Light Paddles Food Water

6. Radio: Yes/No Frequencies _____ _____ _____ _____ _____

7. Trip: Leave at Time ______________ From ______________
Going to ______________________ or ______________
Expect to return by ______________ and in no event later than . . .
______________.

8. Any other information ____________________________________
____

9. Automobile license ______________ Trailer license ______________
Type ____________ Color ____________ Make ______________

10. If not returned by ______________ call the Coast Guard, or
______________________ (local authority), Rescue Center
______________________ (Telephone Number); or ____________
______________________ at ______________________

BASIC SEAMANSHIP AND SAFE BOAT HANDLING

Come, my friends,
'Tis not too late to seek a newer world.
Push off, and sitting well in order smite
The sounding furrows; for my purpose holds
To sail beyond the sunset. . .

"Ulysses"—Tennyson

GUIDE TO CORRECT USE OF MARINE RADIOTELEPHONES

156.8 MHz, designated Channel 16 in the VHF/FM Marine Radiotelephone service, is a required channel for all VHF/FM equipped vessels. Channel 16 must be monitored at all times that the station is in operation, except when actually communicating on another channel. This channel is monitored by the Coast Guard. Calls to other vessels are normally initiated on Channel 16, then, except for distress, you must switch to a working channel.

Tips for proper use of Channel 16:

1. Calls on Channel 16 should be brief and to the point.
2. Using the calling and distress channel for casual or social communications is by far the most dangerous abuse of all. Remember, Channel 16 is a "HOT LINE" to Search and Rescue units. Don't use it for idle chatter.
3. Avoid excessive calling. You may call three times at two-minute intervals and then must wait fifteen minutes before calling again.
4. When the receiving party answers, switch immediately to an appropriate channel.
5. Avoid CB language on your radiotelephone. It is not acceptable in the VHF/FM marine radio service.
6. Schedule calls to other vessels in advance. This will help you avoid calling persons who are not listening.
7. Repeating-back information given by sending vessels or stations is unnecessary and usually superfluous.
8. Use courtesy when calling. Wait until the channel is clear. Listen, especially for distress calls.

Radiotelephone operators are also reminded to use the government Channel 22A when calling the Coast Guard for nondistress information. If you desire communications of this nature on Channel

22A, you must first establish communications on Channel 16. As a final reminder, all boaters are encouraged to equip their vessels with NOAA Weather Radio. There are three weather frequencies now in use in the United States; WX 1 (162.-550 MHz), WX 2 (162.400 MHz), and WX 3 (162.475 MHz).

GUIDE TO SAFE FUELING

One pint of gasoline is as explosive as 30 sticks of dynamite. The Coast Guard reports increasing numbers of fires and explosions occurring due to carelessness while fueling. Follow these rules:

1. Make sure all electrical equipment on boat is turned off. Don't turn on any switches while fueling.
2. Fuel in good light. Gas spills may pass unnoticed in the dark.
3. Don't smoke or allow anyone in the boat to smoke while fueling.
4. Close doors and hatches to keep gas fumes out of boat while fueling. Remember, fumes are heavier than air; they drift downward.
5. Don't fuel your portable tanks near the boat. When they are full, cap them tightly and wipe off any gas which has dripped.
6. While fueling, keep the metal nozzle of the hose in contact with the tank or fill–pipe at all times to prevent static explosion.
7. Watch it. Don't let your attention stray while fueling. If any gas does spill, wipe it up quickly before vapor forms and discard the rag in a safe place.
8. As soon as you have finished fueling, open all doors and hatches to air out any possible fumes. Make a sniff test, especially down near bilges and cabin sole.
9. Don't start engine until your boat has aired for several minutes.

BASIC SEAMANSHIP AND SAFE BOAT HANDLING

Based on the U.S. Coast Guard Auxiliary Instruction Courses

by Blair Walliser, Captain, U.S.C.G.R.

A Rutledge Book

DOUBLEDAY & COMPANY, INC.

CONTENTS

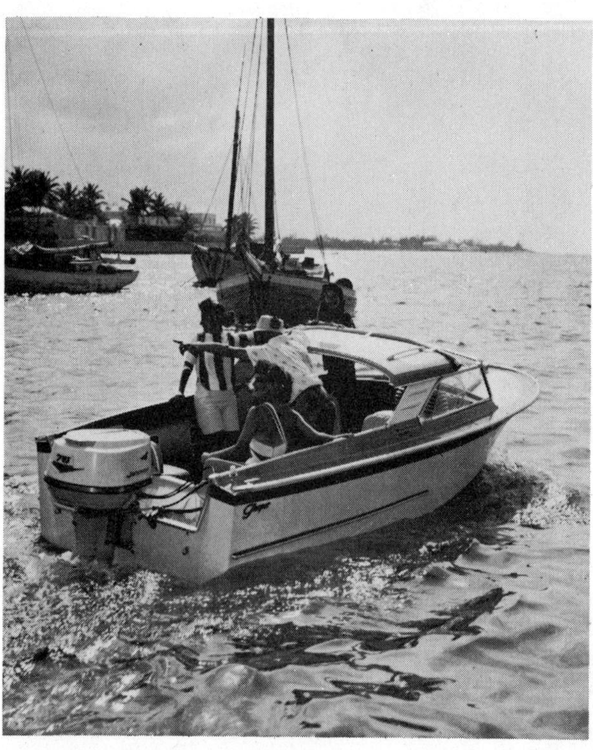

R

Prepared by Rutledge Books
published by Doubleday & Co.

ISBN No. 0-385-14289-7
Library of Congress
Catalog Card Number 62-19528
Sixth Printing 1981

WELCOME ABOARD

As a boatman you are a member of an elite society. You are the envy and despair of landlubbers. You are part of a tradition whose origins go back to primitive man, a tradition with a reputation for daring and adventure rivalled by few other sports or professions.

As a yachtsman you have special status. The natural habitat of man is dry ground and when you go to sea, even in a small boat, you achieve mobility, freedom and a degree of escape not known to the landbound.

On board a boat, you are in direct and personal contact with the forces of nature. The wind opposes you; the waves discomfit and threaten you; the tides and currents impede you. When you surmount the obstacles and reach your goal —even though it may be only crossing a lake and returning— you achieve a sense of mastery over nature.

Most activities of modern man are so removed from the past that we lose contact with tradition. But when the yachtsman looks back, he recalls that in the time of Noah the fine art of ship construction was already far advanced. Did not the Almighty Himself act as naval architect for the patriarch and did not Noah have the benefit of the first long-range weather forecast?

Egyptian tombs indicate that boats were considered the

most suitable form of transport for the journey to the Other World. Later, according to Homer, Ulysses carried a crew of 100 men as he started his long voyage home. By the time of the Romans, naval vessels were powered with up to sixteen banks of oarsmen and the ship on which St. Paul was wrecked not only carried a full cargo but some 275 passengers as well.

Yet almost 1500 years later, the Santa Maria in which Columbus crossed the Atlantic was only some 90 feet long and the Pinta and Nina not much above 50 each. The Mayflower was about the same size as the Santa Maria and crossed the Atlantic at less than 3 miles an hour.

Meantime, on the Pacific, those incredible mariners, the Polynesians, had skillfully navigated and colonized a wilderness of ocean in their outrigger canoes!

In the second century B.C., some of the Greek city-states sent their most promising young men to sea as we send ours to college. The career of mariner has always been held in honor and esteem.

This, then, is the tradition to which the modern yachtsman falls heir. In a world in which man becomes increasingly dependent upon punch cards and data computers, the sea still offers escape to individuality. Small wonder if the yachtsman thrills to the challenge and strives to perfect himself.

1

KNOW YOUR BOAT

The sea is at once the mariner's best friend and his most ruthless enemy.

When wind and water smash at the small craft in a storm, skipper and crew must understand each other promptly and precisely.

Compare these lookout reports: "Swing her around! There's something in the way, off there to one side!" And: "Hard to port! Rocks awash on the starboard bow!"

In the second warning, the man at the wheel knows exactly where and what the danger is and has been told precisely what to do to avoid it. In the first vague alarm, no information is conveyed.

The boat you sail today is a direct lineal descendent of primitive rafts and dugout canoes. Everything on, in, or about a vessel has a historic and correct name. A good boatman is proud of being able to teach the language of boats to his family and friends.

SECTION 1 ■ LEARNING TO KNOW YOUR BOAT

You are now a boat owner, a skipper.

Your first duty to yourself and to those who will be aboard with you, as crew or guests, is to learn the basic terms of boating. Start by familiarizing yourself with the parts of your boat.

To begin: imagine yourself standing on the deck of your boat. Face toward the front, which is the ***bow.*** Behind you, the rear of the boat, is the ***stern.*** The bow end of the deck is the ***foredeck,*** the stern end the ***afterdeck.*** The center is ***amidships.*** To your left is ***port,*** to your right, ***starboard.*** The side of the boat which faces the direction from which the wind is blowing is the ***windward*** side. The opposite is the ***leeward*** side.

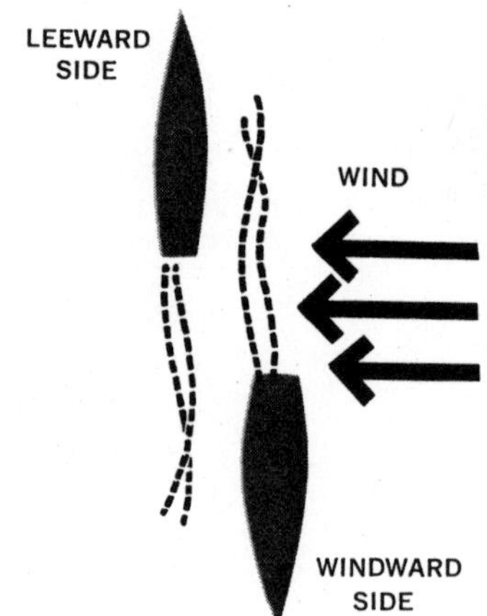

The Hull

The ***keel*** is the backbone of a boat.

The ***ribs*** or ***frames*** extend upward from keel to deck.

The ***planking*** extends fore and aft and covers the hull. (On Fiberglas or aluminum boats, of course, there are no planks, but the areas referred to are identified generally, as on wooden vessels.)

The lowest plank, next to the keel, is the ***garboard strake.***

The topmost plank on the side is the ***sheer strake.***

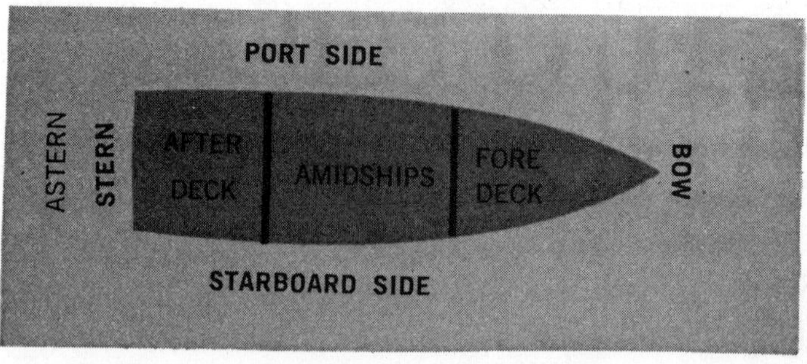

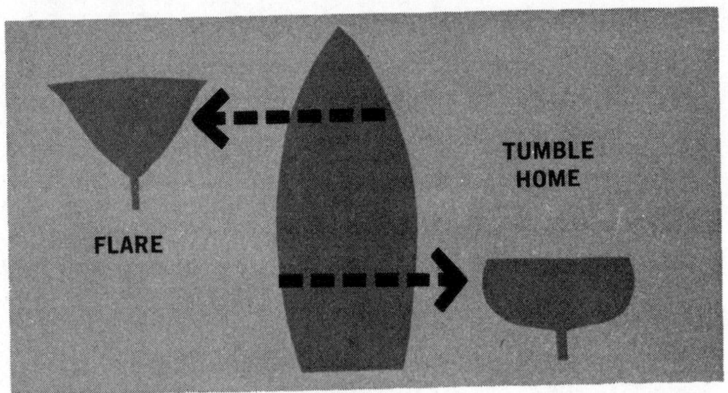

The Deck

The fore and aft planks topside form the ***deck.***

The planks at the outer edge of the deck form the ***covering board.***

The raised strip at the outer edge of the deck forms the ***toe rail*** or ***cap rail.***

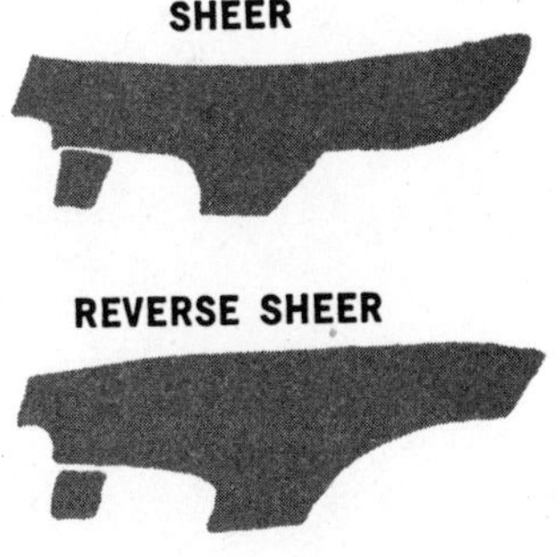

The fence-like protective structure of stanchions and wire is called the ***life rail*** or ***man rail.***

The water-tight entries from above decks to below are the ***hatches.*** The main types of yacht hatch are:

The ***forward*** hatch (to foc's'l).

The ***main*** hatch (to main cabin or stateroom).

The ***lazaret*** hatch (to after stowage space).

The line from bow to stern cut by the surface of the water is the ***waterline.***

The contrasting paint stripe at the waterline is the ***boot top.***

The hull from the waterline upward is the ***topsides.*** The height of the topsides above water is the ***freeboard.***

The vertical depth from the surface of the water to the bottom of the keel is the ***draft.***

The leading edge of the boat is the ***stem.***

The planking that forms the stern, usually varnished and left as "bright-work" on motor-boats, is called the ***transom.*** Some boats are designed as "double-enders" with pointed or canoe sterns.

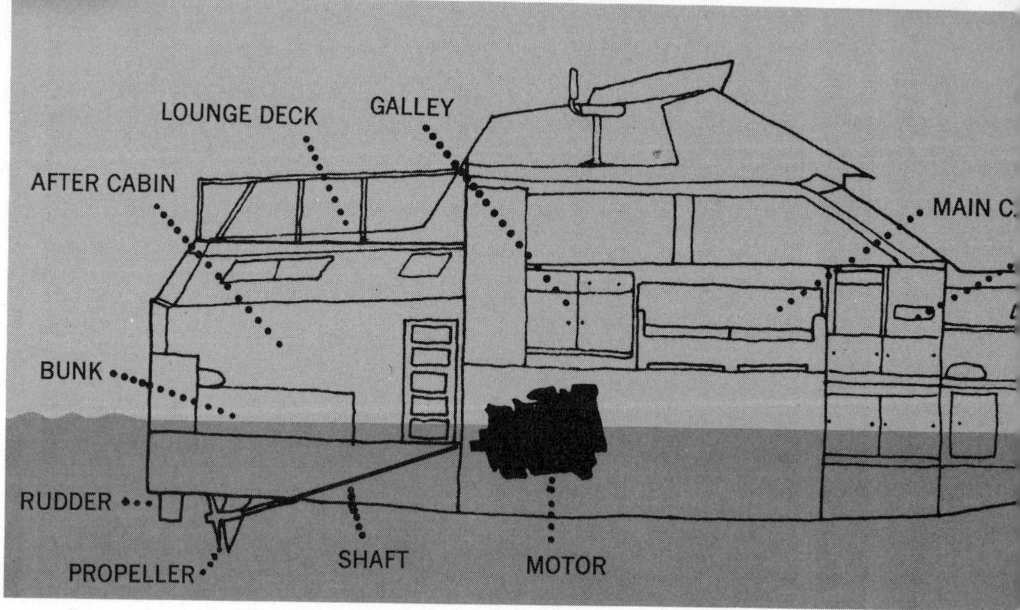

On single-crew craft, the ***rudder post*** is secured to the ***horn timber*** above and the after end of the keel below. The ***propeller shaft*** projects from this same after section of the keel, known as the ***deadwood.***

Below Decks

The planks forming the flooring, or cabin sole, of the cabin are the ***floor-boards***.

The deep parts of the hull beneath the floorboards are the ***bilges.*** A mechanical or hand bilge pump may be used to pump water from the deepest bilge. The water from the shallower bilges flows through ***limbers*** or small holes in the frames to the deep part of the bilge.

A ceiling in a boat is known as an ***overhead.***
All stairs on a boat are referred to as ***ladders.***
"Downstairs" is always ***below deck.***
"Upstairs" is always ***above deck.***
Going toward the bow is ***going forward.***
Going toward the stern is ***going aft.***
Partitions below deck are ***bulkheads.***
Closets and cabinets are ***lockers.***
Full length closets are ***hanging lockers.***
Round, heavy glass windows are ***portholes.***

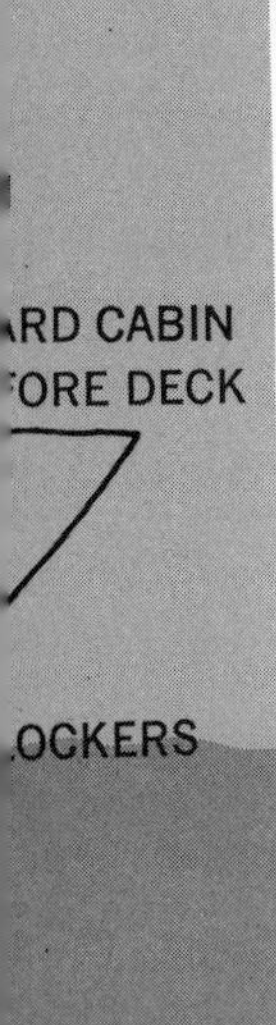

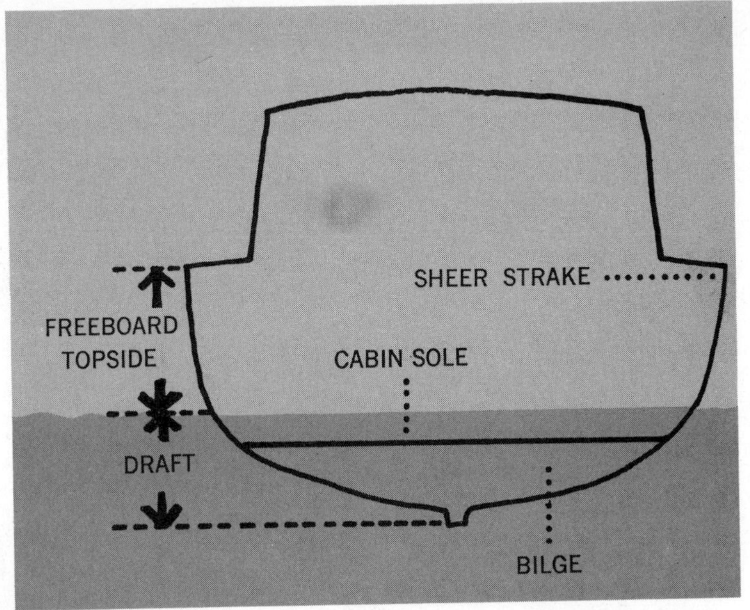

Portholes which do not open are ***port lights.***

The round scoops which pick up fresh air on deck and channel it below are ***ventilators.***

Sails and Rigging

Standing rigging is generally wire (galvanized or stainless steel). It includes the ***headstay*** or ***forestay, shrouds, jumper stay,*** when one is used, and ***permanent backstay*** or ***preventer.*** It is tightened or set up by the use of ***turnbuckles.***

Running rigging is generally manila, cotton, or one of the synthetics such as dacron. ***Running backstays*** are usually wire with rope lower sections to facilitate trimming. Running backstays usually run from the mast at the upper spreaders to the deck and are set up on the weather, or windward, side to provide additional support to the mast. They are slacked on the leeward side to permit the boom free movement outward. ***Sheets*** are lines secured to sails to adjust their angles to the wind. ***Halyards*** are lines which hoist sails.

Sails are of Egyptian cotton, dacron, or other synthetics. They are adjusted to the wind by the sheets which run from the ***clew*** of the sail through ***blocks*** on deck to ***cleats.*** On larger boats, addi-

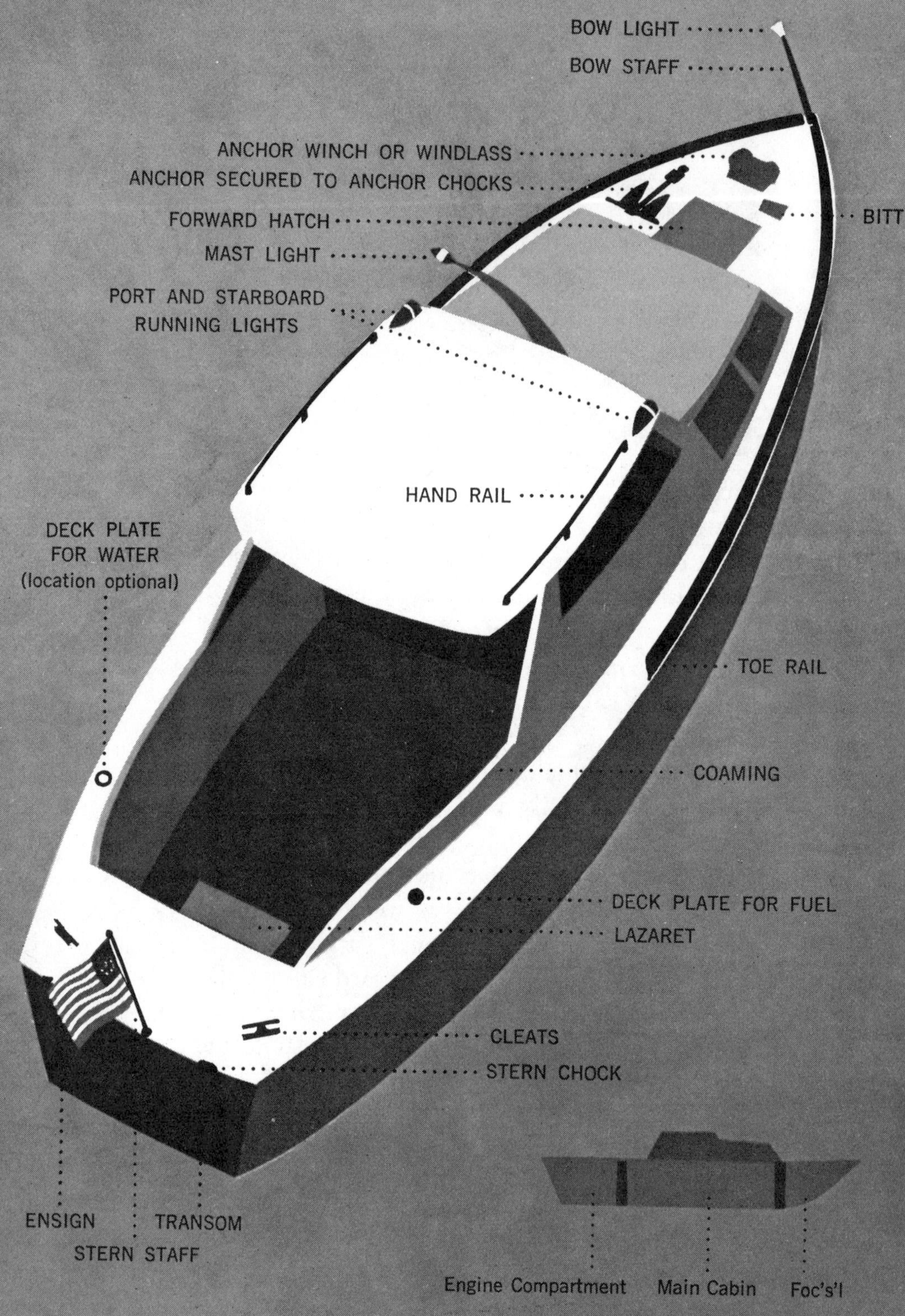
THE POWER BOAT
BOW LIGHT
BOW STAFF
ANCHOR WINCH OR WINDLASS
ANCHOR SECURED TO ANCHOR CHOCKS
FORWARD HATCH
BITT
MAST LIGHT
PORT AND STARBOARD RUNNING LIGHTS
HAND RAIL
DECK PLATE FOR WATER (location optional)
TOE RAIL
COAMING
DECK PLATE FOR FUEL
LAZARET
CLEATS
STERN CHOCK
ENSIGN
TRANSOM
STERN STAFF
Engine Compartment
Main Cabin
Foc's'l

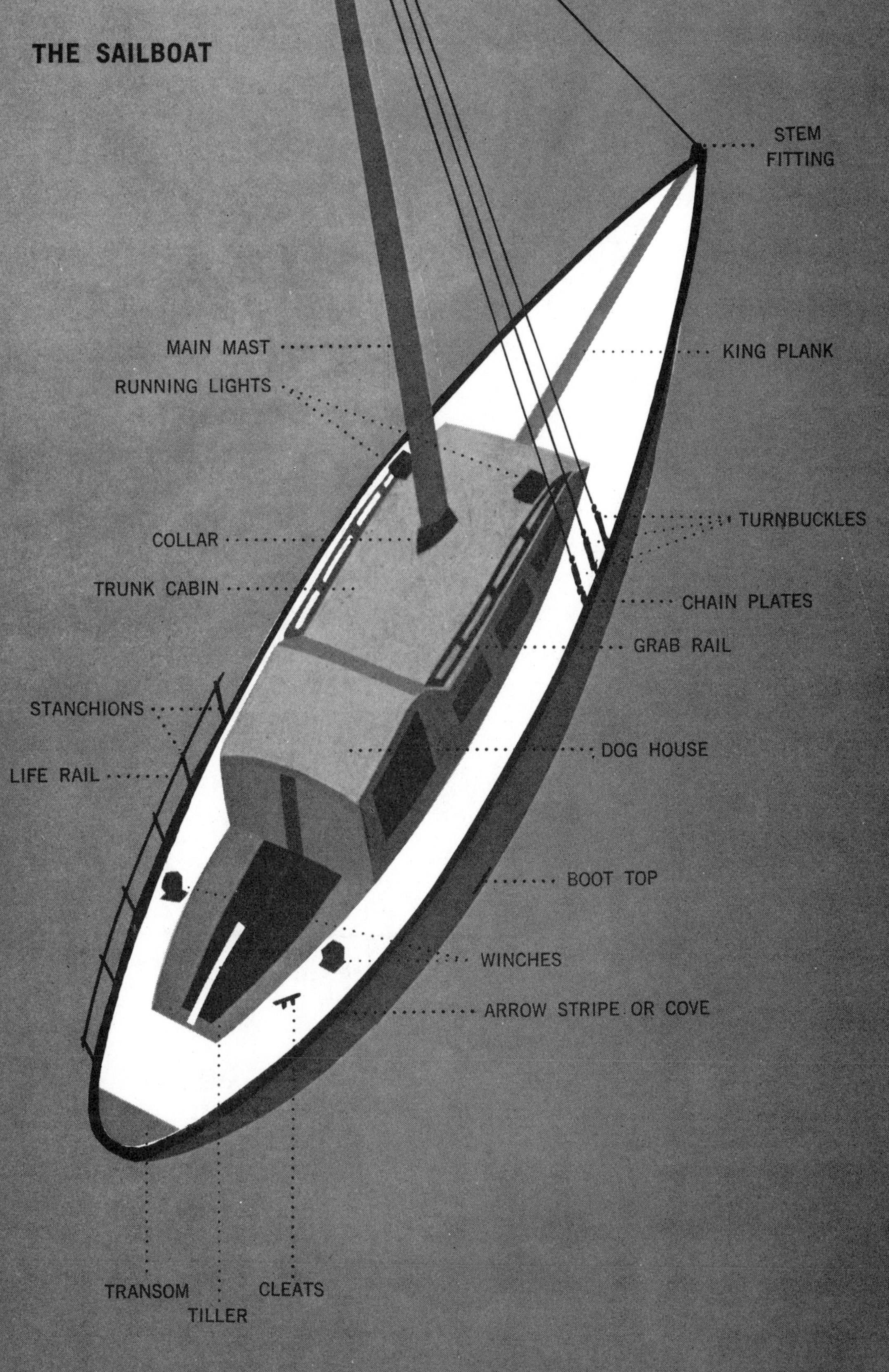
THE SAILBOAT
STEM FITTING
MAIN MAST
KING PLANK
RUNNING LIGHTS
TURNBUCKLES
COLLAR
TRUNK CABIN
CHAIN PLATES
GRAB RAIL
STANCHIONS
DOG HOUSE
LIFE RAIL
BOOT TOP
WINCHES
ARROW STRIPE OR COVE
TRANSOM
CLEATS
TILLER

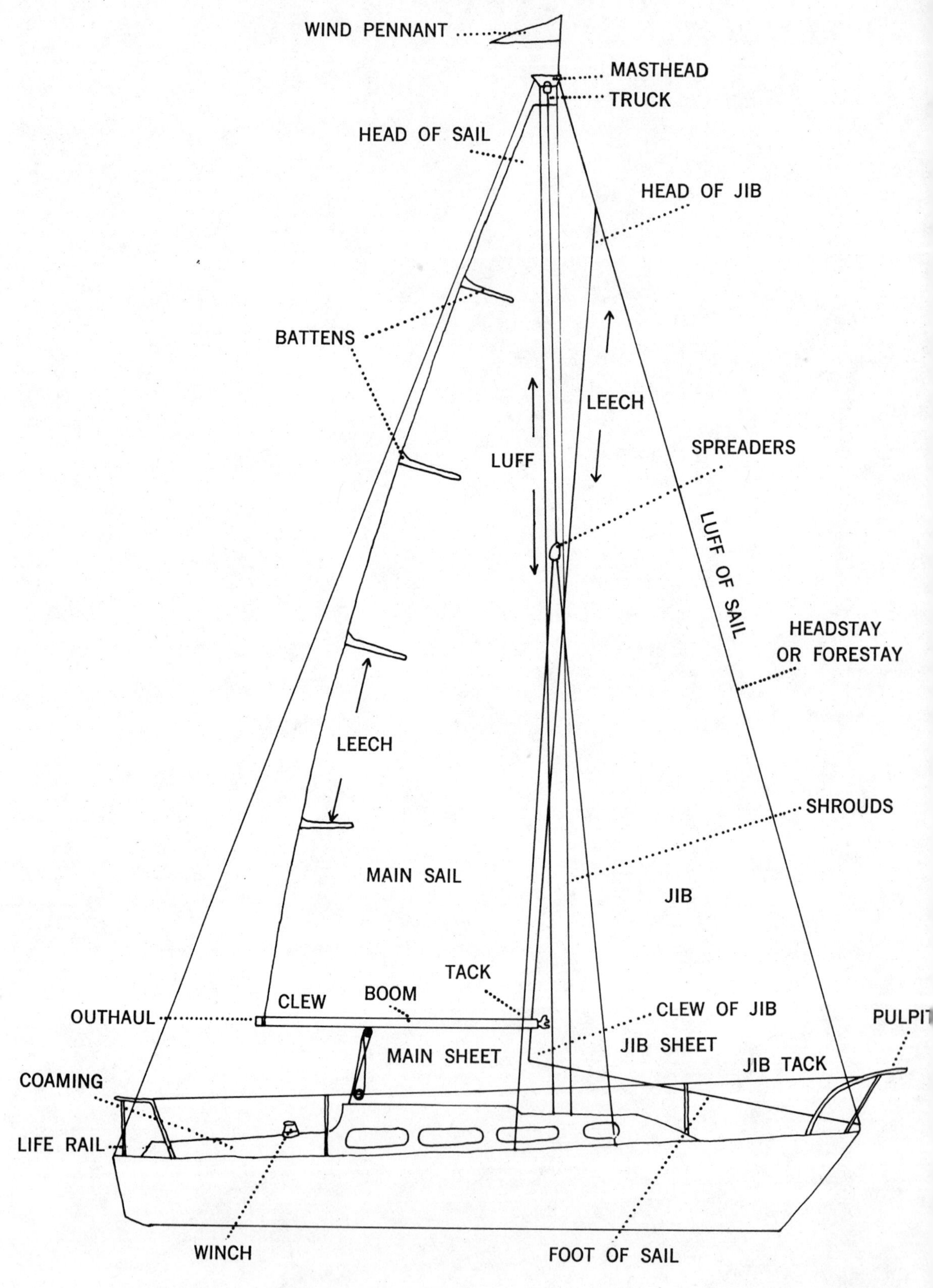
WIND PENNANT
MASTHEAD
TRUCK
HEAD OF SAIL
HEAD OF JIB
BATTENS
LEECH
LUFF
SPREADERS
LUFF OF SAIL
HEADSTAY
OR FORESTAY
LEECH
SHROUDS
MAIN SAIL
JIB
TACK
CLEW
BOOM
OUTHAUL
CLEW OF JIB
PULPIT
JIB SHEET
MAIN SHEET
JIB TACK
COAMING
LIFE RAIL
WINCH
FOOT OF SAIL

tional purchase for ***trimming*** or hauling in is obtained with ***winches.***

Jibs, staysails, mainsails and mizzensails are known as ***working canvas.*** Spinnakers, genoas, ballooners, drifters, mizzen staysails, fishermen topsails, mules and other light sails are known as ***light canvas.***

TYPES OF BOAT ■ SECTION 2

Part of the fun of boating is the pleasure of being able to identify by name the wide variety of power and sail craft that populate the rivers, lakes and seacoasts of the nation. For ease of recognition, the following outlines have been reduced to the simplest forms and divided among outboards, inboards, and sailboats (which may or may not have engines). Reference to the accompanying illustrations will further simplify understanding.

Power Boats

- Displacement type: Pushes through water with large wetted surface.
- Planing hull: At planing speed, forward part rises out of water and boat skims along surface with smaller wetted surface.

Outboards

- Dinghy or pram: Usually 6 to 10 feet long, motor under 5 h.p. Frequently used as a tender for a larger craft.
- Rowboat: Usually flat-bottomed, up to 14 feet long, with 1 or 2 sets of oars. Motor to 10 h.p.
- Utility boat: For fishing, water-skiing, and general use. Up to 16 feet long, with motor up to 35 h.p.
- Runabout: Fast and sporty. Good for water-skiing. Motors to over 100 h.p. Usually planing-type hull.

BASIC RIGGING FOR SAILBOATS

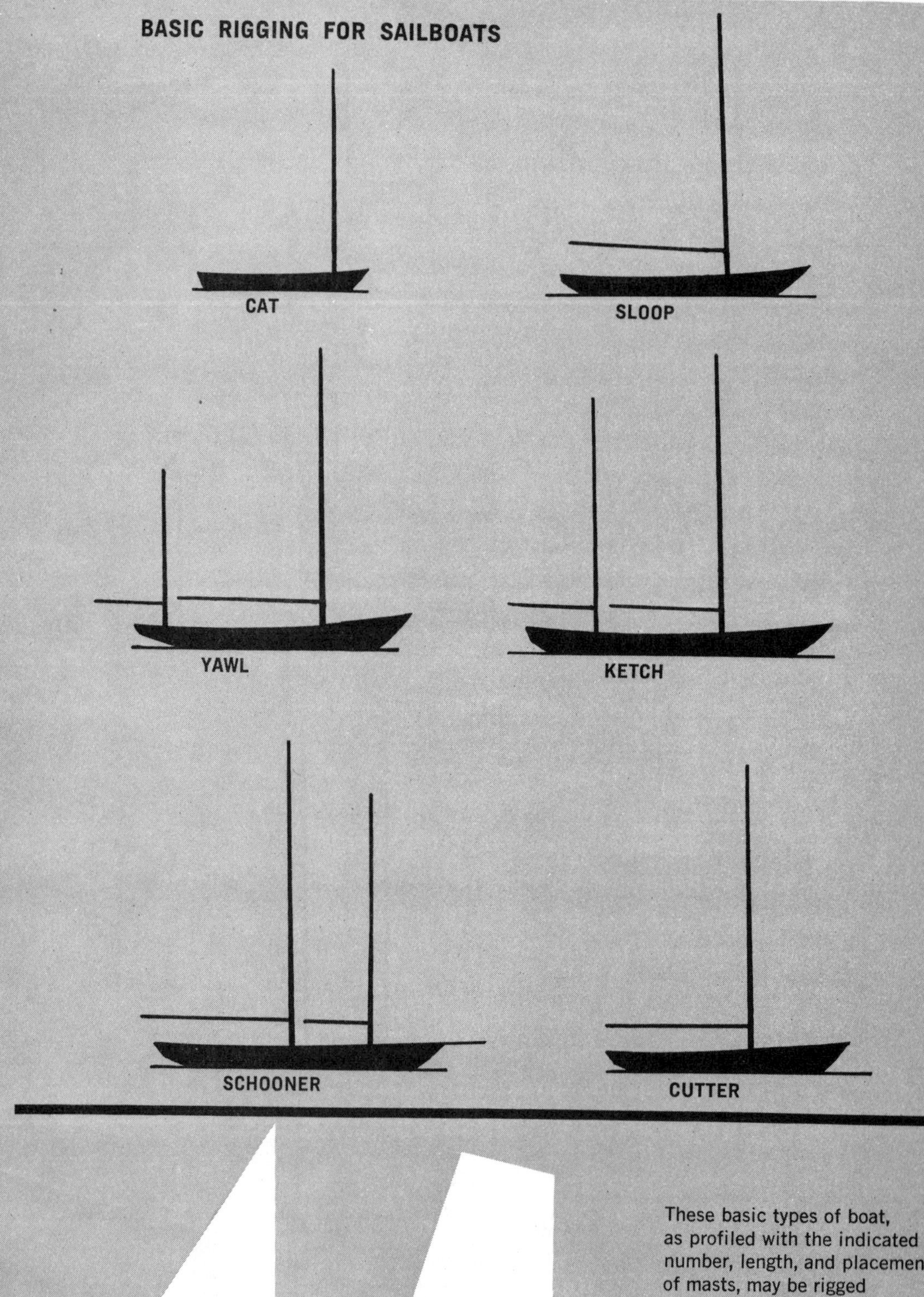

These basic types of boat, as profiled with the indicated number, length, and placement of masts, may be rigged with either jib- (triangular) or gaff-style sails

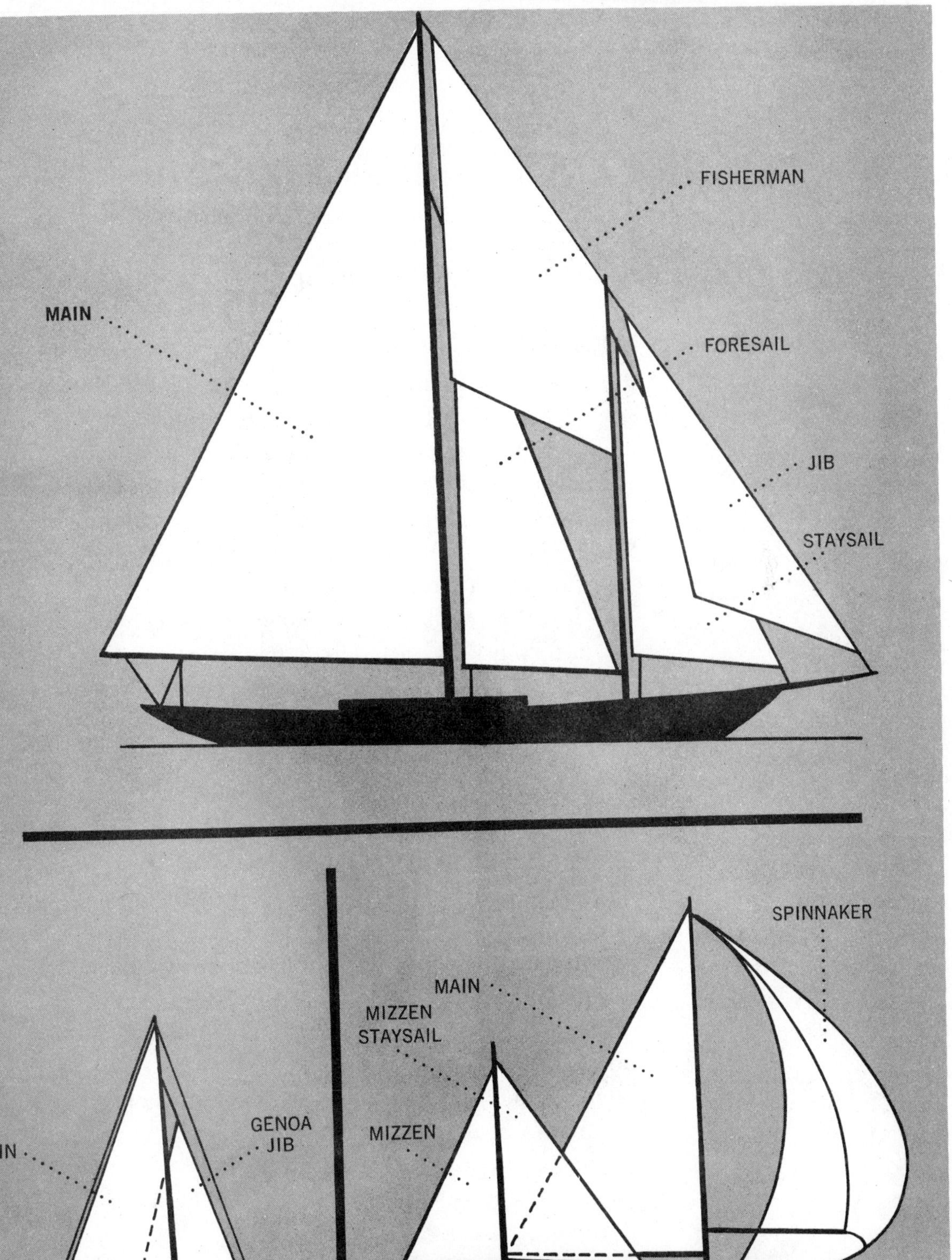
FISHERMAN
MAIN
FORESAIL
JIB
STAYSAIL
SPINNAKER
MAIN
MIZZEN
STAYSAIL
MIZZEN
GENOA
JIB
MAIN

- Outboard cruiser: Has sleeping and cooking accommodations. Single or multiple engines; h.p. depends on size and weight of hull.
- Houseboat: Comfortable living quarters. Single or multiple engines.

Inboards—Inboard–Outboard (Outdrive)

- Runabout: Swift and sporty. Sixteen to 30 feet long. Up to 400 h.p. in single and twin engines.
- Raised-deck or express cruiser: Luxury boat with accommodations for six or more, high h.p., single or twin engines with speeds to 30 knots or better.
- Sport fisherman: Adapted for deep-sea fishing. Operates at both fast and trolling speeds.
- Double cabin cruiser: For two or more couples. Heads forward and aft. Often has crew quarters.
- Convertible sedan: Canvas cover converts from open to closed deckhouse.
- Flying bridge cruiser: Dual controls. May be operated from upper bridge for extra visibility.

Sailboats

- Catboat: Single mast near bow of boat.
- Marconi sloop: Single mast forward, with jib and triangular mainsail.
- Gaff sloop: Single mast forward, with jib and quadrilateral mainsail.
- Cutter: Single mast almost amidship. Double headsail optional.
- Ketch: Two masts, taller forward; smaller stepped forward of wheel or tiller.
- Schooner: Two masts, the taller aft.
- Yawl: Two masts, taller forward; smaller stepped aft of wheel or tiller.
- Motor sailer: Any of the above rigs with large deckhouse, powerful engines and less sail.

BASIC POWER BOATS

OUTBOARD BOATS

PLANING

RUNABOUT

DISPLACEMENT

INBOARD CRUISERS
Showing displacement hull

CABIN AREA

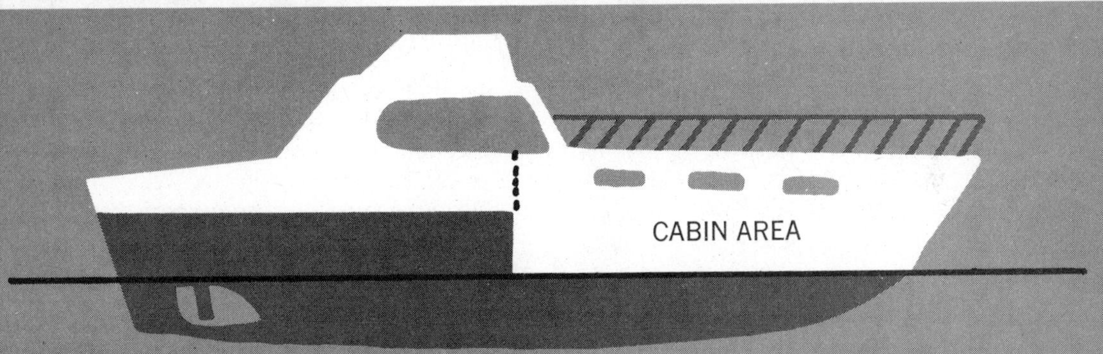

RAISED DECK CRUISER

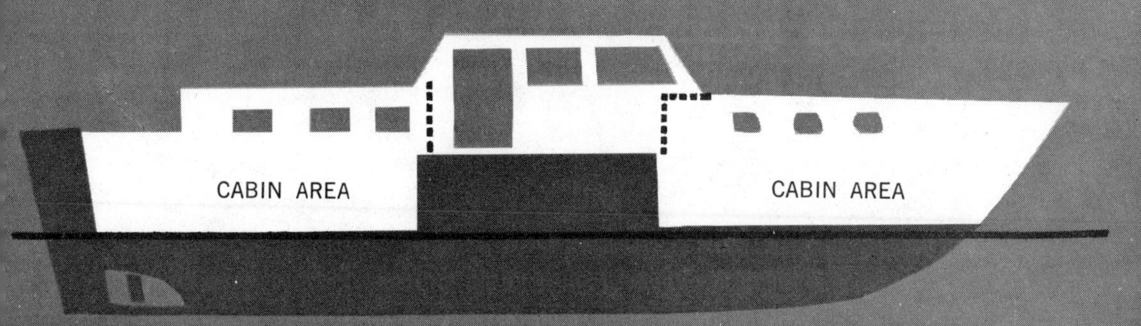

DOUBLE CABIN CRUISER

Other boats: on any large body of water, the three types of vessel shown will be familiar sights. The luxurious cabin cruiser has double staterooms, crew's quarters, ship-to-shore telephone, radio direction finder, and is powered by twin diesels. The outboard utility craft features a speedy, planing type of hull. The author's racing cutter is shown flying a huge parachute spinnaker

SAFETY TIPS

- Know the name for every part of your boat. Know the name and proper operation of all items of equipment. Know the proper nautical terms for all maneuvers. Teach the important ones to your guests so that they can help out intelligently in an emergency.
- On board, always wear shoes—preferably skid-resistant yachting shoes which do not slip on wet decks. Bare feet often result in badly stubbed or broken toes.
- Do not leave loose lines on deck. Stepping on a loose line in a choppy sea may cause the line to roll under foot, pitching you overboard.
- When in doubt, ask. Yachtsmen are notably courteous. Besides, they would much rather give you ten minutes of explanation at the dock than two hours of rescue at sea.
- Never be ashamed to take lessons or seek instructions. Handling a boat is more akin to flying or skiing than to tennis or golf: you can't "pick it up" in the doing.
- Know the exact draft of your ship as well as the depth of the water you're sailing. Many a good ship lies beneath the surface today because her skipper didn't know what lay beneath the surface while he sailed her.
- The word "yacht" is derived from the Dutch "yat," a term originally applied to privateers. There are few pirates in our waters today, but the yachtsman who puts to sea without knowing the basic rules of boat handling and boat safety hardly deserves any better fate than walking the plank.
- If you are a powerboat man, try to go out occasionally with your sailboat friends and vice versa. Each type of sailor will profit by a better understanding of and respect for the other kind of craft.
- Part of this understanding will result in sailboat men holding a steady course when approaching a powerboat bow-on and in power-boaters passing sailboats to leeward rather than windward whenever possible.

5443

2

STEERING AND PROPULSION

What moves a boat? How is that movement guided? A seaman need know only how to do it. The responsible skipper knows why it is being done.

A rowboat's progress is swifter and smoother if the oarsman learns to feather his oars. The expert canoeist avoids the need to paddle first on one and then on the other side of his craft by giving his paddle just the right fillip at the end of his stroke.

A beginning skipper, looking aft, will often note that his wake looks like a "worm line" because he keeps correcting the wheel. As he acquires skill, he learns to meet the swing of the bow by adjusting his wheel before the boat pivots beyond the course.

A good skipper should also understand the construction of his boat's steering mechanism so that he can make repairs at sea. Safety is the underlying necessity for maximum enjoyment of boating and, to steer a smooth course in yachting, you must know your boat!

SECTION 3 ■ RUDDER, WHEEL AND TILLER

The first concern of a good skipper is to handle his boat safely and skillfully. A boat does not steer like a vehicle with wheels. Land craft steer at the forward end; vessels steer at the after end. In other words, a turning car or bicycle follows in the approximate path of its front wheels. A boat turns because the force of the water acting against the rudder swings the stern to port or starboard. The bow changes direction only in response to the movement of the stern.

In this respect, a boat turns much like a wheelbarrow. If the handles are thought of as the stern, it will be observed that they describe a wide arc while the front wheel turns through a narrow arc. Note the distinction between the way a boat turns and the way a car turns.

A boat's turning is also affected by the action of the propeller or propellers, as will be explained.

Boats are steered by a wheel or a tiller, except for outboard and inboard-outboard craft which are steered by turning the propeller–rudder unit.

The modern boat ***rudder*** is a refinement of the old-fashioned steering oar. A steering oar was simply a blade held beneath the surface of the water and guided by a long handle. Similarly, a rudder is a blade affixed to the boat, with an upright extension known as the ***rudder stock.*** The stock may be turned by tiller or wheel.

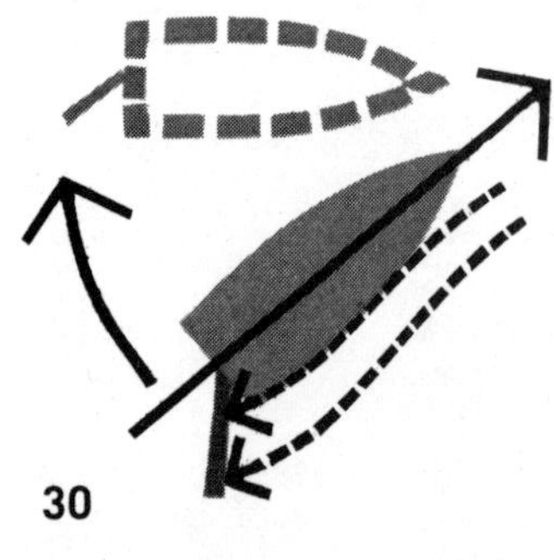

The ***tiller*** is a handle extending into the cockpit and affixed to the rudder stock. Pushing the tiller to port forces the rudder to starboard. The forward motion of the boat through the water causes water pressure against the rudder, forcing the stern to port. The resultant movement of the bow is to star-

Rudder and tiller as a unit. The rudder pintles fit into gudgeon fittings on the transom.

A twin inboard-outboard or "outdrive" installation.

board, producing a right turn.

The ***wheel*** is connected with the rudder by cables. When the wheel is swung to starboard, the rudder is turned to starboard. The water pressure forces the stern to port, resulting in a direction turn of the bow to the right.

A third method of steering is used in small outboard craft. The whole motor is turned, including the propeller which forces the stern to port or starboard, changing the direction of the bow.

ENGINE AND PROPELLER ■ SECTION 4

Under way, the water pressure on the rudder which swings the stern for steering results from two forces: the movement of the vessel through the water, and the stream of water forced astern by the propeller. The latter is known as ***screw current.*** It is sometimes mentally pictured as a cylinder of water of the same diameter as the screw. Its force is proportional to the size and pitch of the propeller and to the number of revolutions per

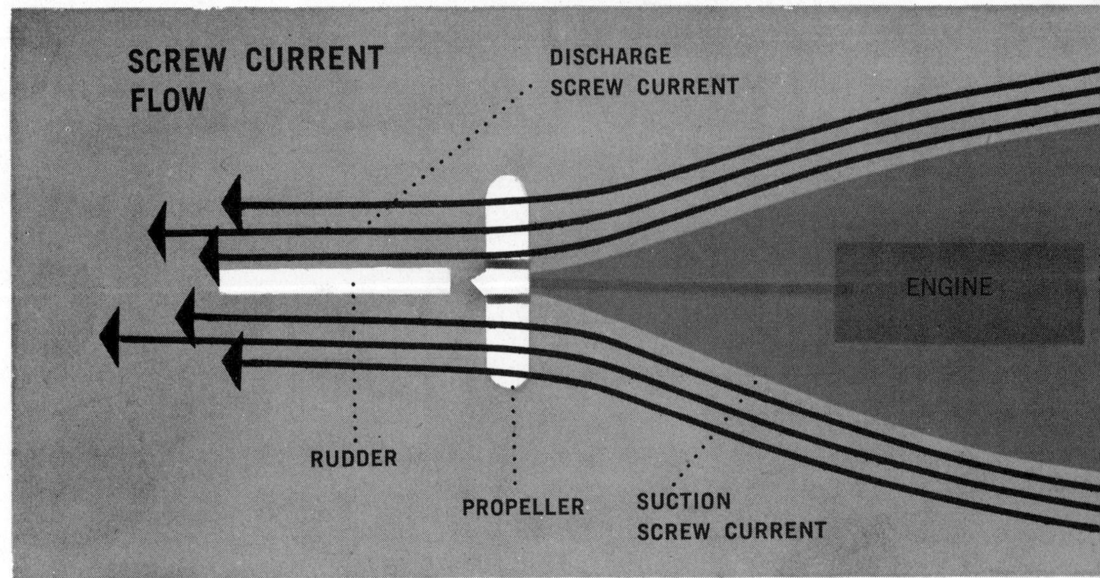

minute at which it turns.

The speed of the boat through the water is likewise proportional to the screw's size (diameter), pitch (angle at which the blades are set) and RPM (revolutions per minute). Pitch is measured by the distance the propeller would travel forward in one revolution if there were no slip.

There are two elements to the screw current, or water set in motion by the turning of the propeller. The water forced aft of the screw is known as the ***discharge screw current.*** The water pulled from forward of the propeller is known as ***suction screw current.***

At high speeds, the movement of the boat through the water is the dominant factor acting on the rudder. But at low speeds, the screw current is more important, since the water forced aft by the propeller can be controlled by the throttle. In confined areas, a vessel can be maneuvered more readily by using short bursts of power with the rudder hard over. The boat responds more rapidly in a sidewise direction than in moving ahead or astern.

Most single-engine craft have right-hand propellers. When moving ahead through the water, the boat's screw current flows under the hull and astern. When in reverse, however, the stream is forced against the starboard side of the keel and hull, tending to push the stern to port. For this reason, most single-engine boats will back to port even when the rudder is amidship. If the skipper wants to back to starboard, he must use considerable right rudder.

With an inboard-outboard installation, the screw and the rudder turn together so that tight turns can be made. This allows for positive control in forward or reverse.

In backing, it will be helpful to remember that you point the rudder in the direction in which you want to back.

However, the rudder action does not begin to take effect until the boat gathers headway through the water when reversing. Therefore, with a single-engine vessel, stopped in the water and rudder amidships, the reversing screw will put the stern to port because the screw current is being forced forward and against the starboard side of the boat. With the rudder to port, of course, the boat will back even more definitely to port.

With the single screw backing and the rudder to starboard, however, the skipper will note a curious situation. Until the boat gathers way, she will back to port. As soon as she starts to move through the water, the rudder will take effect and she will then swing to starboard as she moves astern. The accompanying diagrams should be carefully studied.

An extension of the above principle will explain

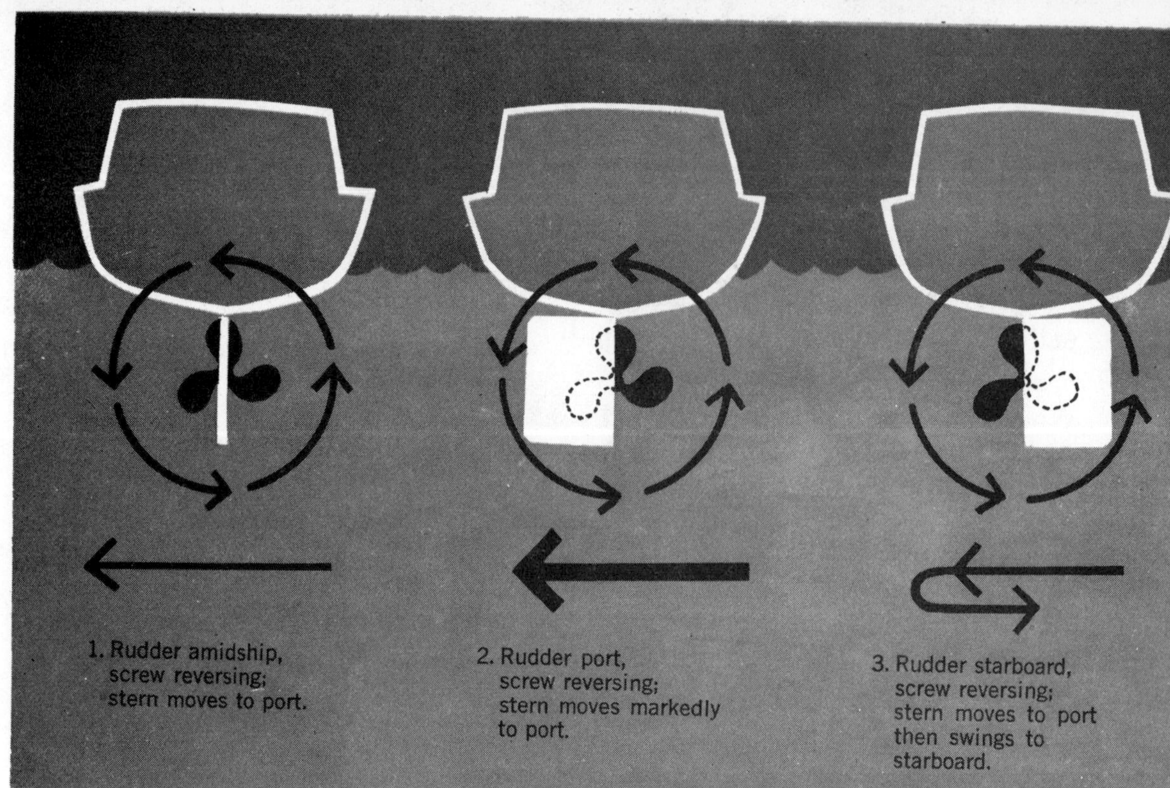
1. Rudder amidship,
screw reversing;
stern moves to port.
2. Rudder port,
screw reversing;
stern moves markedly
to port.
3. Rudder starboard,
screw reversing;
stern moves to port
then swings to
starboard.

what most skippers will note early in their experience: that it is easier to bring a boat in to a dock on the port side. As the boat glides in, the skipper reverses his engine to bring her to a stop. The push of the reverse screw stream on the starboard side of the hull will push the stern in to the dock as the craft comes to a stop.

SECTION 5 ■ WIND AND SAIL

Sailing can no more be taught from a book than ski jumping or tight-rope walking. The only way to learn sailing is to sail. Ideally, the beginner should start in the simplest rig with the best possible teacher. However, a knowledge of the basic principles by which boats sail can and should be studied in advance. When a few basic concepts are known, practical learning will be simpler.

Let us begin with a leaf blowing across a pond. It sails with the wind and only where the wind carries it. A raft with a sail is also carried forward by the wind. However, the occupant of the raft can exercise some control by changing the ***trim*** of the sail, the angle at which it faces the wind. If he now installs a rudder, he can change and guide the direction of his craft. If he goes another step forward, he will exchange the raft for a dugout canoe which is much better shaped than the raft to move forward through the water. Eventually he will learn to do one other thing: he will devise a keel for his boat to keep it from sliding sideways.

We now see that he is able to control his sailboat in three ways: by the design which enables it to slide easily forward through the water without too much leeway or sideways slippage, by the rudder which gives him control over the course he sails, and by trimming the sails so that he does not have to depend solely on a following wind. A final sophistication is achieved by dividing a single square sail into several triangular sails which can be trimmed individually and thus more efficiently.

The most common and familiar sail arrangement today is the ***sloop rig.*** This is composed of a single mast with a large or mainsail aft of the mast and a smaller sail (jib) forward of the mast. The accompanying diagrams indicate how the two sails are trimmed on the basic points of sailing; that is, with the wind aft, with the wind abeam, and with the wind forward of the beam.

Individual sailboats have different characteristics and sail trim will vary slightly, but the difference between a little Comet or Lightning class boat and an America's Cup defender is one of refinement, not of basic principle.

The principle of ***running*** before the wind is the simplest and most easily understood: the sail is

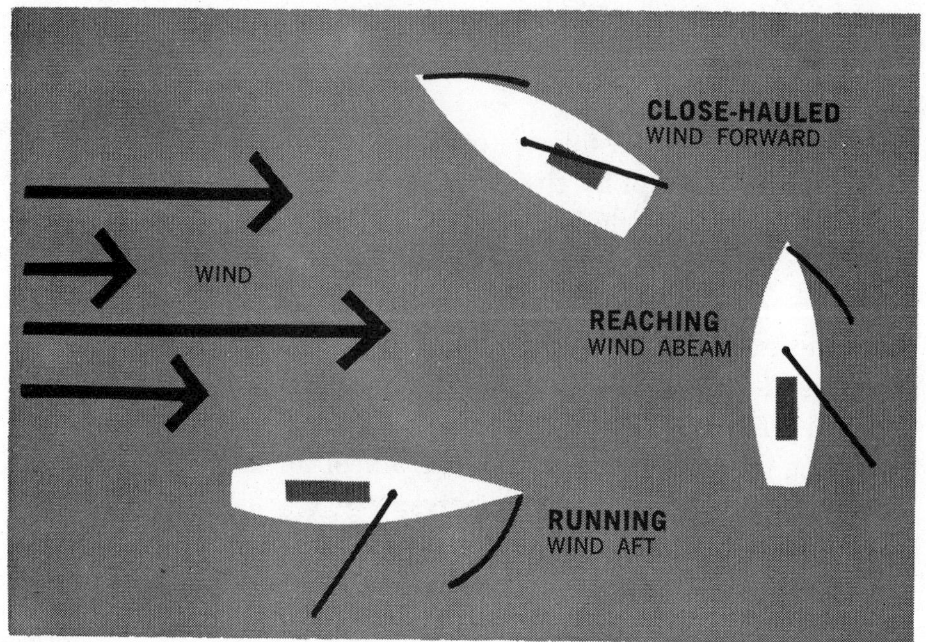

"Down East"—these two gaff riggers, ketch and sloop (foreground), are shown in service on Penobscot Bay. They afford their owners many happy hours of sailing

squared off to the wind as far as possible and the wind pushes the boat as it does a leaf on a pond. The skipper exercises control and can sail toward his objective more or less directly down wind.

Let us now consider ***reaching,*** or sailing with the wind abeam. This the leaf and the raft cannot do because they would be blown sideways. But the hull shape and the keel of the sailboat are so designed as to permit it to slip readily forward through the water, but only with considerable resistance sideways or to leeward.

In the illustration, we omit the jib for simplicity. The force of the wind is AB. It blows onto the mainsail, AC, at an angle. Hitting the mainsail, it is deflected and flows aft, parallel to the sail. The force that is deflected aft, AC, blowing parallel to the sail is not effective and is lost. But DB, the effective part of the force on the sail (whose power can be observed by the fact that it causes the boat to heel over) divides into two other components. One, AB, is sideways or to leeward and this is resisted by the keel and hull design. The remaining component, DE, acts in a direction parallel to the keel to push the boat forward through the water.

The single most difficult concept for the beginner to understand in sailing is how the boat can sail ***close-hauled***—that is, into the wind. Actually no sailboat sails directly into the wind. However, almost all well-designed sailboats are able to sail at an angle of 45 degrees to the wind. This effect is achieved by bringing the mainsail well in, so that it is as flat as possible. In the accompanying illustration, note the difference in AB, the wind direction, and AC, the mainsail trim from the "reaching" diagram.

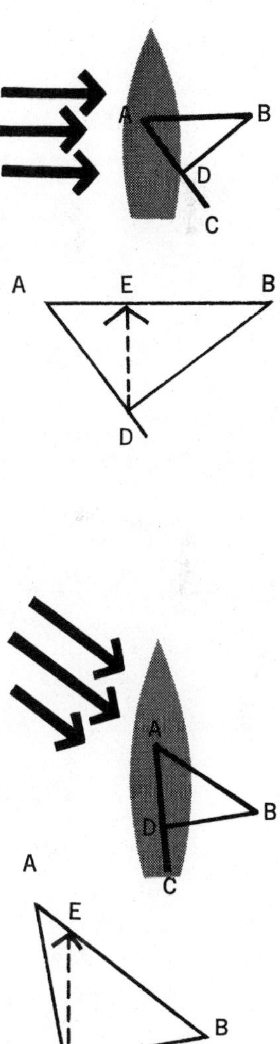

Although the best-designed sailboats cannot hold closer to the wind than 45 degrees, they are still able to attain the effect of sailing into the wind by a process known as ***beating.*** This consists of a series of courses, first 45 degrees to one side of the wind and then 45 degrees to the other. Although the boat's track shows a series of right-angle turns, the ultimate effect is to allow the vessel to make good a course to a point directly to windward of its start.

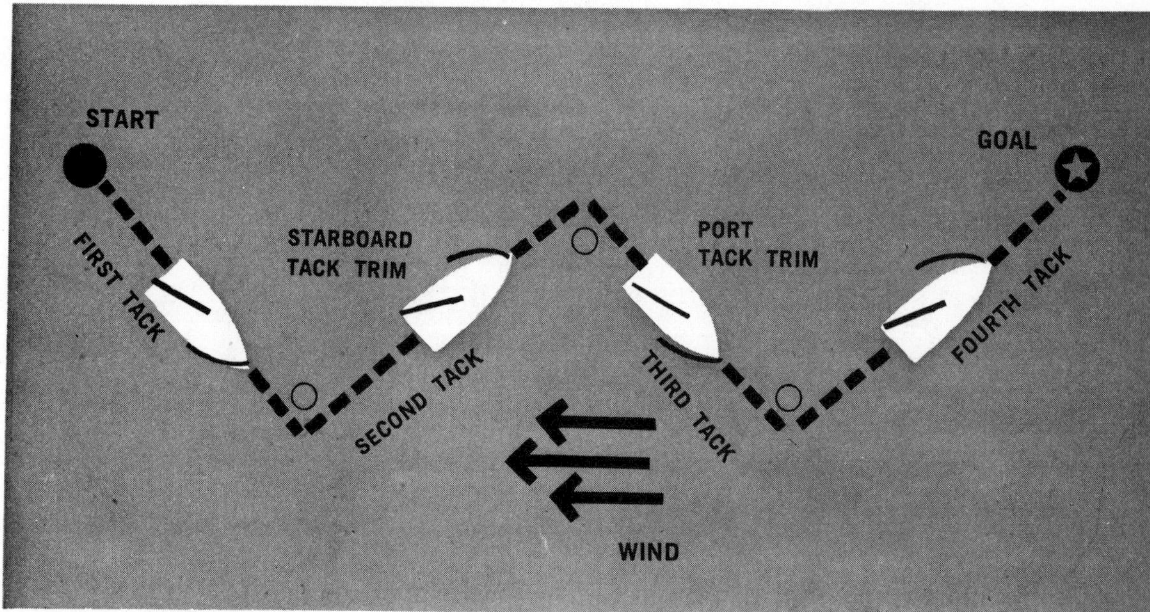

Each of the above courses is known as a ***tack.*** The boat is on the ***starboard tack*** when the wind comes from the starboard side and on the ***port tack*** when the wind is from the port side. Complete maneuverability is obtained because the sails are arranged to trim equally well on the starboard and port sides of the vessel.

SAFETY TIPS

• Check all components of your steering assembly each spring before launching. At the same time, check the propeller stuffing box against possible leaks.

• Guard against a worn or straggling wiring system. Wiring should be waterproof, well insulated and of adequate size. Connections should be as short as possible and wires should not wear due to contact with moving parts.

• When learning to sail a small boat, hold the mainsheet in hand or at least have it ready to run out on an instant's notice in event of a strong puff of wind.

• Never make half hitches around cleats with manila or cotton sheets or halyards. They may jam when wet.

• Do half hitch dacron or nylon lines to prevent slipping.

• Halyards should be coiled and secured neatly but ready for quick action if sails have to be dropped fast.

• Skill in boat handling is achieved only through constant practice under all conditions. Roll up newspapers into large balls and throw them overboard. Then practice coming up to them, steering between them and around them.

• Accuracy of steering may be checked by observing the boat's wake from time to time. A wriggly "worm-line" wake usually indicates inattentive helmsmanship.

• While checking your wake, observe its effect on other boats. If you are causing noticeable waves and badly rocking small craft at anchor or under way, slow down promptly!

• When turning sharply in confined waters, watch your stern as well as your bow. Remember—the stern swings wide.

• Some boat-owners adjust their carburetors to idle at minimum RPM in order to save gas. This is a mistake. An overslow idle causes spark plug fouling, risks stalling when the throttle is closed and results in poor maneuverability at the same time. Check your engine manufacturer.

3

BASIC SEAMANSHIP

In fair weather, any millpond mariner can look like a salty sailor. But when the wind swings into the north quadrant and the seas rise, Father Neptune quickly separates the men from the boys.

The secret of meeting the challenge of a hard blow lies in knowing what your boat can do and having confidence in your own ability to make her do it.

Skill at tying a half dozen or so knots is as vital to safe boat handling in this push-button age as it ever was. Automation engineers have yet to devise a machine that will make a boat fast with the proper breast and spring lines. With all the latest advances in electronic equipment, a skipper must still have a thorough knowledge of right-of-way rules. Starboard and port passing and overtaking require a practiced skipper.

Sound seamanship remains the cornerstone of safe boat handling.

SECTION 6 ■ GETTING UNDER WAY

New yachtsmen often feel that fire hazards on a boat are exaggerated. Yet year after year, Coast Guard statistics show that many serious boating accidents are due to fires and explosions. The boatowner is therefore urged to review the *Skipper's Check List For Getting Under Way* included with this book. Check off each item faithfully until you know the routine by heart. When your engine is warm, with oil pressure at a steady satisfactory level and water cooling system properly functioning, your family and guests safely stationed, you are ready to get under way. Let us assume you are leaving:

From a mooring

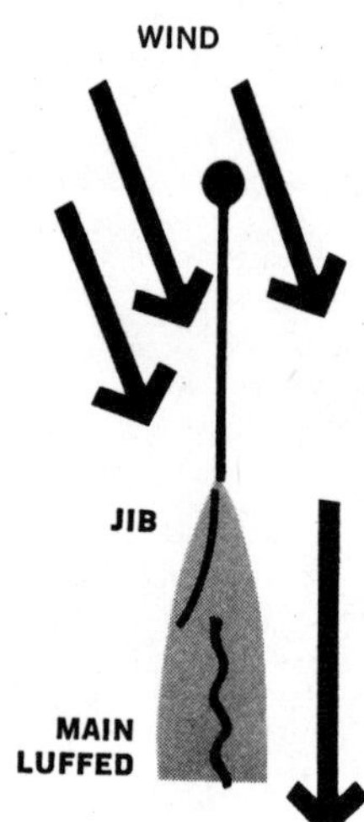

Your boat will be headed into wind or current, whichever is stronger. Take in all fenders and boarding ladder. Station a man forward to cast off your mooring line. Make sure the dinghy painter is up short and not likely to foul the propeller. Cast off the mooring hawser, nudging the boat forward a foot or two if necessary to slack the line. Now drift back or reverse slowly to prevent running over your mooring line and buoy. In a sailboat, raise your mainsail first, being sure the main sheet is free to run and the backstays are cast off. Decide which tack you want to fall off on. Then raise your jib and, when you are ready to cast off, weather the jib to insure falling off on the proper side as you leave the mooring.

From riding at anchor

Haul in on your anchor line until it is tending straight up and down. Normally, this will break

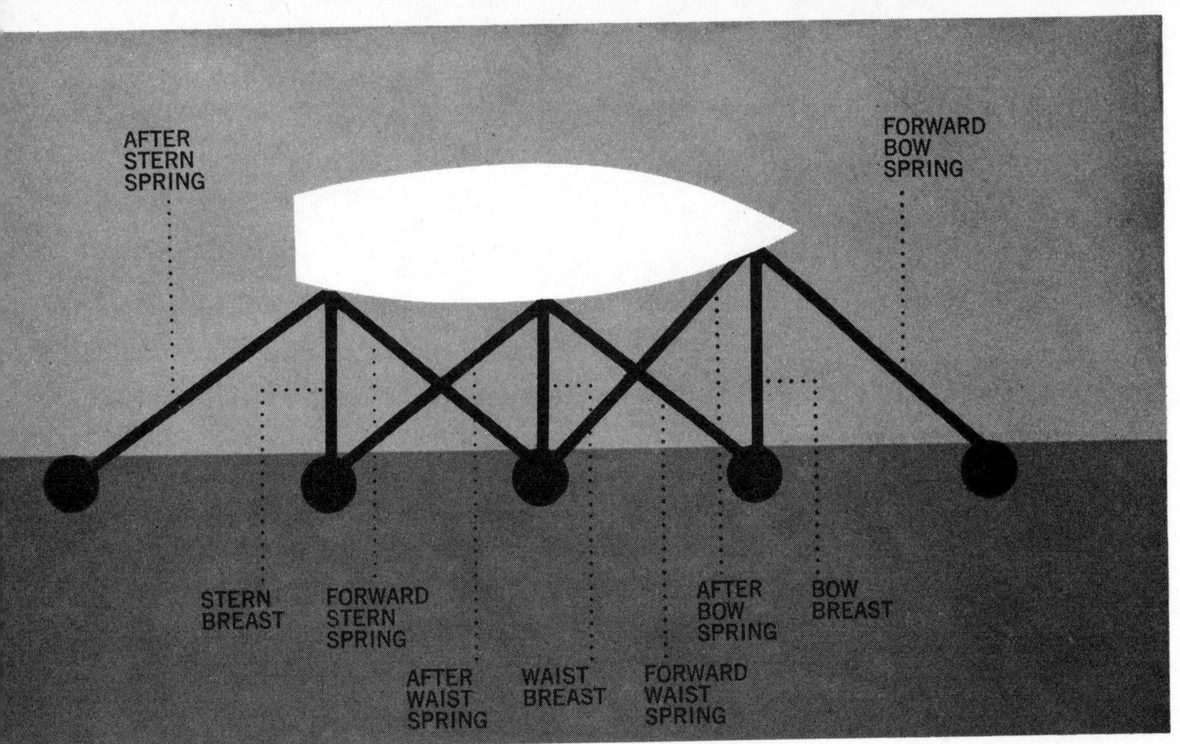

out or free the anchor. If it does not, this can be accomplished by securing the anchor line and running forward a few feet under power or circling the anchor. Depending on the size of boat and anchor, the latter will be hauled up to the surface by windlass or by hand. The careful skipper will then see that it is cleaned of mud either by swab hose or by running forward through the water with the anchor slightly submersed but well secured. The anchor should always be fully secured in the anchor chocks before the boat heads out into open water.

From a dock

The skipper should know the correct names of all dock lines even though he will probably never have occasion to use more than a few at once. They divide into combinations of the following: bow, waist or stern (quarter), depending on the part of the ship to which the line runs; forward or after—the direction the line runs from the ship; and

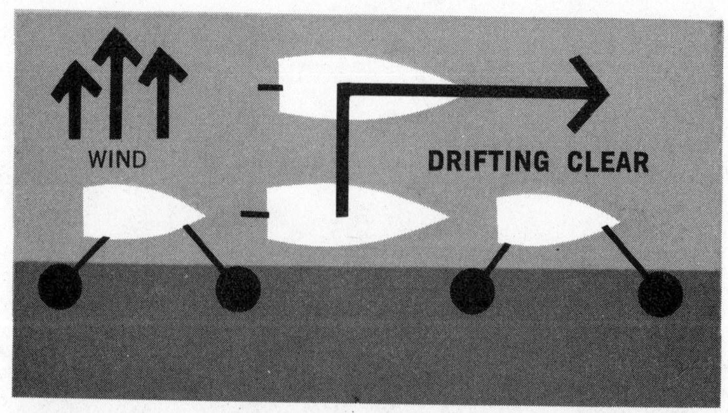

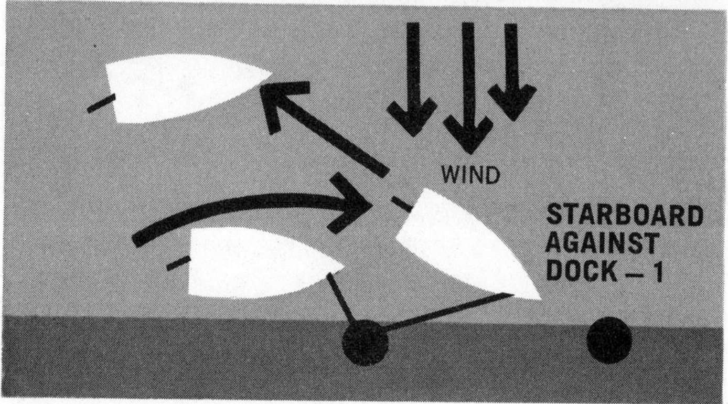

breast or spring. A ***breast line*** runs at right angles between ship and dock. A ***spring line*** runs forward or aft from the ship. It prevents forward or aft motion, tends to hold the ship off the dock and, if long enough, allows for the rise and fall of the tide.

In clearing a dock, the skipper notes wind and current. He may do this by slacking all dock lines slightly. If his vessel tends away from the dock, he may simply cast off lines and proceed ahead when he drifts clear. If he is on the weather side with his starboard being pushed toward the dock, he has two options: cast off the stern line and go forward slowly with right rudder, forcing the bow into the dock and the stern out. Then reverse and back out. Or: reverse the engine. With a right hand screw, the stern will swing out. To prevent the bow from

being forced into the dock, use right rudder as the boat goes astern. This will allow the ship to back out and clear the dock. If the port side of the ship is against the dock, use an after bow spring line and proceed ahead slowly with left rudder to throw the stern out. Then cast off and back slowly, using right rudder until clear.

72 COLREGS (RULES OF THE ROAD) ■ SECTION 7

The navigation rules at sea are far older than traffic laws ashore. They do not provide the skipper constant reminders as traffic signs and stop lights do the motorist. The basic Regulations for Preventing Collisions at Sea must therefore be memorized. Local rules divide into rules for the Western Rivers and Great Lakes, and the Pilot Rules for coastal waters. Inquire about an appropriate rule book for your area from your local Coast Guard office (see Chapter 7).

The time-honored Rules of the Road were replaced in July of 1977 by the new 72 COLREGS. These regulations are now the international standard. Every boat operator should obtain a copy of the new CG 179 which carries the new rules, and notes changes and clarifications over the old Rules of the Road. As before, the rules are directed to the prevention of collisions.

Boats run the risk of collision when meeting, crossing, or overtaking.

Meeting (Inland Rules)

When two power boats are approaching head on, each must alter his course to starboard so they may pass ***port to port*** well clear. A signal of ***one short blast*** should be sounded and returned by the other vessel with a similar signal.

When two boats are approaching but will clearly pass ***starboard*** to ***starboard,*** they must hold course and exchange whistle signals of ***two short blasts.***

Passing signals should never be given except when vessels are in sight of each other. In fog or reduced visibility, ships must sound prescribed fog signals.

Crossing

The boat having right of way, formerly known as the ***privileged*** vessel, is now known as the ***stand-on*** vessel.

The boat having to keep clear, formerly known as the ***burdened*** vessel, is know known as the ***give-way*** vessel.

Sailboats or rowboats normally have right of way over motor boats.

A boat's ***danger zone*** is the area from dead ahead to two points abaft of the starboard beam. Any vessel approaching within this ten-point arc is privileged and has right of way over your boat.

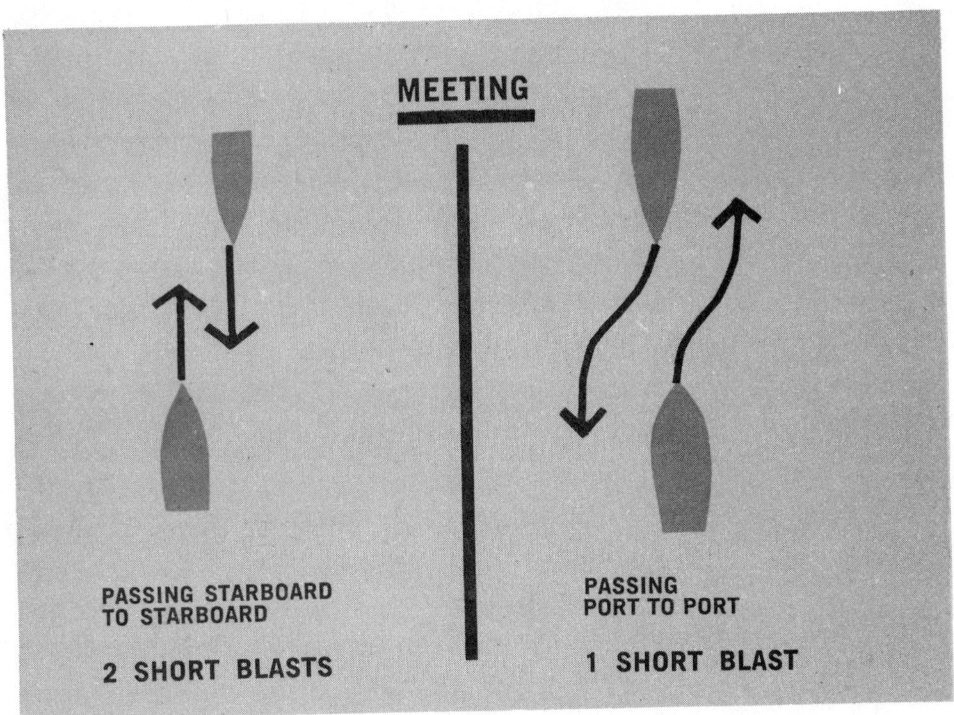

Stated in simple, rememberable terms, a boat approaching from your ***right*** has ***right of way.*** A boat approaching from your ***left*** may be ***left*** to pass ***astern.***

The good skipper knows that if a boat approaching from either right or left is clearly going to pass ahead or astern, he may hold course and speed. But if the bearing of the approaching vessel does not change, then danger of collision must be presumed. Watching the bearing is particularly important at night, when the course and speed of the approaching boat are difficult to judge. ***The stand-on vessel is obliged to hold course and speed except to avoid collision. The give-way vessel is obliged to keep clear.***

Overtaking

The rule is simple: ***The overtaking boat must keep clear.*** However, the stand-on vessel must hold course and speed. If the give-way vessel wants to pass on the starboard side, she sounds ***one*** short blast. You then answer with ***one*** short blast to indi-

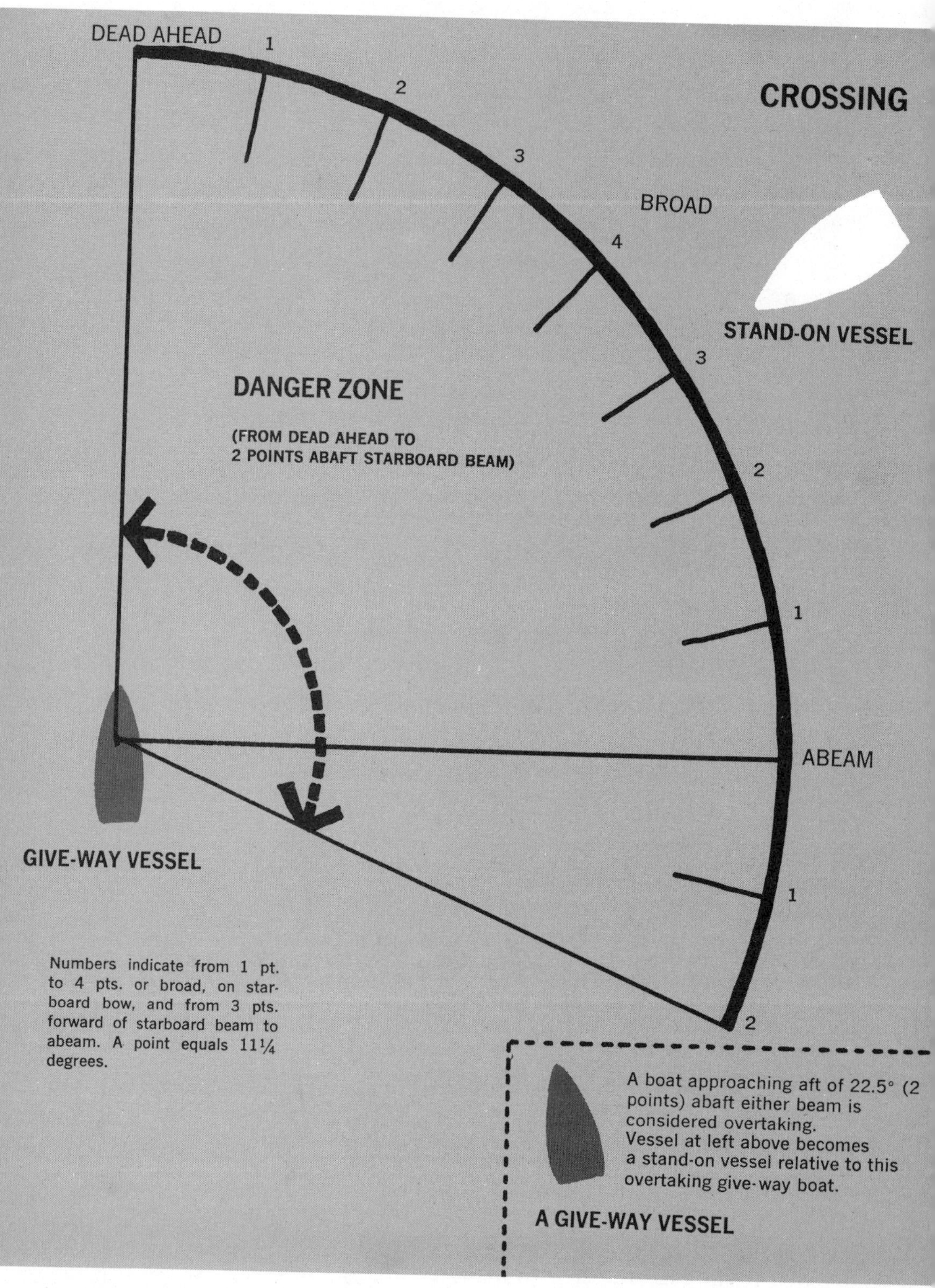
CROSSING
DEAD AHEAD
1
2
3
BROAD
4
3
2
1
ABEAM
1
2
STAND-ON VESSEL
DANGER ZONE
(FROM DEAD AHEAD TO
2 POINTS ABAFT STARBOARD BEAM)
GIVE-WAY VESSEL
Numbers indicate from 1 pt. to 4 pts. or broad, on starboard bow, and from 3 pts. forward of starboard beam to abeam. A point equals 11¼ degrees.
A boat approaching aft of 22.5° (2 points) abaft either beam is considered overtaking.
Vessel at left above becomes a stand-on vessel relative to this overtaking give-way boat.
A GIVE-WAY VESSEL

cate that you understand and agree. If the overtaking boat wishes to pass to port, she sounds ***two*** short blasts. Again you repeat her signal to indicate that you agree.

If you do not agree, you should sound the danger signal—***five*** or more short blasts. A single blast must never be answered with two blasts or vice versa. The only alternative to accepting the other vessel's signal is to sound the danger signal. The danger signal, which may be supplemented by five short and rapid flashes of light, should be given any time doubt exists as to danger of collision.

Sailing Vessels

All rules that apply to motor boats apply to sailing vessels under power. A sailboat is regarded as being under power when she has her engine going, even though the sails may be up. The following special rules apply to sailboats *not* under power when meeting, crossing and overtaking:

A sailboat on the starboard tack (boom out to

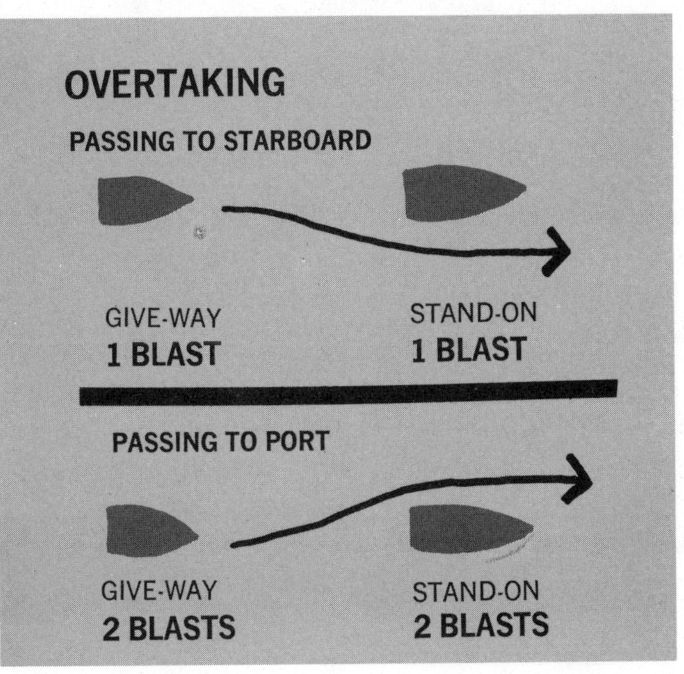

Note: In narrow channels where overtaken boat must take action to permit safe passing, the overtaking boat sounds: ——— ——— —— (two long and one short for intent to pass to starboard) and ——— ——— —— —— (two long and two short for intent to pass to port). The vessel to be overtaken indicates her agreement to either signal by sounding ——— —— ——— —— (one long, one short, one long, one short).

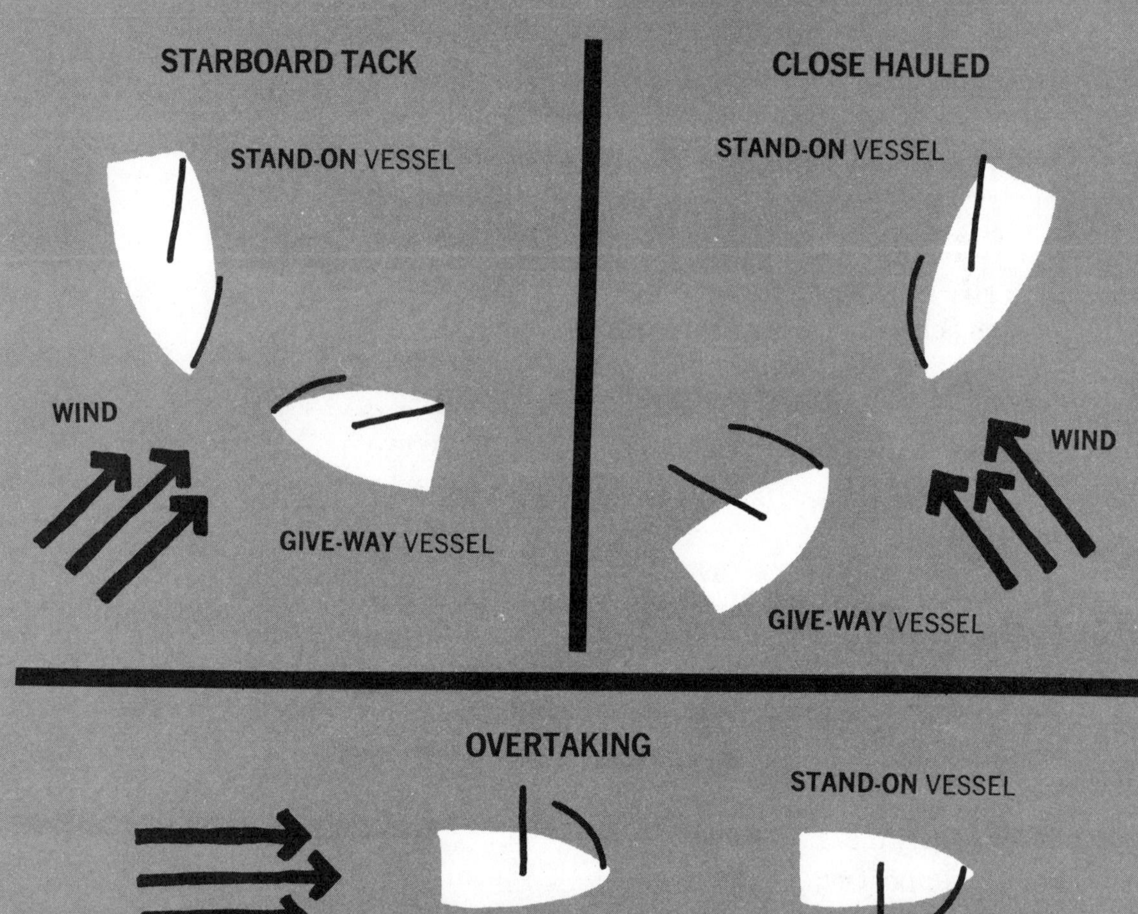

port and wind from starboard side) has right of way over a sailboat on the port tack (boom to starboard and wind from port side) if both are close-hauled or neither is close-hauled.

A sailboat close-hauled has right of way over a sailboat reaching or running free, regardless of tack. The overtaking boat must keep clear.

Whistle signals are never exchanged between sailboats. However, sailboats are required to use

WHISTLE SIGNALS

Signal	International Rules	Inland Rules
▬ ONE SHORT	I am directing my course to starboard	• As privileged vessel, I am holding course and speed. • As burdened vessel, I am maneuvering to give you right of way. • As overtaking vessel, I wish to pass you on your starboard. • Overtaken craft: you may pass me safely to starboard.
▬ ▬ TWO SHORT	I am directing my course to port.	• As overtaking vessel, I wish to pass you on your port. • Overtaken craft: you may pass me safely to port.
▬ ▬ ▬ THREE SHORT	My engine(s) are going astern.	• My engine(s) are full speed astern.
▬ ▬ ▬ ▬ SEVERAL, FOUR OR MORE, SHORT	Danger Signal. (5 or more may be sounded by privileged vessel required to hold course and speed if it believes burdened vessel not holding safe course and speed)	• Danger signal. (On Great Lakes—**5** short blasts) • Lack of agreement on signals. • Other craft's intentions not understood.
▬▬▬▬ ONE LONG (8-10 SECONDS)	Sounded within .5 mile of bend in channel where approaching vessels are not visible. *	• Sounded as a warning by a vessel leaving a dock. * • Sounded as a warning when within .5 mile of a bend in channel.
	* (NOTE: This warning signal is preliminary to passing signals and should not be confused with a passing signal)	

their horns to sound fog signals.

In narrow channels neither sailboats nor power boats can hamper the movements of large vessels.

It should be noted that all Rules of the Road are subject to emergency conditions. If shoal water or obstructions prevent a boat from observing strict rules, she must sound the danger signal. Exercise good judgment.

SECTION 8 ■ MOORING AND ANCHORING

In mooring or anchoring, the boat should always approach its mooring or the spot at which it wishes to anchor with its bow into the wind or the current, whichever is stronger. In a mooring area, this can easily be determined by noting how other ships lie. Station one man forward with a boat-hook, and proceed ahead dead slow toward the buoy.

The mooring consists of a mushroom anchor (preferably), a railroad car wheel (occasionally) or a concrete block (less desirable) sunk into the soft mud or sand on the bottom. From this anchor, a chain or cable is attached to a buoy at the surface. Ample chain should be provided to allow for rise and fall of the tides and a substantial excess

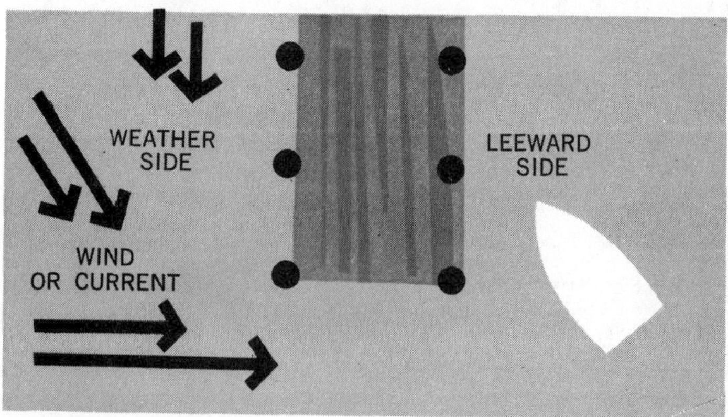

to lie buried on the bottom. To the buoy is attached a mooring hawser which is hauled aboard the ship through bow chocks or hawse holes. To facilitate picking up this hawser, a pick-up buoy is made fast to the bight at the end with a light rope pennant.

It is to the pick-up buoy that the man on the bow addresses his efforts with the boat-hook. Having snared the buoy, or the pennant affixing it to the bight of the mooring, the bow man signals the skipper to disengage the engine, and the bight of the mooring hawser is hauled aboard and affixed to the forward bitt or cleat. In approaching a mooring in a sailboat, the skipper drops or slacks his jib and rounds up when he judges that he has enough head reach to "coast" up to the mooring. The main sheet is slacked so that the mainsail luffs in the wind, and sails are dropped as soon as the mooring is made fast. If it is necessary to approach the mooring downwind before rounding up, speed may be reduced by strapping down the mainsail—that is, hauling in the sheet until the boom is almost amidship.

In anchoring either a motorboat or a sailboat, the vessel should be maneuvered to the spot where the anchor is to lie and the anchor held ready to let go. The anchor is dropped (not "cast") at the instant the ship loses headway. As the craft drops back, enough scope is paid out to equal five to seven times the depth of the water. In a blow, fifteen times the depth is considered a safer margin. The careful skipper must be certain, however, that in the event of a wind change he will have ample room at the anchorage to swing in an arc of 360 degrees or else that someone will be stationed

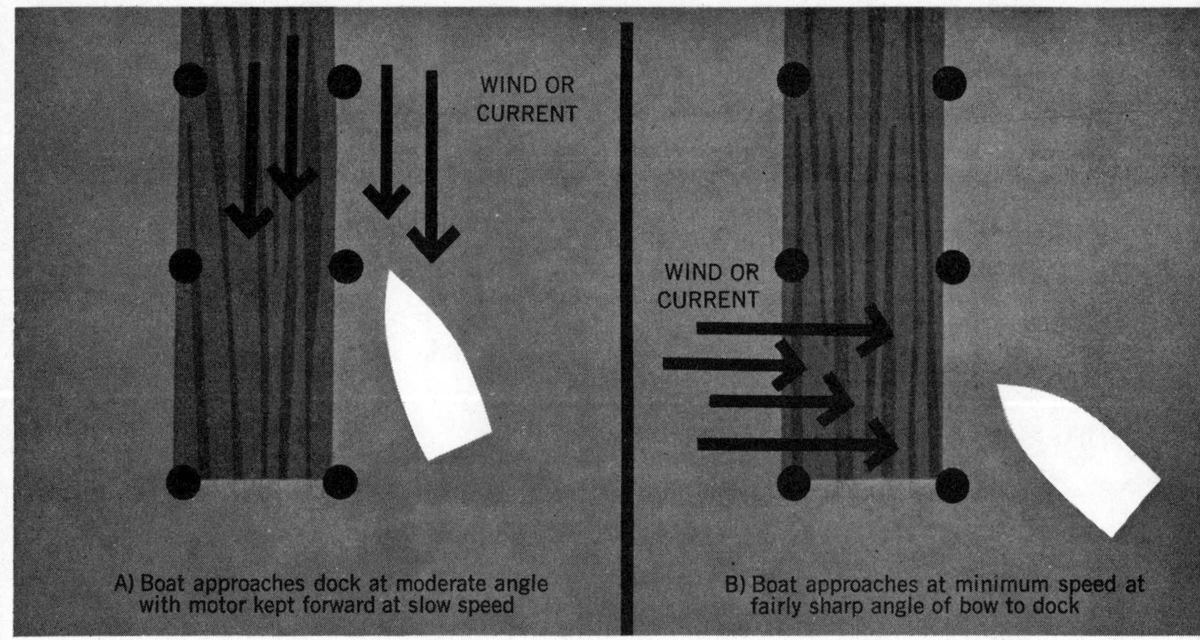

A) Boat approaches dock at moderate angle with motor kept forward at slow speed

B) Boat approaches at minimum speed at fairly sharp angle of bow to dock

on watch to guard against swinging into other vessels, breakwaters or shoal water as the wind or tide changes. Many an otherwise peaceful slumber has been rudely broken by well-separated vessels swinging at their anchors and suddenly banging into one another or even some less-yielding obstacle.

Mooring alongside a dock offers more difficult problems than unmooring, or clearing, a dock. In making a dock, the skipper of motorboat or sailboat must remember that he has greater control of his vessel if he comes in against wind or current (whichever is stronger) than with a fair wind or current setting him forward. Also, if he has a choice he should prefer the lee side of the dock to the weather side, since he may back off and make fresh approaches to the lee side but will be without much margin for error on his first try on the weather side.

For these reasons, it is well to have the dock lines on deck and free to run, and to have the fenders rigged at the proper height on the ship's topsides to afford best protection from the pilings or planking along the docks. A fender board is most useful

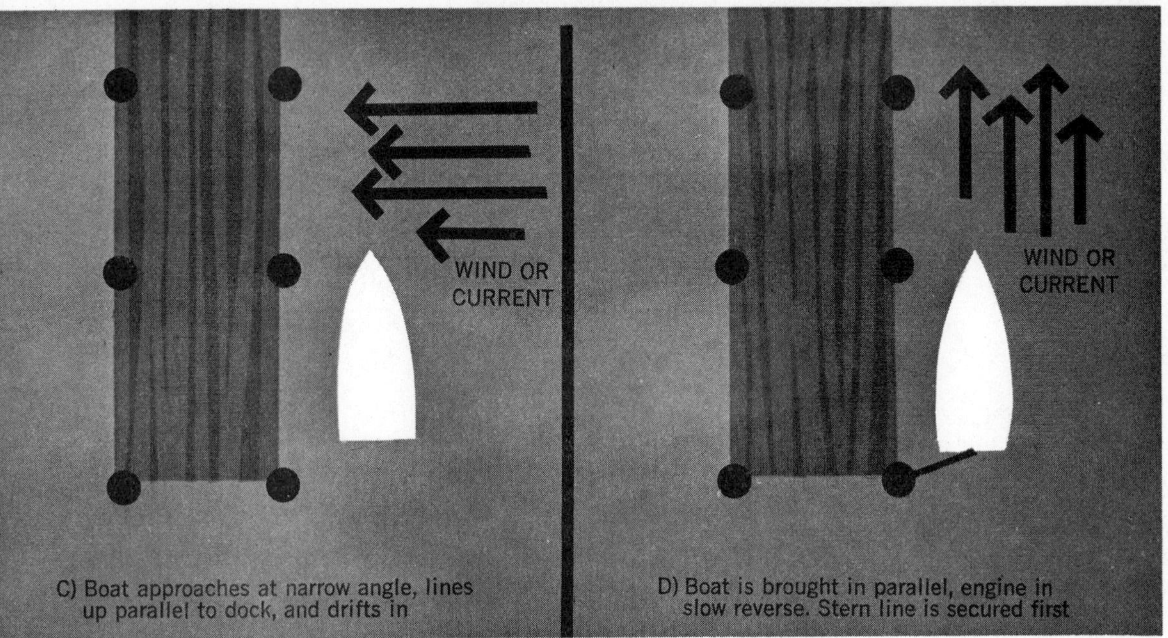

C) Boat approaches at narrow angle, lines up parallel to dock, and drifts in

D) Boat is brought in parallel, engine in slow reverse. Stern line is secured first

when the ship must lie alongside piling. Last but not least, able-bodied members of the crew should be prepared to fend off by hand in an emergency.

Assuming wind or tide is off the dock, the skipper will make his approach at minimum speed at a fairly sharp angle so that his bow comes in to the dock first. If there is a man on the dock, the bow line should be heaved up and secured to a piling bollard or cleat ashore. If not, the man on the bow should carry the line onto the dock. Once the bow line is secured, the stern line is passed onto the dock and the engine disengaged.

If the wind or tide is dead ahead, the boat approaches at a less sharp angle and the motor may be kept forward at slow speed until both bow and stern are secured.

If the vessel is being set onto the dock by wind or current, it should come in at a narrow angle and line up parallel to the dock about a boat-length off and then drift in. A boat-hook or oar may be used to fend off as the craft closes with the dock. This is the riskiest way of tying up and, unless a weather line can be run out to another slip or piling to hold the ship off, it may be advisable to drop an anchor amidship as the craft stands off the dock and keep a taut breast line to hold it off from grinding away fenders, rub rail and topsides.

If the boat must be brought into the dock with the current, keep the engine slowly in reverse to maintain control. Pass the stern line ashore first, and when it is secured the bow will drift in close enough to get a bow line ashore.

A single-engine boat makes dock more easily on the port side, since the stern will go in toward the dock once she is close in and the engine is reversed.

The method of tying up to the dock will depend on such factors as the size of the boat, length of intended stay, strength of wind and current, and availability of mooring line or lines on the outboard side. Assuming a short tie-up under favorable conditions with a light craft, simple bow and stern lines with properly-rigged fenders will suffice.

Assuming an overnight stay in tidal waters with no outboard mooring lines, a bow line, after-bow spring line, forward-quarter spring and stern lines will provide good protection. The height of the tide when tying up should be noted. On a falling tide, provision should be made to slack the lines as the

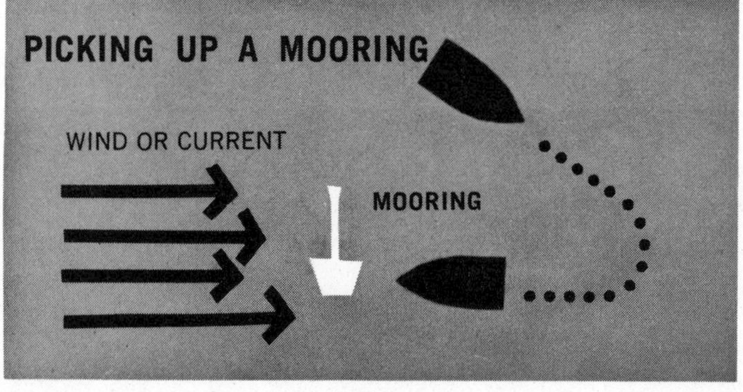

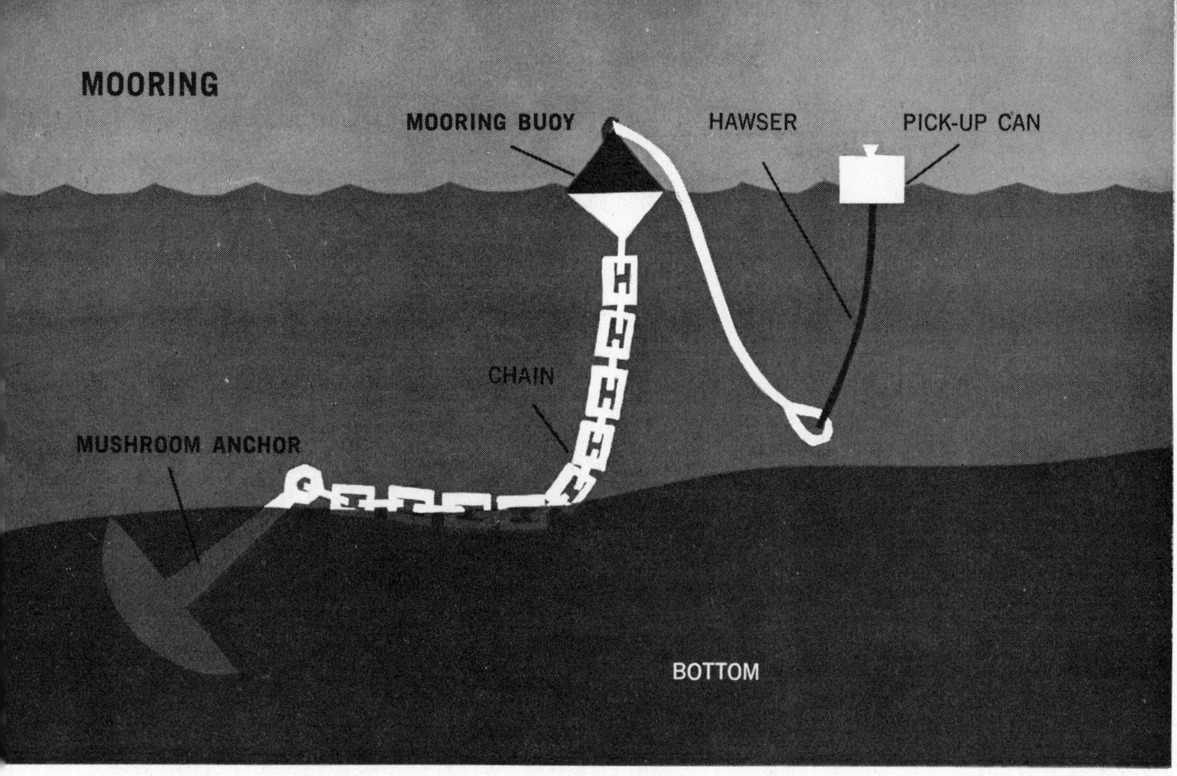

tide falls. On a rising tide, they should be taken up as the tide comes in. Much minor damage can be done to a boat by tying up securely at high tide, leaving the craft, and having the mooring lines literally holding the vessel out of the water as the tide falls beneath her.

Only through observation and experiment will the good skipper learn the most effective way of tying up his boat under varying conditions at various types of dock.

In backing out of a slip, the skipper should always remember that the stern becomes the bow in respect to right of way rules.

WEATHER ■ SECTION 9

The city dweller and office worker are constantly surprised by "sudden" changes in the weather. A rain shower, a wind squall, an overcast sky seem to appear unexpectedly and without warning.

To the experienced seaman, weather changes virtually never appear without considerable advance notice. In former times, the sailor relied almost exclusively on the barometer, wind direction and the appearance of the sky. Today, with a vast network of meteorological observation and reporting stations around the world, with electronic computers working for the weather man, and with the constant availability of weather reports by radio, the yachtsman has swifter and more accurate weather information than was ever available before.

Yet, in spite of all of the magic of contemporary science, the weather bureau is again and again embarrassed by its failure to predict a sudden severe local storm or by over-warning for a blow that misses the local area entirely. In the interests of safe boating, there is no substitute for a sound understanding by the yachtsman of the principles of weather judgment.

In the United States, most weather moves from west to east at about 500 to 600 miles a day. Television viewers who watch the highs and lows on the weather maps will recall that these weather centers move across the country from left to right at about this rate, although the winds within each system may blow in any direction.

It is this eastward trend that forms the scientific basis for the often-quoted weather verse: "Red at night, sailor's delight. Red in the morning, sailor take warning!" The redness of the sunset is caused by dusty dry air in the west, indicating a dry day ahead. But when the dry dusty air is in the east, as at sunrise, it usually means that the fair weather has passed and will be succeeded by clouds.

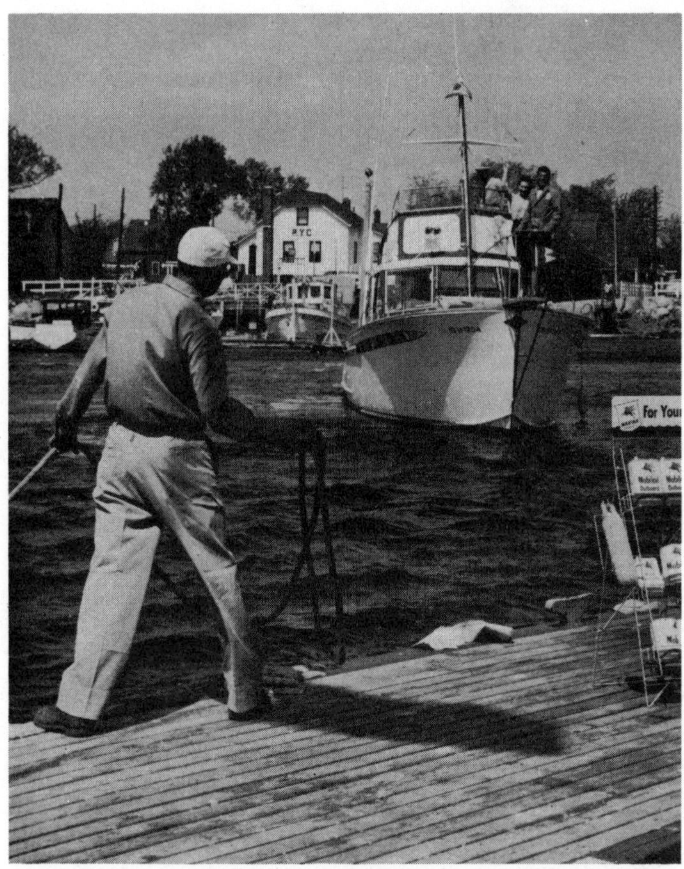

There is no substitute for your sound weather judgment. The safe skipper makes for port when a bad blow is forecast. The crew is at the bow, ready to receive a helpful line

The modern meteorologist prefers to speak in terms of warm fronts and cold fronts but, basically, these "fronts" are associated with high-pressure areas and low-pressure areas respectively. The winds making up a high pressure area blow around it in a clockwise direction. The winds making up a low-pressure area blow about it in a counter-clockwise direction. The approach of a high is indicated by a rising barometer, the approach of a low is signalled by a falling glass.

Storms seldom take place within the central areas of highs and lows. It is along the leading edges of the warm air mass or cold air mass that turbulence breaks out. Storms along the cold fronts are intense and often destructive, but usually of short duration. Storms along the warm fronts are vaster and slower, normally taking from 24 to 48 hours to pass over. The terms "cold front" and "warm front" do not refer to any absolute scale of temperature but merely indicate that the air masses are cooler or warmer than the air they displace.

The two illustrations (pp. 62-3) should be carefully studied. An understanding of their principles will contribute more to the skipper's weather knowledge than pages of description.

The cold front hugs the ground, pushing the warm air up and forming thunderheads or anvil tops. Winds roar and rain pours down. As the squall passes, the sky may clear and good visibility prevail.

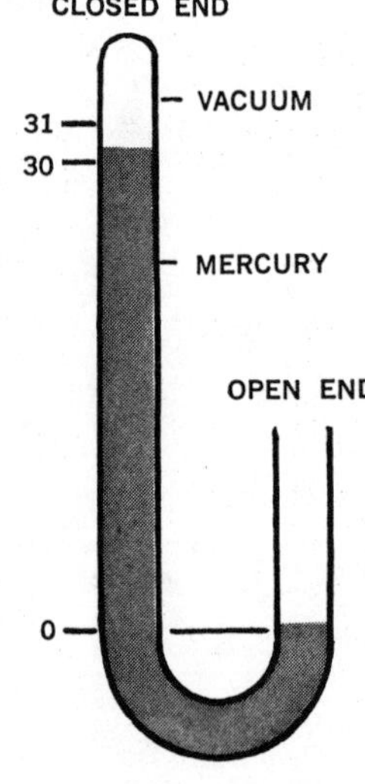

The solid lines on a weather map are called ***isobars*** or lines of equal barometric pressure. Where the isobars are well-spaced, the winds are usually light; where they are close together, indicating a rapidly rising or falling barometer, the winds are higher. Pressure is usually calibrated in inches. In the days of mercury barometers, this measurement represented the number of inches the mercury would be raised by atmospheric pressure acting on the open surface of a cup of mercury in which the open end of a sealed tube of mercury was immersed. The modern aneroid barometer operates on the simple principles of air pressure on a diaphragm activating a spring which moves the needle.

The aneroid barometer should be tapped lightly before reading, since there is normally a slight lag in the needle movement. After each reading, the adjustable needle should be re-set.

VISIBILITY SCALE			
0	50 yards and less	**5**	1-2 nautical miles
1	Over 50 yards and up to 200 yards	**6**	2-5 nautical miles
2	Over 200 yards and up to ¼ nautical mile	**7**	5-10 nautical miles
3	¼-½ nautical mile	**8**	10-25 nautical miles
4	½-1 nautical mile	**9**	25 nautical miles and above

On weather maps such as those issued by the Department of Commerce and reprinted in certain newspapers, long lines running between highs and lows will indicate warm and cold fronts. The ***cold front*** advances like a wedge, usually southward and eastward, pushing under a mass of warm air. The ***warm front*** normally advances eastward and northward over a retreating wedge of cold air. When pressures balance, a front may come to a halt. It is then labeled a ***stationary front,*** usually bringing little wind but often sustained rainfall. When a cold front overtakes a warm front and forces it upward, heavy rains and winds may occur; this is known as an ***occluded front.***

As you study the diagrams of the two fronts, note that the cold front has a sharp, steep leading edge. The storm band, often less than twelve miles deep, may pass in a few hours. The clouds accompanying the cold front are readily identifiable as low, ominous cumulus clouds, topped by a cumulonimbus

or thunderhead, with its anvil shape stretching out ahead of the storm as a high, misty overcast. The front itself moves in swiftly with squalls and gusty, shifting winds.

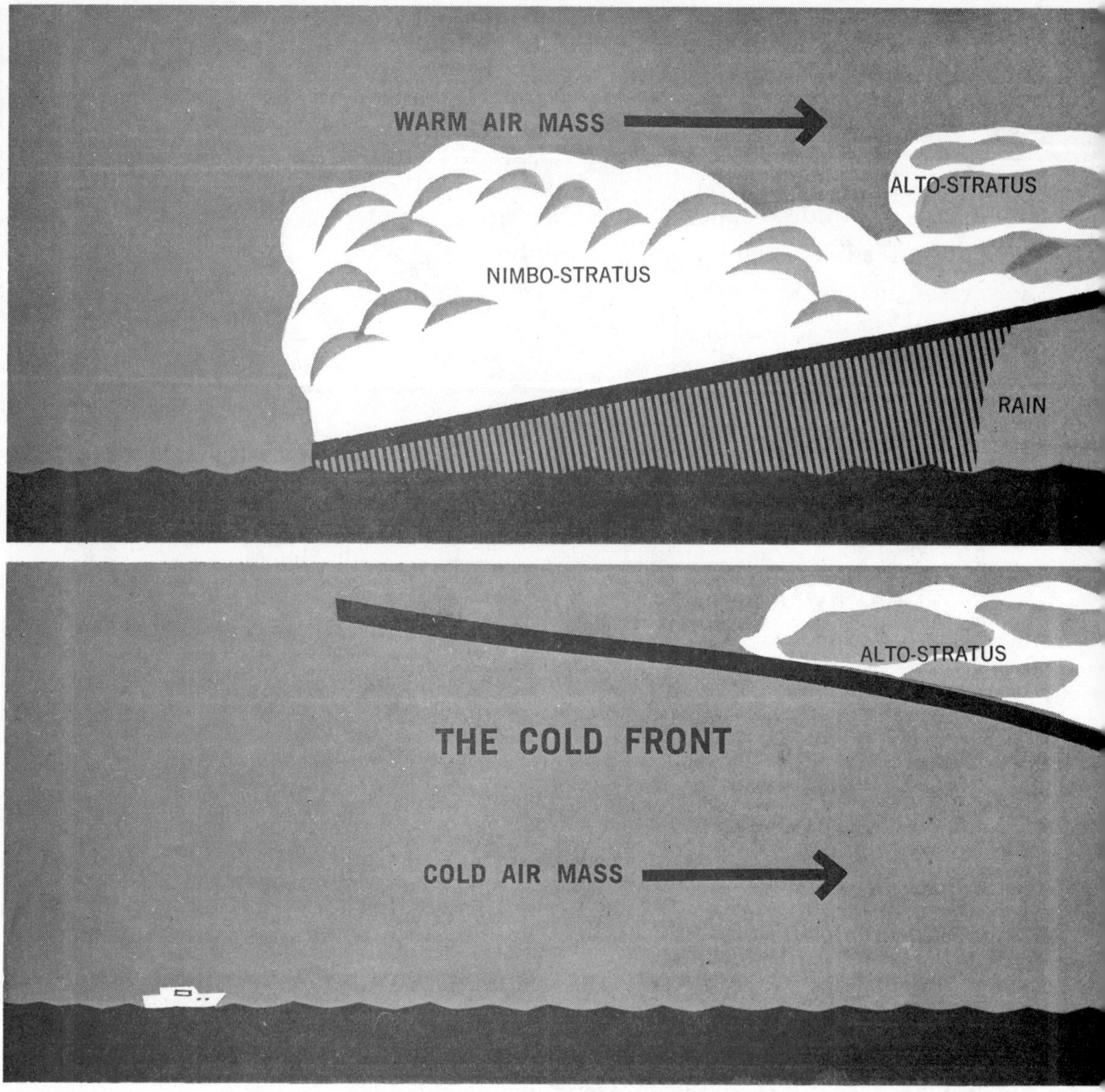

The clear weather that follows the passing of a cold front is frequently accompanied by high, small, white cumulus clouds, bright and sharp against a clear blue sky. Then, as the high cirrus and alto-stratus clouds of the warm front begin to move in over the cold air mass, halos are formed around

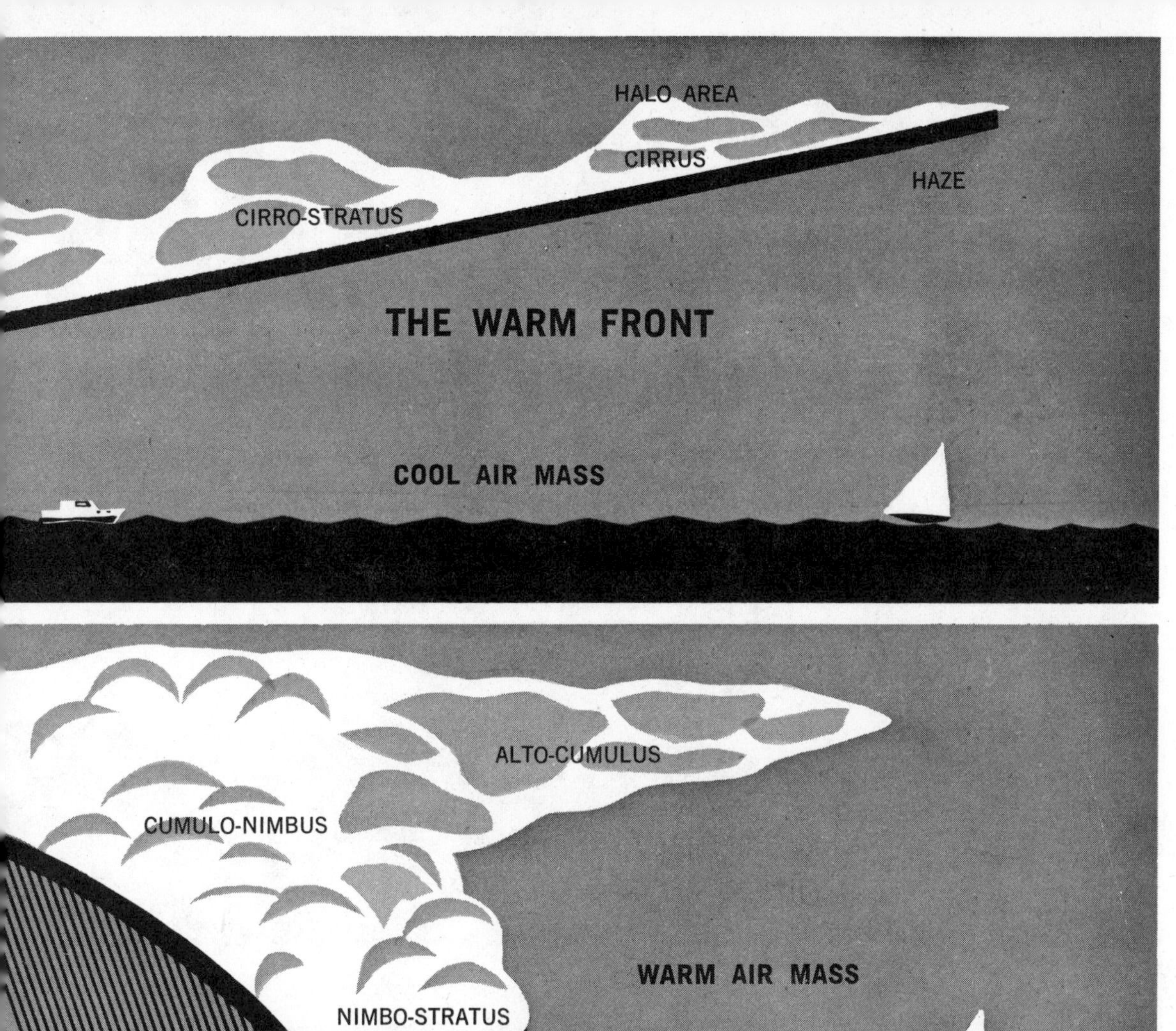

sun or moon. Usually, the bigger the halo, the nearer the rain. As the whole sky clouds over, the appearance of the rain-laden nimbostratus clouds indicates that a sustained downpour is on the way. The rain may be followed by strong winds.

Although the Coast Guard no longer flies weather signals at its stations, many yacht clubs still do. Learn to recognize the signals on page 67. The accompanying weather chart will be found useful in doing your own local forecasting and in checking against radio forecasts.

Heavy weather ahead. Skipper appraises the ominous, low-rolling storm cloud

Cumulo-cirro-stratus storm clouds in that order in foreground, behind, above

hanging heavy above the horizon, knowing that its size and color mean trouble

Flying scud on Lake Michigan. Cold front approaches, probable bad weather ahead

WEATHER CHART

Wind	Barometer at sea level	Probable Weather
SW to NW	30.10 to 30.20 steady	Fair for 1 or 2 days. Little temperature change.
SW to NW	30.10 to 30.20 rising 30.20 & above, steady	Fair followed by rain. Continued fair, no decided temperature change.
SW to NW	30.20 & above, falling slowly	Slowly rising temperature, fair for 2 days.
S to SE	30.10 to 30.20 falling slowly	Rain within 24 hours.
S to SE	30.10 to 30.20 falling rapidly	Increasing winds, rain within 12-24 hours.
SE to NE	30.10 to 30.20 falling slowly	Rain within 12-18 hours.
SE to NE	30.10 to 30.20 falling rapidly	Increasing wind and rain within 12-24 hours.
E to NE	30.10 & above, falling slowly	In summer with light winds, rain may not fall for several days. In winter, rain in 24 hours.
E to NE	30.10 & above, falling rapidly	In summer, rain probable in 12 hours. In winter, rain or snow with increasing winds when wind goes to NE.
SE to NE	30.00 or below, falling slowly	Rain will continue 1 or 2 days.
SE to NE	30.00 or below, falling rapidly	Rain with high winds, clearing within 36 hours (followed by cold in winter).
S to SW	30.00 or below, rising slowly	Clearing in a few hours, fair for several days.
S to E	29.80 or below, falling rapidly	Severe storm imminent, followed in 24 hours by clearing (and colder, in winter).
E to N	29.80 or below, falling rapidly	Severe NE gale and heavy rain.
Going to W	29.80 or below, rising rapidly	In winter, heavy snow and cold wave. Clearing and colder.

STORM SIGNALS

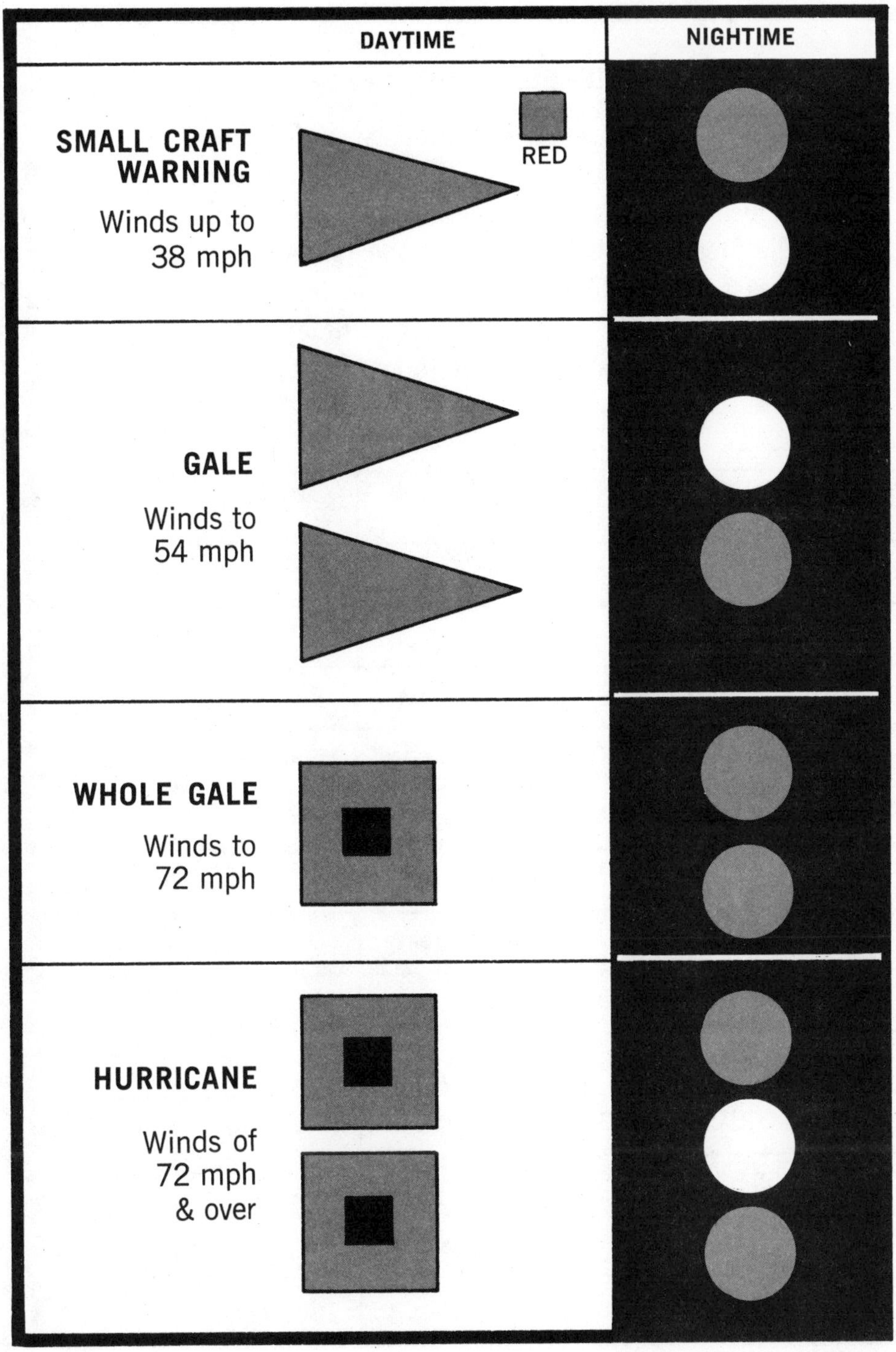

	DAYTIME	NIGHTIME
SMALL CRAFT WARNING Winds up to 38 mph	RED	
GALE Winds to 54 mph		
WHOLE GALE Winds to 72 mph		
HURRICANE Winds of 72 mph & over		

THE BEAUFORT SCALE

In making log entries, in reporting accidents, in exchanging weather information and, occasionally, in swapping lies over a friendly beer while cruising, the Beaufort scale is the authoritative system of measuring and describing wind and sea conditions. Refer regularly to this scale for accuracy in logging wind conditions and for use in interpreting weather forecasts.

Beaufort Number	Wind in miles/hr.	Wind in knots	Description of wind	Description of sea	Height of waves
0	Under 1	Under 1	Calm	Glassy	0 ft.
1	1-3	1-3	Light airs	Calm	0
2	4-7	4-6	Light breeze	Rippled	0-1
3	8-12	7-10	Gentle breeze	Smooth	1-2
4	13-18	11-16	Mod. breeze	Slight	2-4
5	19-24	17-21	Fresh breeze	Moderate	4-8
6	25-31	22-27	Strong breeze	Rough	8-13
7	32-38	28-33	Mod. gale	Very rough	13-20
8	39-46	34-40	Fresh gale	Very rough	13-20
9	47-54	41-47	Strong gale	Very rough	13-20
10	55-63	48-55	Whole gale	High	20-30
11	64-75	56-63	Whole gale	Very high	30-45
12	Over 75	Over 63	Hurricane	Phenomenal	Over 45

Weather Terms

For aid in keeping your log and for assistance in visualizing weather predictions, the following tables are useful. The first refers to the condition of the sky with respect to cloud cover.

Fair — Virtually no clouds. Bright sun during day. Stars and moon unobscured at night.

Partly Cloudy — Noticeable clouds, usually covering between one-tenth to better than one-half of the sky.

Cloudy — Clouds over more than half the sky but less than completely covering the sky.

Overcast — No clear areas visible at all.

Haze — A greying of the sky and obscuring of visibility due to fog, smoke, light precipitation or any combination of these.

Fog — A denser obscuring of sky and limitation of visibility due to high moisture content in the atmosphere. May be characterized by humidity of up to 100%.

The Visibility Scale (which will be found on page 61) is useful to the boat owner for recording the extent of visibility. A copy should be kept near the compass.

Cloud Formations

Although the science of weather forecasting is steadily improving, each of us recalls storms which seemed to break without warning from the weather bureau and other storms or bad weather which were predicted but which never materialized. To the student of weather—and every good yachtsman needs both the desire and ability to anticipate local weather conditions—the sky becomes an open book whose paragraphs are written in clouds. Here, then, are the clouds and their descriptions:

CLOUD FORMATIONS

	UPPER CLOUDS
CIRRUS (Ci)	Very high, feathery clouds, delicate white in color, frequently occurring in wispy rows.
CIRRO-STRATUS (Ci.S.)	A thin film of pale white cloud, sometimes completely covering the sky and giving it a hazy appearance, at other times spread across the sky like fine lacework. Often causes halos around the sun and moon.
	INTERMEDIATE CLOUDS
CIRRO-CUMULUS (Ci.Cu.)	A mackerel sky; groups and often lines of white flakes with few or no shadows.
ALTO-CUMULUS (A.Cu.)	White or greyish blobs of cloud, partly shaded, often so crowded together as to lose definition. Often arranged in crowded ranks.
ALTO-STRATUS (A.S.)	A sheet of cloud, grey or bluish in color, usually covering the entire sky. It may be thick and opaque or it may be thin enough to resemble a heavier form of cirro-stratus.
	LOWER CLOUDS
STRATO-CUMULUS (S.Cu.)	Lumpy masses of dull grey clouds, often filling the entire sky, especially in winter. Usually do not produce rain or snow. They often form in long rolls with dark bottoms.
NIMBUS (N.)	This is the true rain cloud. It is dense, dark and shapeless with ragged edges from which rain or snow falls. When nimbus breaks into detached fragments, or when ragged blotches move swiftly beneath a vaster nimbus cloud, it is often referred to as scud.

ASCENDING CLOUDS	
The familiar large, fluffy white clouds with flat bases and ascending, dome-shaped upper portions.	**CUMULUS (Cu.)**
This is the great thunder cloud—enormous masses of cloud like huge tables or more often like anvils because of their flat tops with pointed ends. There is generally a veil of fibrous cloud at the top and a base cloud similar to nimbus from which heavy local showers of rain or snow, or even hail, will fall.	**CUMULO-NIMBUS (Cu.N.)**
HIGH FOG	
A layer of fog but usually at 3,000 feet or above, thus still permitting reasonable visibility on the ground.	**STRATUS (S.)**

Weather Folklore

The folklore of weather predicting, from Aunt Em's rheumatiz to the dew forming on the highly polished cabin trunk of a Fiberglas yacht, is virtually inexhaustible. Yet much of it does have a scientific basis—and almost none of it is infallible.

For what they are worth, here are some of the more familiar rules of thumb, not for predicting but guessing the weather:

Rainbow before noon—bad weather soon. Rainbow before night—clear skies in sight.

When the mare's tails (high, wispy clouds) are being whipped across the sky, look for the storm wagon to follow soon.

If the trees, especially the maples, are showing

the undersides of their leaves, look for rain within 24 hours.

Big, bright-white billowy clouds mean fair weather so long as they are scattered, but when they start gathering together, bad weather looms.

Heavy dew on grass or deck means fair weather ahead.

At dusk: high clouds red, strong winds ahead; sky bright blue, fair weather due.

Cloudy sunset, falling glass; storm and wind will come to pass.

High clouds and low clouds going different ways —unsettled weather for one or more days.

A favorite among sailboat men is:

If the wind and then the rain,
You may soon make sail again.
If the rain and then the wind,
Topsails lower and mainsail mind.

Also:

First rise after low
Indicates a stronger blow;
When the rise starts after low,
Squalls expect and clear below.

Another:

Red sky in the morning,
Sailors take warning.
Red sky at night,
Sailors'delight.

And another:

A mackerel sky with mares' tails
Makes tall ships carry low sails.

And finally, referring to the length of time taken for warm and cold fronts to pass:

Long foretold, long last;
Short notice, soon past.

SAFETY TIPS

- When you anchor, keep well out of the channel and be sure that you have ample room to swing in *all* directions.
- When you anchor, drop the anchor overboard hand over hand. Never throw it. If you or anyone on board gets caught in the line, real danger may result.
- Carry two anchors, plenty of line. Judge proper scope by *indicated* weather, not by weather when anchoring.
- Always carry an anchor light at night.
- When fending off with a boat-hook, never brace it against your body. A sudden surge may cause internal injuries. Hold pole or bar to one side of body.
- When fending off, don't get caught between boat and dock. Carry a fender by a line and drop it where contact between boat and dock is indicated. In many cases, it is better to hang the fenders from pilings or bollards on the docks.
- Always watch the sky for change of weather. Plan your trips after you have checked the local forecast.
- Many local radio stations have special weather broadcasts for mariners. Have a written schedule on board, showing time and dial spot for marine weather broadcasts.
- Be alert for danger signals such as sudden changes in wind or rapidly gathering clouds. In a small boat, head for port as quickly as possible.
- Slack your halyards if rain is expected, whether sails are up or down.
- Change your mooring hawser in midseason. It will be safer to re-use in spring, whereas hawsers renewed in spring are at their weakest when autumn storms hit.
- On a sailboat, always flake your mainsheet as you haul it in, letting the coils fall at random. There is less danger of this mainsheet fouling than one carefully coiled.
- Never half hitch sheets or halyards on cleats. Once around and then successive figure eights will hold safely. Half hitches often jam when you most need to free them.

• When you drop anchor, it is sometimes desirable to tie a float or even a large wad of paper on a light line tied to the anchor to indicate the exact position of the anchor.

• If you carry pets aboard, it is always desirable to keep a harness on them. If they fall overboard, they can frequently be hauled in with a boat hook.

• As soon as bad weather threatens, have all passengers on deck don life jackets. Wearing a life jacket in stormy going is the mark of a good seaman, not of a coward.

• Know the limitations of your boat. Don't attempt off-shore cruising in outboards or day sailers.

• Have your engine well warmed up before leaving your mooring, slip or dock. Tight quarters such as these often require split-second maneuvering with quick bursts of speed that can stall a cold motor.

• Many charming shore-side hosts turn up an unexpected streak of sadism when they get guests aboard on a choppy day. However much it may inflate the skipper's ego to defy sea and spray, the really thoughtful owner will hold close to a weather shore and stay under the lee of the land until he is sure that his guests share his sturdy bravado and solid digestion.

• In tidal waters, when exploring strange waters and out of the way inlets, try to do so at low tide (and in any case not at high tide) so that you'll have a safety margin in case of grounding. When cruising new waters in rivers and lakes, watch the local boats and follow the parts of the channel they use. In general, the safest craft to follow are fishing boats, work boats and well-maintained old-timers. The riskiest to follow are the over-powered hot-rods.

• If you have trouble backing your single-screw powerboat, try shifting to neutral and then giving a short, sharp burst forward with full right or left rudder. The effect will be to impel the stern to port or starboard without imparting much forward motion to the boat.

LINES, KNOTS AND SPLICES

Knots, lines and splices help to dictate the ways a man handles his craft. Basic knowledge for the seaman

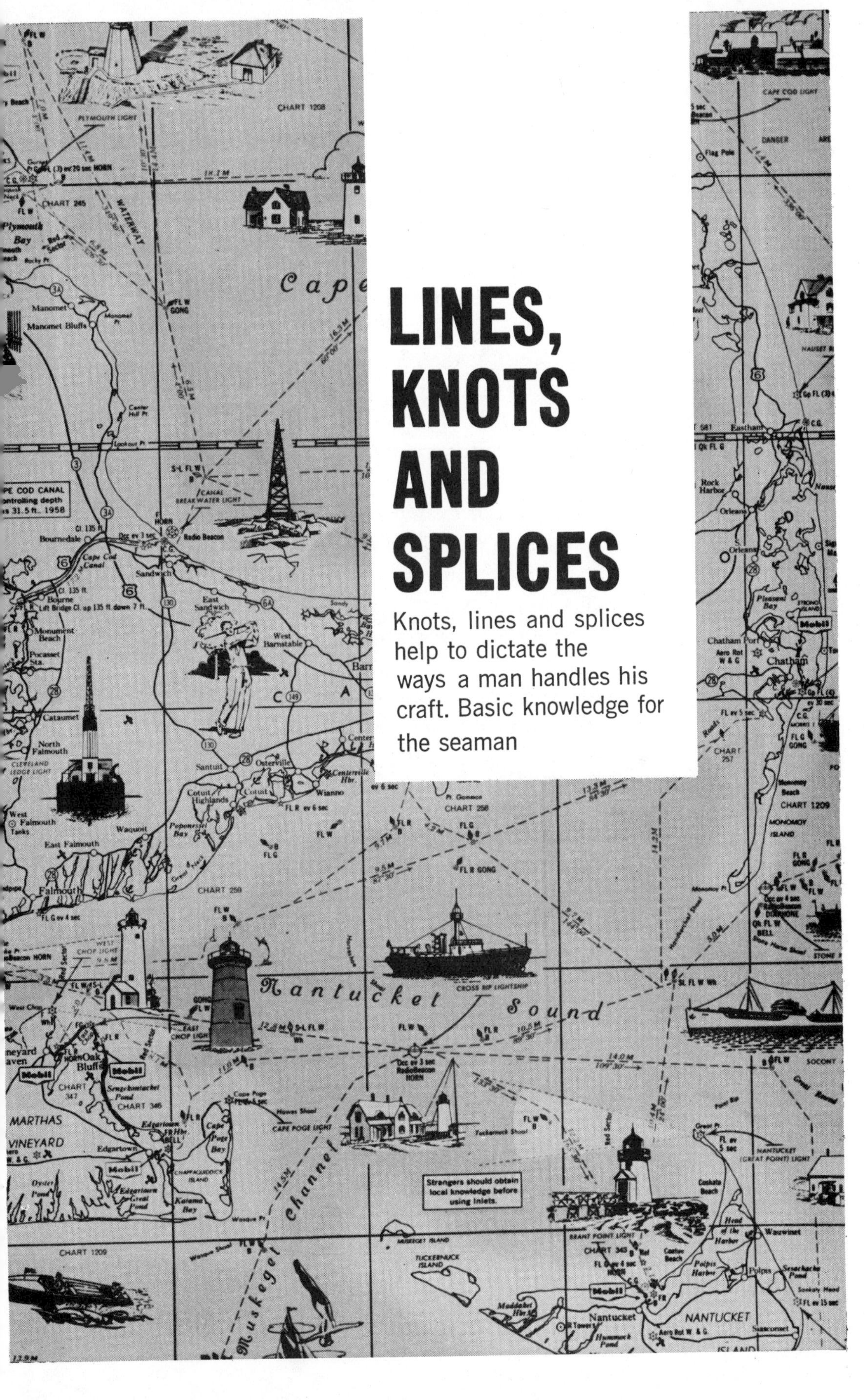

What cloth is to a suit, rope is to a line. It is an old naval riddle that there is only one rope on board a ship—the bell rope. Normally, ropes are referred to as ***lines.*** In turning a rope into a line, it may be served (bound), spliced and/or knotted.

There is perhaps no better index to a man's seamanship than his facility with knots. The landlubber regards the essential purpose of a knot as staying tied. The seaman knows that a good knot serves two functions: staying tied so long as that is necessary and coming rapidly untied when that is desired. For example, the granny or false reef knot may be as tight a knot as the reef. But it is a fingernail-breaker to untie when wet and after it has taken a strain.

Following are the most important knots. The good seaman should be able to tie them in total darkness or with his eyes closed. Practice and practice with a six foot length of line until you can make them automatically.

The ***Overhand*** and ***Figure Eight*** knots are chiefly useful to keep an unserved line from fraying or to keep any line from pulling through a block or other aperture.

The ***Reef*** — or ***Square*** — knot, probably the most useful of all knots, is strong, won't slip, is *easily tied* and *readily opened* by pushing the standing parts and ends toward the center of the knot. If the skipper wants to make it so that it will untie even more quickly, as when used for reefing sails, he will pass one end back through the bight. Like the half bow shoelace knots, it can then be untied simply by pulling on the loose end.

The ***Bowline*** is an eye knot, useful for putting a temporary bight or loop in the end of a line.

It is the best and most useful knot for fastening the end of a line to another object. It does not slip and is readily untied. It is a good knot to pass through a ring-bolt in towing a dinghy and it is a favorite knot for securing a sheet to a sail. Its other uses aboard ship are numberless.

The knot most used for securing dock lines to bollards and pilings is the ***Clove Hitch.*** The illustration shows how the hitch is made. In actual practice, the experienced sailor will make a pair of bights and flip them over the top of a piling as fast as one can say the words. Another simple, much-favored method is the ***Eyesplice*** bight.

In tying to a dock over night, the ***Towboat*** and ***Magnus Hitches*** enjoy some advantages over the Clove Hitch in that they do not jam or slip sideways and are less tempting for another skipper to tamper with in case he decides to use one of your bollards for one of his dock lines too.

Among the other major working knots, the ***Sheepshank*** is best for shortening up a line. As long as there is a strain on the line, it will not slip, yet lets go readily when the strain is relaxed.

For marrying two lines of different sizes, the ***Sheet Bend*** is a traditionally-accepted knot. It is rarely used now for its original purpose: bending a sheet onto the clew of a sail.

The ***Rolling Hitch*** is useful in securing a smaller line to a larger one when the latter is under strain. It is also a first-class knot for securing a line to a spar. It is easily tied wrong, in which case it will almost certainly let go or jam.

The ***Carrick Bend*** and more particularly the ***Double Carrick Bend*** is most useful when marrying two heavy lines such as hawsers. Its chief

OVERHAND

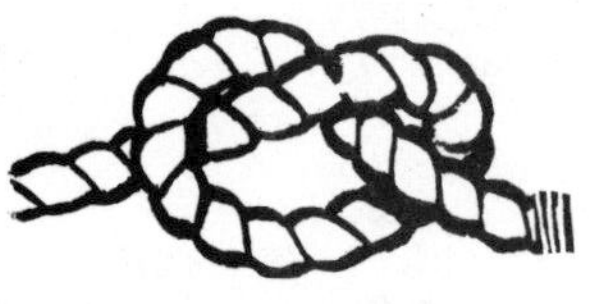

FIGURE EIGHT

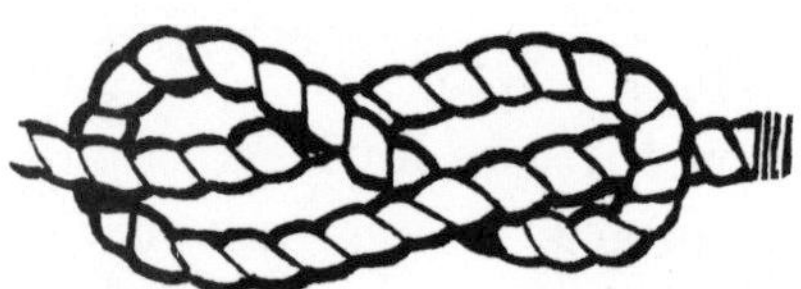

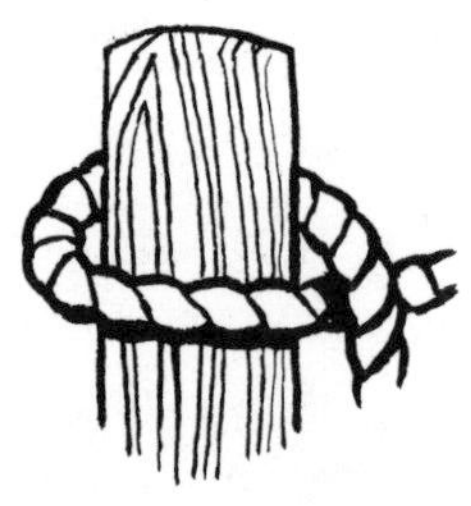

REEF or SQUARE KNOT

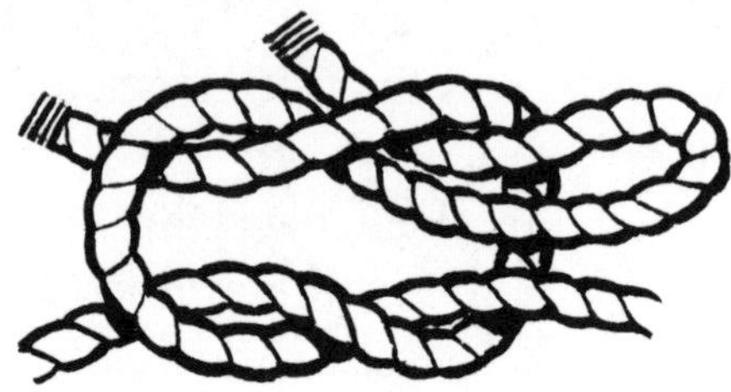

BOWLINE

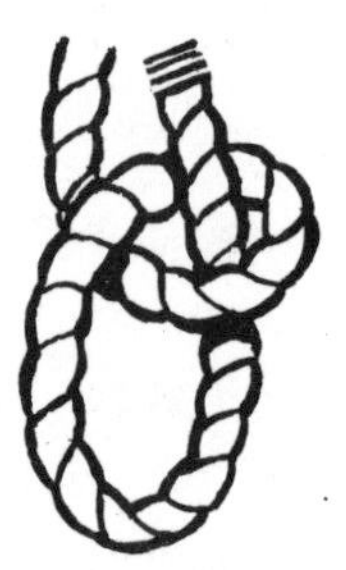

CLOVE HITCH

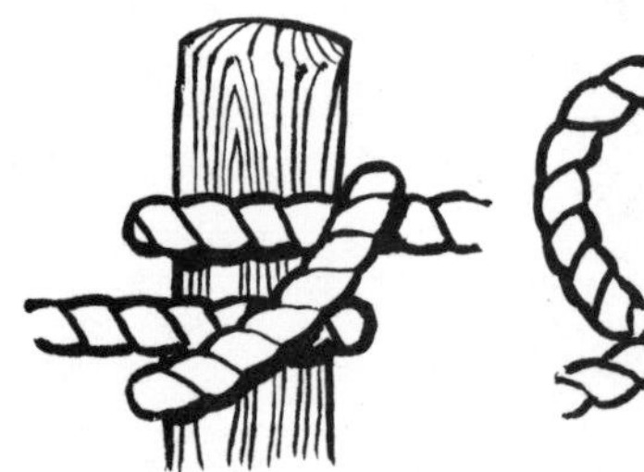

EYESPLICE BIGHT

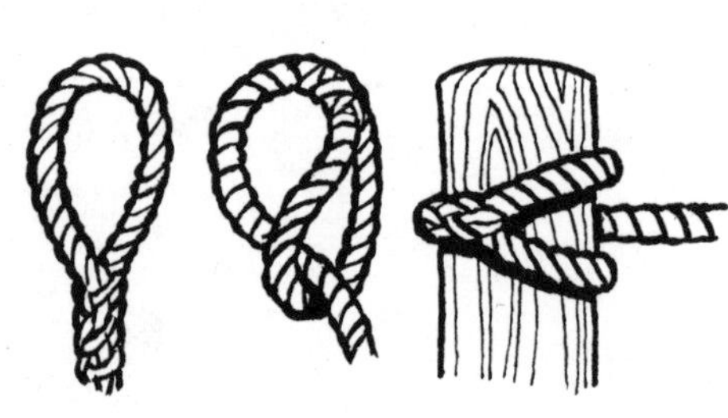

TOWBOAT HITCH

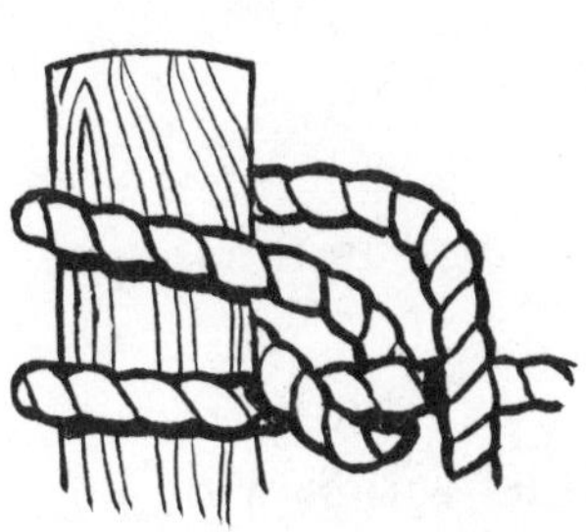

MAGNUS HITCH

SHEEPSHANK

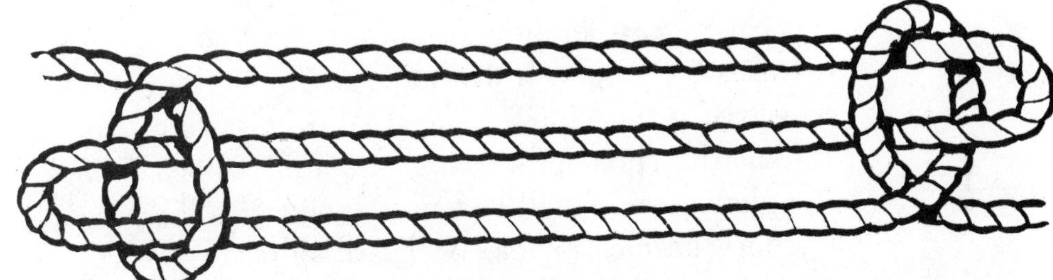

SHEET BEND

DOUBLE SHEET BEND

ROLLING HITCH

CARRICK BEND

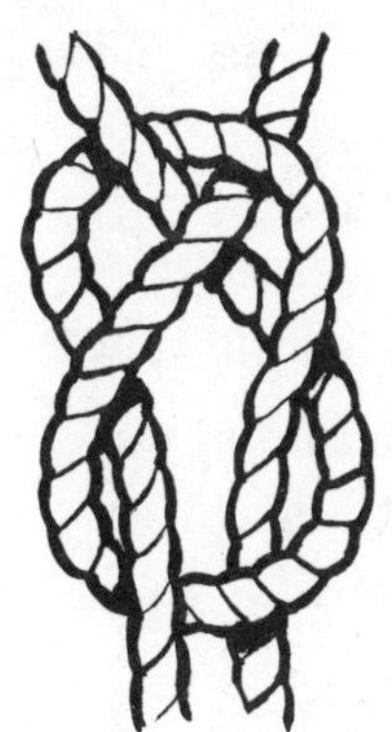

DOUBLE CARRICK BEND

WHIPPING

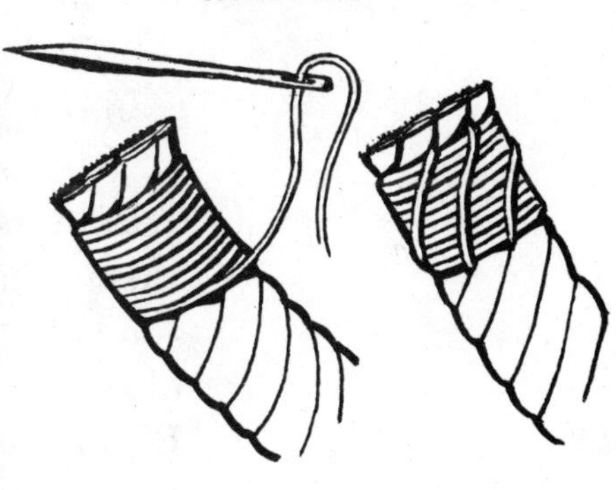

virtue is that it avoids sharp turns in the line which would fray or deform it.

Serving, or ***whipping,*** keeps the ends from unlaying. It is best accomplished with sewing needle, waxed linen line and a sewing palm. One of the wise early investments that a good skipper will make is in a sewing kit. Sewing equipment, together with canvas for patching sails in the case of a sailboat, or tarps or awnings in the case of power, linen thread, beeswax for waxing, a ball of marlin (heavy waxed twine) for seizing, needles, a sewing palm, a marlin spike for splicing, and a fid for heavy line splicing, should all be kept together in a ditty bag. Since needles for use on board ship are normally triangular in shape and much heavier than regular darning needles, the palm is used instead of the housewife's thimble.

There are many ways of whipping or serving the end of a manila, nylon or dacron line, but the most satisfactory is to wrap ten to fifteen turns of thread around the freshly-cut end and then sew diagonal bindings with the lay of the rope. The purpose of waxing thread or marlin is to keep it from slipping or fraying.

Splicing consists in bending a line back upon itself to form a loop or bight, or marrying two lines together at the ends. Although some rope is braided, we shall assume that the rope which forms our lines is three-strand manila or synthetic fiber.

It is desirable to wrap a couple of turns of electrical tape around each of the strand ends to keep them from fraying as the splice is being made. Dacron or nylon may be singed. The most common way of securing two lines together is with a **short splice.** Begin by unlaying the strands of each line from

SHORT SPLICE

LONG SPLICE

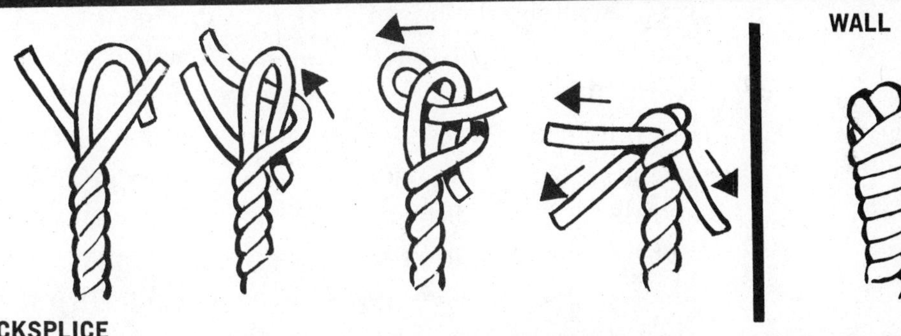

BACKSPLICE

EYESPLICE

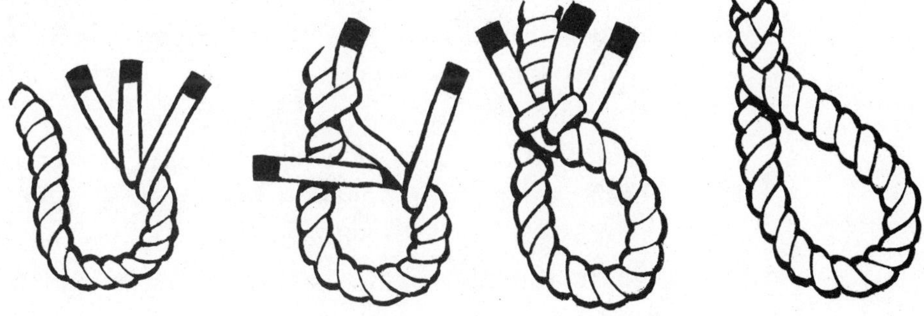

three to six inches in proportion to the thickness of the rope. Intertwine the strands, as indicated in the illustration. Bring the lines snugly together. Now temporarily fasten the lines in this position with a piece of strong thread or yarn wrapped tightly outside the joining. Now tuck one strand first over, then under, two strands of the opposite line. The tucking should be across the lay of the line. Take the next strand and tuck it over and under the opposite strand adjoining. Do the same with the third strand. Then repeat the process, continuing to weave the lines together and pulling each tuck slightly as you go. A short splice consists of at least three rounds of tucks.

A ***long splice*** is used when the splice must pass through a block or other aperture where a short splice would be too thick. For this splice, the two rope ends should be unlayed for quite a distance and then snugged together as in the short splice. Next, unlay one of the strands even farther than the others and, as it is unlayed, slip one of the strands from the opposite line into the open groove, spiraling along the line and keeping the strand tightly twisted so that it appears to take the exact place of the unlayed strand. Now cut off all but about three inches of the displaced strand. At this point, reverse the process in the opposite direction—that is, unlay a strand of the previously whole rope. You will now have three pairs of ends about three inches long. Each pair should be married with a simple overhand knot. The ends are then tucked under and over as in a short splice, the ends of each pair going in opposite directions. Each strand is subsequently divided into thirds and tucked, and finally the line is pulled and pounded by mallet, or rolled under foot, to smooth and tighten it.

Some skippers like to finish the end of a line with a ***Backsplice*** or ***Crown knot*** instead of whipping. With the end upward, separate the three strands. Now loop the center one back and down. The right-hand strand is twisted behind the rope to hold the loop firm and the left-hand strand is run through the loop. The other strands are now tucked into the rope in order, over and under.

The ***Eyesplice*** is used to provide a permanent bight or loop in the end of a line. With the end of the line in the right hand and the remainder (or standing part) leading away from you and held in the left, separate the three strands of the end. As always, start tucking the center strand under an opened strand of the standing part. Now take the left-hand strand and tuck it under the strand to the left of the one under which your center strand was tucked. The right-hand strand now goes under the next strand. Pull each tuck cleanly snug as you splice, always tucking from right to left against the lay of the standing part of the line.

The knots and splices described here are only an introduction to the subject, but they cover the major uses that the average yachtsman will require. To those who find the subject interesting, the literature is enormous, the diversion endless.

A rope is made of ***strands*** which are in turn made of ***yarns*** which are made of ***fibers.*** Each successive unit is twisted in a direction opposite to the previous one, allowing rope to hold its twist.

Wire rope is usually made up of six twisted strands, each of which contains a varying number of twisted wires. Jibstay and preventer stay wires are usually single strands made up of seventeen wires, giving the rope a smoother surface. Modern yachts use either galvanized or stainless steel wire rigging, solid or rod-rigging is used on racing craft.

Fiber rope is measured by ***circumference.***

Wire rope is measured by ***diameter.***

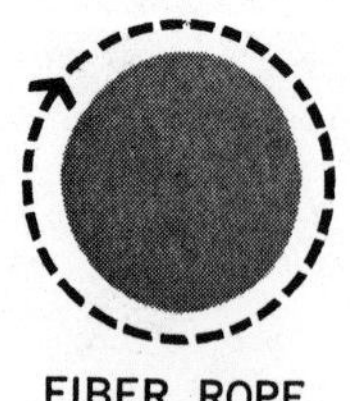

FIBER ROPE MEASURE

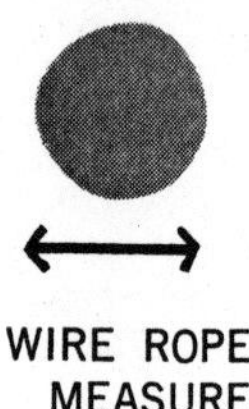

WIRE ROPE MEASURE

Fiber rope may shrink when drying after being wet. Lines which are belayed taut should be slack when wet; otherwise they are weakened by strain if they become too taut as they dry.

Rope may deteriorate if allowed to remain wet. For this reason it should be coiled and hung by a loop to dry. Many boat owners like to flemish a line (coil it in a tight, flat spiral) on deck be-cause it presents an attractive appearance. This is not recommended since it allows both line and deck to remain damp for considerable time after rain.

Wire rope should be stowed in reels. It should never be allowed to kink. Turns should never overlap on a winch or drum. If the wire rope is run through blocks, the sheaves of the blocks should be of larger diameter than those used for fiber rope. Wire rope should not be made to turn sharply. Once broken wires appear, the wire rope should be replaced.

When heaving a line onto a dock or another ship, the best technique is to hold the line coiled in the left hand, coils being about the size of the bight or loop in the end of the line. Now take the bight and about three coils in the right hand and heave only this much, while holding the rest of the coil in the left hand free to run. If the first heave does not succeed, the whole line should be drawn back aboard and recoiled before a second heave is attempted. An infallible mark of a landlubber is the heaving of a fouled or tangled line. Another lubber's mistake is to heave a line without having the ship's end made fast on deck.

Most rope is right-handed and should be coiled, or flemished, in a clock-wise direction. As the rope is coiled, twists should be shaken out so that the coil lies smoothly without bights or twists.

Flemishing

If new rope kinks badly, it may be freed by trailing it in the water astern. Great care should be taken that the line does not foul the propeller.

With the advent of the synthetic fibers, yachtsmen have discovered certain notable advantages in strength, rot- and mildew-resistance, as well as ease of handling, over natural fibers. Manufacturers claim that nylon lines are about twice as strong as natural fibers and dacron lines about 1½ times as strong. They also claim up to double the wear. Needless to say, the synthetic lines are more expensive than those of natural fibers.

Nylon lines are recommended for mooring lines and other uses where resiliency is important in resisting sudden strains. Their tendency to stretch makes them undesirable to use as sheets or halyards.

Dacron lines are preferable where minimal elasticity plus durability are important. They are ideally suited for sheets and other running rigging.

Dacron and nylon lines are spliced the same as natural fibers, except that at least two extra tucks are recommended because of the smoothness of the fibers. Properly-spliced lines have 90% or more of the strength of unspliced lines.

Lines of synthetic fibers may be cleaned by a vigorous application of soap or detergent and fresh water. Soaking in a detergent solution overnight will loosen grime and grease. They should be thoroughly rinsed in fresh water after washing.

BASIC NAVIGATION

To separate seamanship, navigation, boat handling and upkeep is a matter of convenience in presenting facts, but the separation is arbitrary. The good yachtsman dedicates himself to the whole subject of boats and boating. He is learning constantly—almost as much so after two decades as after two months. He could not be happy being an expert seaman and knowing nothing about navigation. Nor could he be a first-rate navigator without knowing about boat handling and upkeep.

The progression from seamanship to navigation is not like the progression from arithmetic to algebra. The study of seamanship continues long after the skipper has acquired skill in navigation. And although good equipment helps, perfection in navigation and seamanship does not depend on having the most modern or expensive equipment. The alert mind and body of the skipper are still the important elements in safe boat handling.

SECTION 10 ■ CHARTS AND COMPASS

Every skipper who wants to take his boat beyond local, familiar waters needs to know how to navigate. Navigating skillfully is one of the greatest satisfactions of owning a boat. Basically, it consists of overcoming a series of obstacles and winning a victory over wind, wave and shoal.

Navigation is the science of safely conducting a vessel from a point of departure to a destination, along known courses at known speeds.

On long off-shore trips, the navigator may use celestial navigation, taking observations of sun, stars and moon, or he may combine this with electronic devices such as radar, loran, consolan and radio direction finders.

By far the most frequent form of navigation used by yachtsmen is called ***piloting.*** Piloting is concerned with guiding a vessel along coasts and waterways from one recognized, fixed point to another. Piloting requires knowledge of the boat's position, its course, its speed and the potential hazards along the way.

Position is determined by the use of a chart. The vessel's location on the chart can be fixed by bearings on two or more known points, or bearing and distance from a single known point.

The ***course*** is the best route to follow from a point of departure to a destination. Usually it is the shortest safe line. Course is laid out on the chart and kept by following the compass.

Charts are the mariner's road maps. Where a road map is two-dimensional, however, the chart supplies a third dimension: water depths and land heights.

The vertical lines on a chart represent imaginary

circles around the earth through the North and South Poles. They are called ***meridians of longitude.***

The horizontal lines, all running parallel to the equator, are called ***parallels of latitude.***

Measurement of longitude begins arbitrarily at Greenwich, England. All meridians west from Greenwich to a point in mid-Pacific, exactly half way around the world, are West Longitude. All meridians east from Greenwich to the same line are East Longitude. Parallels north of the Equator are North Latitude, south of the equator are South Latitude.

Any point on the earth's surface can be accurately located in terms of latitude and longitude. A degree is subdivided into 60 minutes. A minute is divided into 60 seconds. For instance, the location of Fort Sumter (the site of a marine radio-beacon) is: lat. 32° 45′ 12″ N., long. 79° 53′ 02″ W.

A ***nautical mile*** is 6080 feet long. It is longer than a land mile in order that it may correspond to one minute of latitude.

A ***knot*** is a rate of speed—not a distance. It is equal to one nautical mile per hour. Never say "knots per hour."

For use in navigating, the spherical grid of latitudes and longitudes is transferred onto a flat sheet or chart. Since a globe cannot be precisely represented on a flat surface, two chief types of projections are used:

The ***Mercator projection*** is used along the coasts. This method assumes the earth to be a cylinder which is unrolled. Distortion occurs in high latitudes but in most waters the charts are quite accurate.

The ***polyconic projection*** is used in the inland lakes. This divides the earth's surface into a series of cones which are opened out. For use on the lakes, the method is completely reliable.

Charts usually bear a distance scale. For quick reference with dividers, a minute of latitude may be picked up from the side of the chart and used as a mile. Never use minutes of longitude at the top and bottom of the chart.

When checking depths, be sure to note from the legend whether the figures represent feet or fathoms. A ***fathom*** equals six feet.

The symbols and abbreviations are also interpreted in the legend. For a complete description of all symbols used on charts, obtain the National Ocean Survey Chart #1 called "Nautical Chart Symbols and Abbreviations."

Coastal charts and the handy new Small Craft Charts can be ordered from the National Ocean Survey, Riverdale, Maryland 20840.

Lakes charts may be obtained from the U.S. Lake Survey Office, Detroit, Michigan.

Charts are also available at official prices from

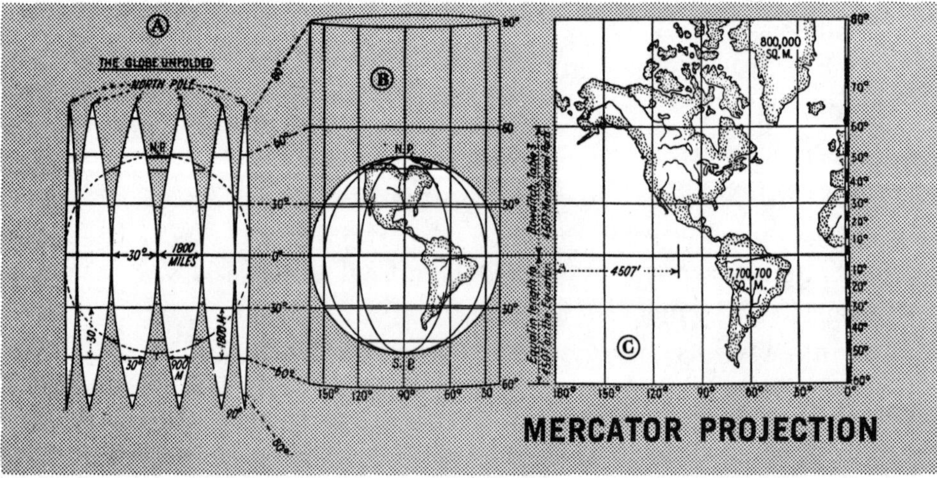

MERCATOR PROJECTION

certain marine suppliers and map stores. Catalogues may be obtained from the government without charge. Charts are corrected annually. Use only up-dated charts.

Notices to Mariners, containing current information on navigational matters, are available from the U.S. Navy Hydrographic Office, Washington. Local notices may be had at nearest Coast Guard office.

Charts issued by oil companies are useful for planning itineraries, estimating distances and locating points of interest. They should not be used for navigating.

The ***compass*** is the most important piece of navigational equipment on your boat. The principle of the compass may best be understood if the earth is thought of as a huge magnetized sphere. A magnetized needle, held anywhere on its surface, will tend to line up with the magnetic lines of force of the earth. If the North Magnetic and South Magnetic Poles were exactly at the North and South Poles, magnetic compasses would indicate true directions.

However, in actual fact, the North Magnetic Pole

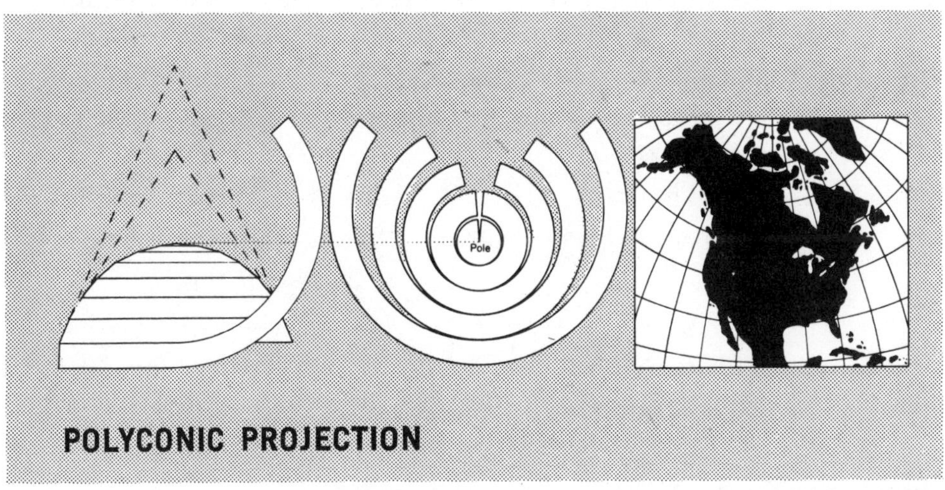

POLYCONIC PROJECTION

is over a thousand miles from the North Pole and situated to the north of Hudson Bay. The South Magnetic Pole is located far south of Australia. Because the North Magnetic Pole and the True North Pole are almost in a line from Lake Michigan, sailors in those waters have virtually no variation. In the North Atlantic, however, magnetic variation may range as high as 30 degrees and more.

Variation changes slightly from year to year, but for most purposes may be thought of as virtually constant. Each government chart has one or more compass roses indicating the local variation. On large-scale charts, the variation will usually be the same over the entire chart.

The principle of the compass has been known since long before the time of Columbus. A magnetized needle, if free to pivot, will line up in the earth's lines of force, that is, with one end pointing toward the North Magnetic Pole. The correction to True North is then made by allowing for the local variation.

The simplest compass is a magnetized sewing needle, carefully rested on the surface of a glass or dish of water, so that it floats. It will line up pointing to the North Magnetic Pole. The woodsman's compass is the next simplest. This watch-like apparatus is simply a magnetized needle free to pivot on a bearing.

The yachtsman's compass is the most complicated of these three. It consists of not one but a bundle of magnetized needles, bound together and mounted on a pivot in a sealed container called a compass bowl. Attached to the needles, but free to rotate in the bowl, is the round compass card showing all 360 degrees and 32 points. As you

will note from consulting the sample rose, North is actually 000°, East is 090°, South is 180° and West is 270°.

The sealed compass bowl is filled with liquid—usually 55% water and 45% alcohol to keep it from freezing. The liquid buoys up the compass card so that it pivots easily and also damps the movements of the card to keep it from swinging rapidly or picking up engine vibrations.

On the inside of the compass bowl is scribed a vertical mark called a ***lubber's line.*** The lubber's line is precisely parallel to the fore and aft line of the ship. The direction indicated by the compass card at the lubber's line is the ***heading*** or direction of the ship's course.

The compass bowl is mounted to remain level regardless of the ship's heel or pitch, through an ingenious arrangement of ***gimbals.***

Compasses are preferably mounted in a shielded, lighted housing called a ***binnacle.***

Compass Errors

The woodsman accepts the reading of his pocket compass uncritically because he is interested only in approximate directions.

The yachtsman requires absolute accuracy; an error could mean damage or loss of ship and lives. He knows that he must correct his compass for two kinds of error.

Variation arises from the fact that the Magnetic North Pole is located a thousand miles from the True North Pole. Compass variations are known for all areas on earth. Each chart contains compass roses showing the variation in the area. In addition to changing from place to place, variation also changes from year to year.

Deviation is caused by metals in the boat which influence the compass to one side or another of North. Deviation may be reduced through the use of compensating magnets near the compass. Compass compensation, however, is a job for an expert.

Since deviation varies on different headings, each vessel should carry a card showing the amount of deviation on each point of the compass.

A third type of error may be introduced when a vessel heels over. ***Heeling*** error is less important in power craft than in sailboats.

There are a number of ways of checking deviation on the yachtsman's compass. The simplest for practical use is to set up a series of ranges or known courses in your local area in as wide a variety of directions as possible. These courses should be

SAMPLE DEVIATION TABLE

	For Magnetic Course	Steer (P.S.C.)		For Magnetic Course	Steer (P.S.C.)
N	0°	010°	S	180°	174°
	15°	027°		195°	188°
	30°	043°		210°	200°
NE	45°	057°	SW	225°	214°
	60°	070°		240°	230°
	75°	084°		255°	248°
E	90°	096°	W	270°	266°
	105°	108°		285°	285°
	120°	120°		300°	302°
SE	135°	132°	NW	315°	318°
	150°	147°		330°	338°
	165°	160°		345°	354°
			N	360°	010°

between such visible navigating marks as towers and lighthouses or identifiable marks ashore. From your chart, figure the magnetic course between a series of these marks as well as the reverse or reciprocal course. By steering a very steady course on these ranges, it is possible to determine the deviation error of the compass from the magnetic course as indicated by the chart. Where a sufficient variety of ranges between buoys does not exist, it is possible to cross the range on different headings and take a bearing on the mark as you cross. The helmsman checks the compass course and an observer checks the bearing of the known marks. By adding or subtracting the angular bearings, the skipper can determine the deviation on his compass heading.

The observations should also be done on reciprocals or reverses of each course. This method is usually somewhat less accurate since bearings must be made exactly as the range is crossed. Running ranges between known marks, where the course may be held until the helmsman and compass are both steady, may be considered more reliable.

SECTION 11 ■ LAYING OUT A COURSE

Before starting out on any trip across waters marked by aids to navigation, it is desirable to lay out a course. Certain articles are indispensable.

The local harbor entrance is usually a good point to take for departure. Now let your eye travel along the route to your destination. If you do not pass near any hazards, it is safe to lay out a direct course. Usually, you will have to break the long course up into shorter legs, each change calculated to avoid a danger or give you a chance to check your position.

A Simple Navigational Example:

A skipper in Little Neck Bay wants to head up Long Island Sound for a visit to Stamford Harbor. He consults his chart of Western Long Island (#1213, price $3.25) or his new Small Craft Chart (price $3.50) and observes that the shortest safe course, taking a departure from Stepping Stones light at the entrance to his harbor, leads him past Execution Rocks light (left to port) and up to Red Bell Buoy #32, off Stamford Harbor.

Since the Stepping Stones lighthouse is clearly visible, the skipper examines the harbor chart and notes that there is good water on a straight course between his mooring and the light. With his protractor, he now fixes a departure point where Stepping Stones light will bear due East. The arm of the protractor shows him that he has a clear course for several miles to Black Bell #25. Using the protractor as directed, he ascertains that this course is 035° True. Near Buoy #25, it will be necessary to adjust course. The course is now clear to #32 ("The Cows") off Stamford. However, the

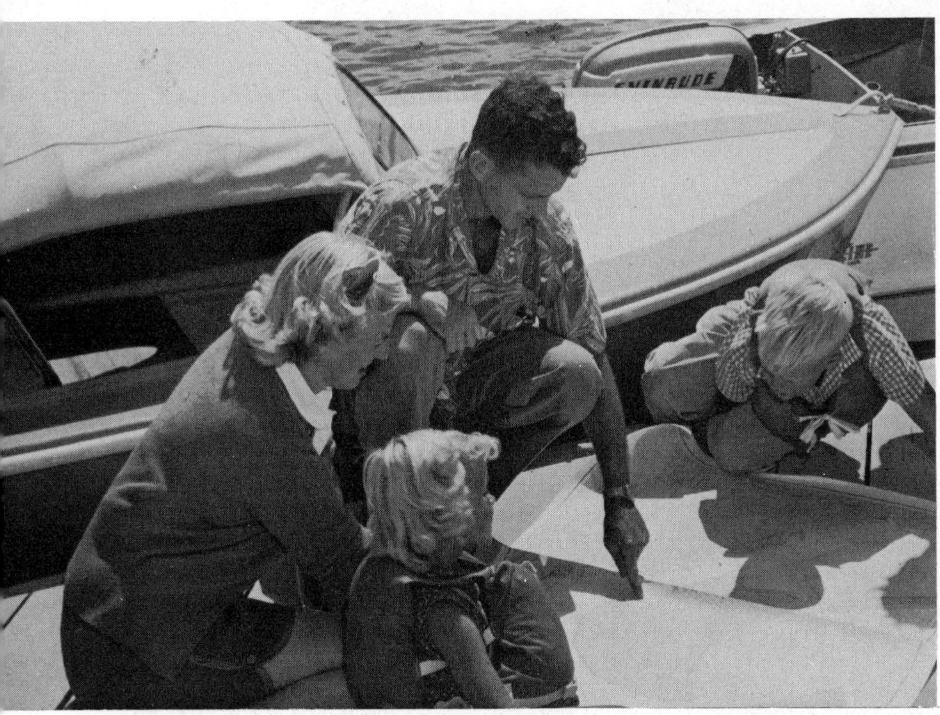

Planning the trip: a pair of boating parents plans a cruise and rendezvous. Note that both youngsters wear life jackets

skipper notes that he will pass about half a mile northwest of Matinicock Buoy #21, a good spot to check his position again. He then checks a point on his direct course where #21 will be directly abeam. At "The Cows" buoy (Red Bell #32), he will alter course to pass between the breakwater lights. This course proves to be 324° True. And once inside the breakwater, the channel course in the harbor is almost True North—357°. He notes that the channel is well buoyed with red nuns to starboard and black cans to port.

Having marked his course line with a good, sharp pencil, the skipper uses his dividers to check distances. Along the course line from Stepping Stones

Taking departure from Little Neck Bay (lower left foreground), skipper bound for Stam

ford Harbor passes Stepping Stones light and Execution Rocks, leaving them left to port

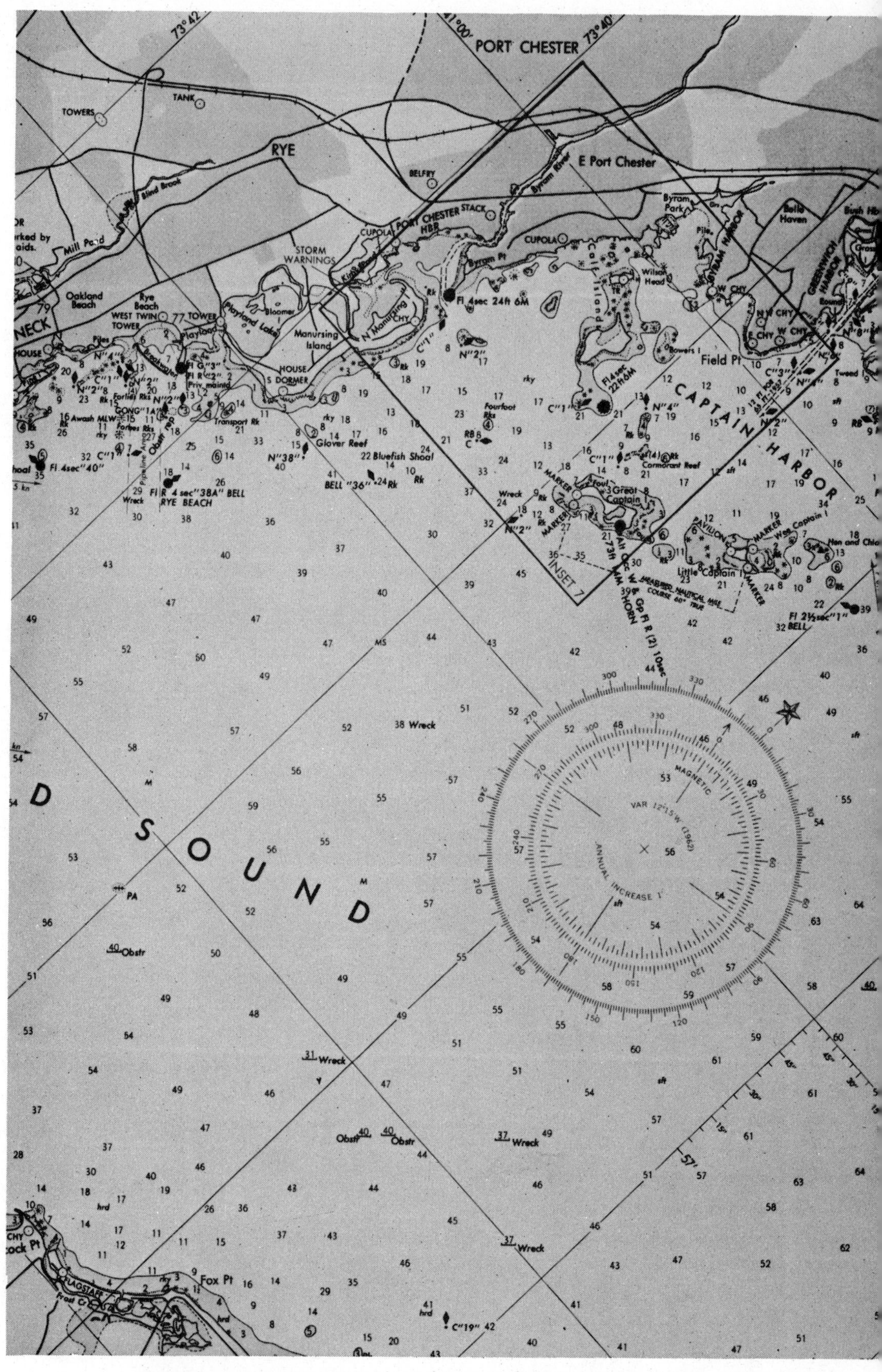

He proceeds northeast, first checking course at Buoy 23, to "The Cows" (Red Bell 3

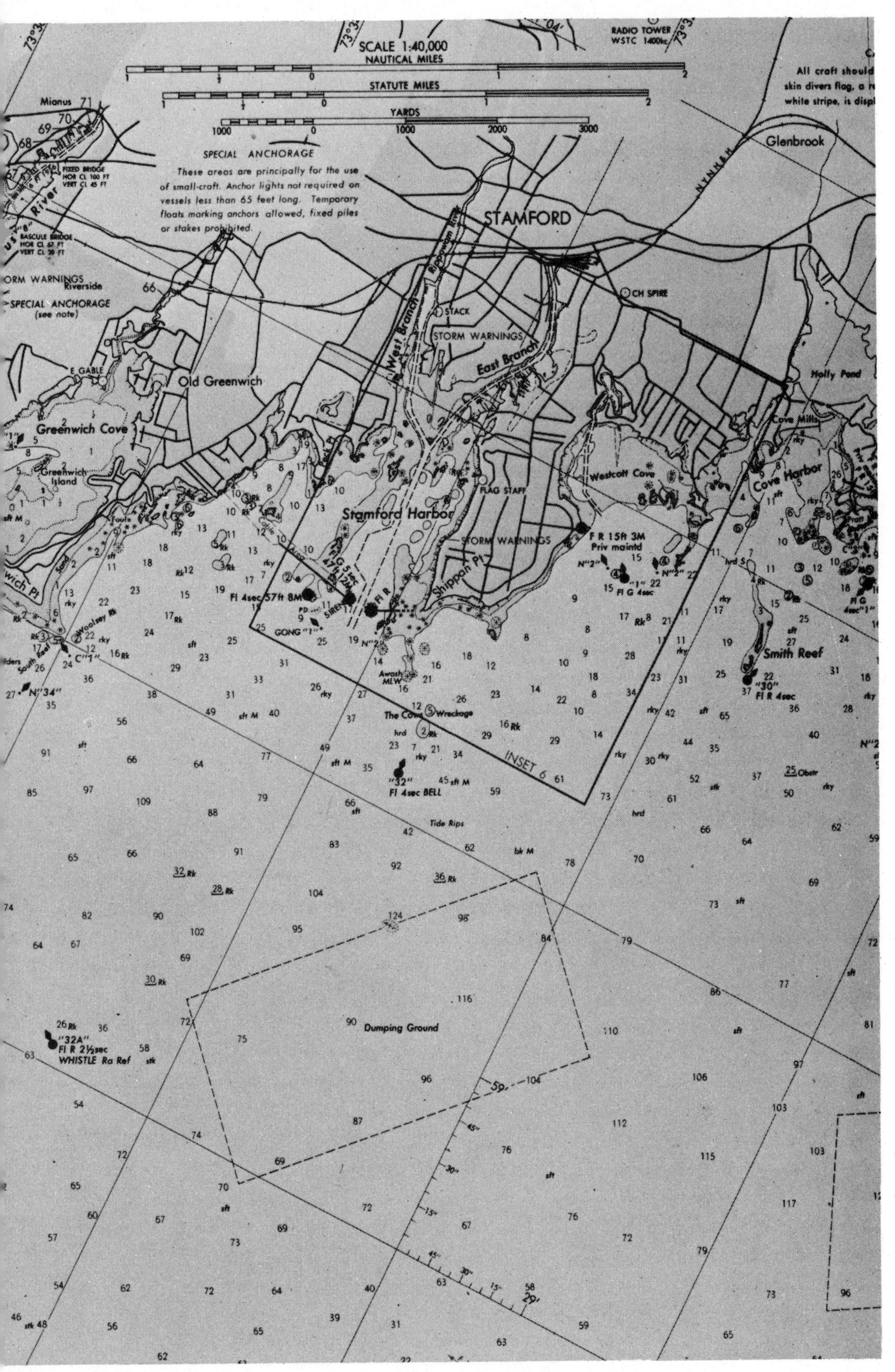

tside of Stamford. There he enters harbor channel, passing between breakwater lights

light to Black Bell #23, he indicates 4.1 miles. Along the course line from #23 to the mid-channel buoy, #21, he marks 4.6 miles and along the continuation of this line, from #21 to #32, he measures 7.1 miles. Finally, from #32 to the breakwater entrance, the distance is .9 mile.

Checking the compass rose, the skipper notes that the variation is 12° West. He then checks his deviation table for compass deviations on the True courses he has marked down. He adds the 12° westerly variation to the True course and adjusts for deviation. He then marks the resultant compass direction on each course line and folds his chart for ready reference under way. He notes that his light list is conveniently at hand in case he wants a more complete identification of any aid to navigation along his way, or in case of fog or darkness.

Ready now to get under way, our skipper turns to his checklist and verifies the precautions necessary for a safe trip.

Position Under Way

At various times while under way along your course line, you will want to check your progress and position. Even the steadiest helmsman will find his boat carried from its course by such influences as wind, sea and current. To know his position at all times between bearings and fixes, or where bearings are not possible, the skipper employs ***Dead Reckoning.*** These are the elements:

Log the time when you are at a known position and indicate the position on your chart.

Log your speed; log time of each speed change.

Log your course; log the time of each course alteration as you change course.

Separately, log direction and force of wind, sea and current.

Here is a simple example:

You get under way at 12 noon. Your speed is 10 knots. At 12:30, you are on course. Your present position? Five miles from your departure point along your course line. If wind and sea are dead ahead, you will be less than five miles along; if astern, more. If abeam, you will be to one side or the other of your course line.

The safe skipper verifies his position as often as possible under way by taking bearings. Let us assume that he looks about for landmarks. Astern, he sees Execution Rocks lighthouse. Abeam, he sees a standpipe in Hempstead Harbor which he locates on his chart. Off his quarter, he sees a tall radio tower which he finds on his chart at Columbia Island.

Lines drawn from these landmarks to his vessel must intersect and the resultant ***fix*** will be his position. The direction of the landmark from the vessel is a ***bearing.***

To take a bearing, it is desirable to have a pelorus on board. Basically, a pelorus consists of two sighting vanes and a compass rose. It is aimed, like a gunsight, at the object from which you desire a bearing. If the pelorus fits on the compass, the compass bearing can be read off directly. If a "dumb compass" or fixed compass rose is used, it must be aligned with the lubber's line, the helmsman must "mark" the course as the sight is taken, and the direction must be figured back to the compass. Assume that you now know the exact compass direction of the lighthouse, the radio tower and the standpipe. These are compass bearings and must be

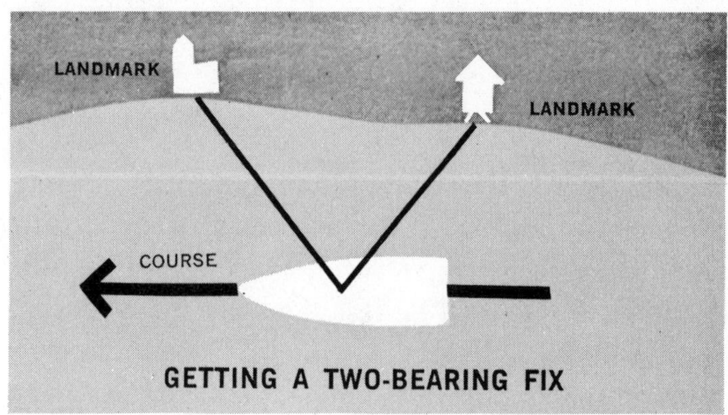

GETTING A TWO-BEARING FIX

figured back to True bearings for use on the chart. In this case, we take deviation and variation and add easterly or subtract westerly.

Here is a memory-aid that will help keep this straight:

From True to Compass,
With AWE you SEE***
From Compass to True,
It's SW—AE.

**Add Westerly Error; **Subtract Easterly Error.*

We now draw a line on the chart from the known position of the lighthouse to the unknown position of the boat. If our bearing sight on the light was exactly west or 270° True from the boat, the boat must be directly east or the reciprocal of 270° from the light. The reciprocal of any bearing is always 180° away or directly across the compass—in this case 090°T.

Now, with the protractor center at the light, draw a line along the reciprocal bearing toward the boat. (Since you know the light is west of you, obviously the line must be extended in an easterly direction.)

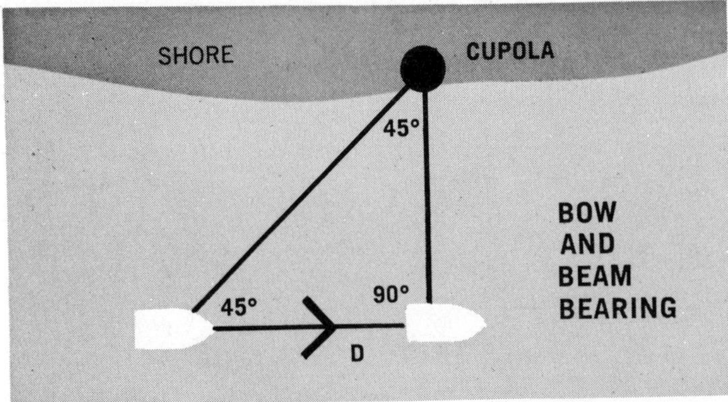

Draw a similar reciprocal bearing from the radio tower and the standpipe.

Your position is where the lines intersect.

N.B. If you take ten minutes to do your paper work, however, you had best run the position along your course line by the distance you have covered in those ten minutes, i.e., 1/6 of your hourly speed.

A fix may be obtained from two bearings, but three will be more accurate. If the observations are accurate, your intersection will be perfect. If not, the bearing lines will form a triangle.

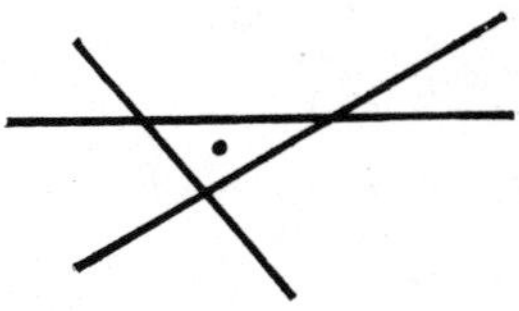

Take the center of this triangle as your position.

For comprehension and skill, the new skipper will want to depend on classwork and discussion with the instructor.

Distance Off Shore

In avoiding rocks and shoals or locating buoys in limited visibility, the skipper will often want to know his exact distance off shore. Let us assume, for example, that only one recognizable landmark is visible—a cupola on a point.

Distance off shore may readily be gauged by bow

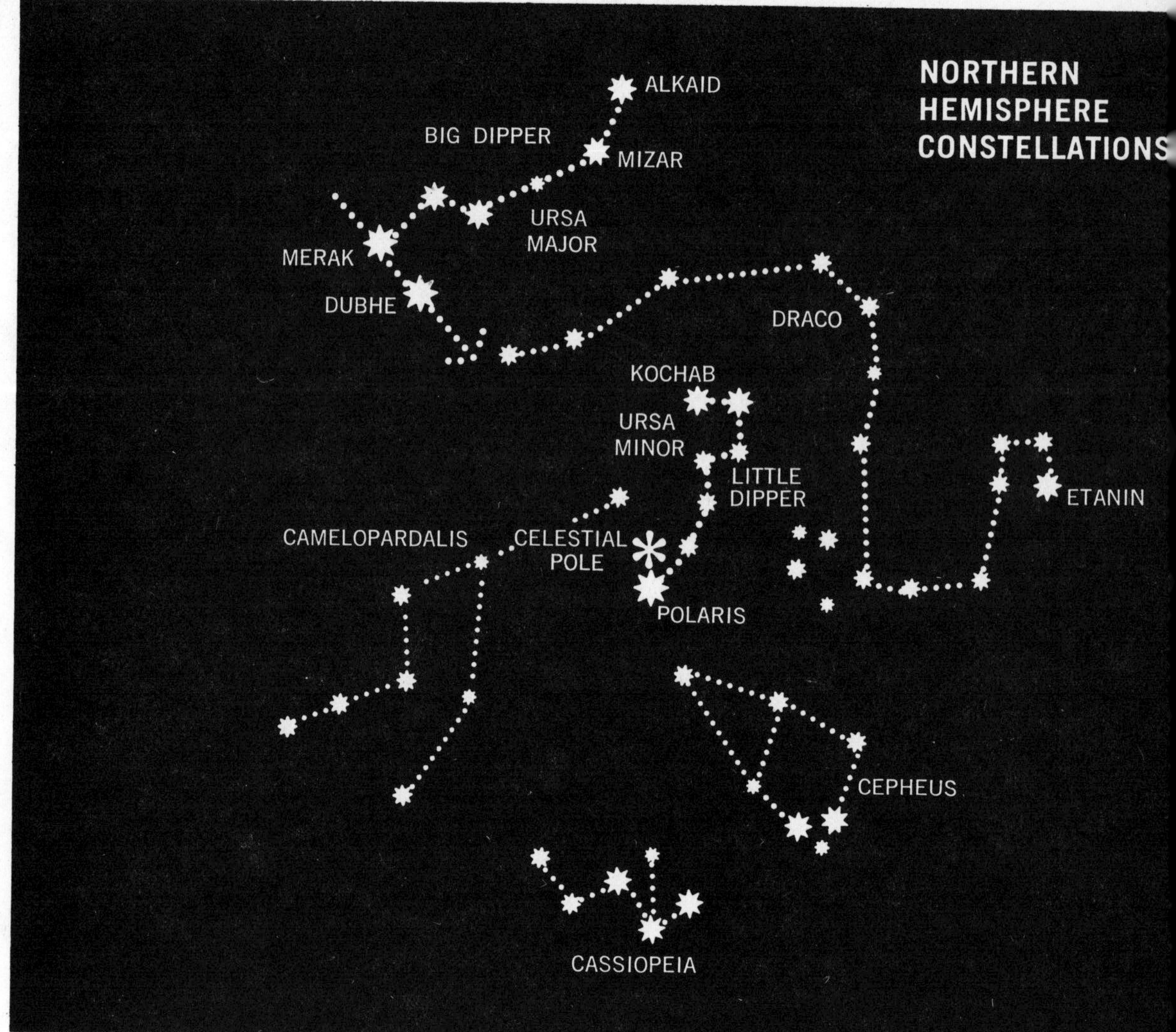

and beam bearings. Clock or watch time is taken as the cupola comes broad on the bow—that is, bears exactly 45° from the ship's heading, halfway between dead ahead and directly abeam. Speed is noted and maintained. When the landmark is directly abeam, the time is taken again. The distance of the vessel off shore is now exactly equal to the distance between observations, because the sides of any 45° right triangle are equal.

Some skippers scribe, paint or mark with studs the 45° and 90° angles on cabin top or on bridge. Similar geometric rules apply for bearings taken at

MISSISSIPPI RIVER BUOYAGE SYSTEM

Left descending bank		Right descending bank
LIGHTED BUOYS These buoys have no special shape. Flashing characteristic usually same as for shore light.		**LIGHTED BUOYS** These buoys have no special shape. Flashing characteristic usually same as for shore light.
LIGHTED JUNCTION BUOYS Mark junctions and obstructions where preferred channel is to right—but may be passed on either hand.		**LIGHTED JUNCTION BUOYS** Mark junctions and obstructions where preferred channel is to left—but may be passed on either hand.
UNLIGHTED BUOYS NUN BUOYS Various types are used, but color and shape distinctions are maintained.		**UNLIGHTED BUOYS CAN BUOYS** Various types are used, but color and shape distinctions are maintained.
JUNCTION BUOYS Mark junctions and obstructions where preferred channel is to right—but may be passed on either hand.		**JUNCTION BUOYS** Mark junctions and obstructions where preferred channel is to left—but may be passed on either hand.
QUARANTINE BUOYS No special shape. Identify quarantine areas. Warning to keep clear.		**QUARANTINE BUOYS** No special shape. Identify quarantine areas. Warning to keep clear.
ANCHORAGE BUOYS No special shape. Identify anchorage grounds and safety harbors.		**ANCHORAGE BUOYS** No special shape. Identify anchorage grounds and safety harbors.
DREDGING BUOYS No special shape. Identify dredging operations. Warning to keep clear.		**DREDGING BUOYS** No special shape. Identify dredging operations. Warning to keep clear.
SPECIAL PURPOSE BUOYS No special shape. Stripes may be either horizontal or vertical.		**SPECIAL PURPOSE BUOYS** No special shape. Stripes may be either horizontal or vertical.

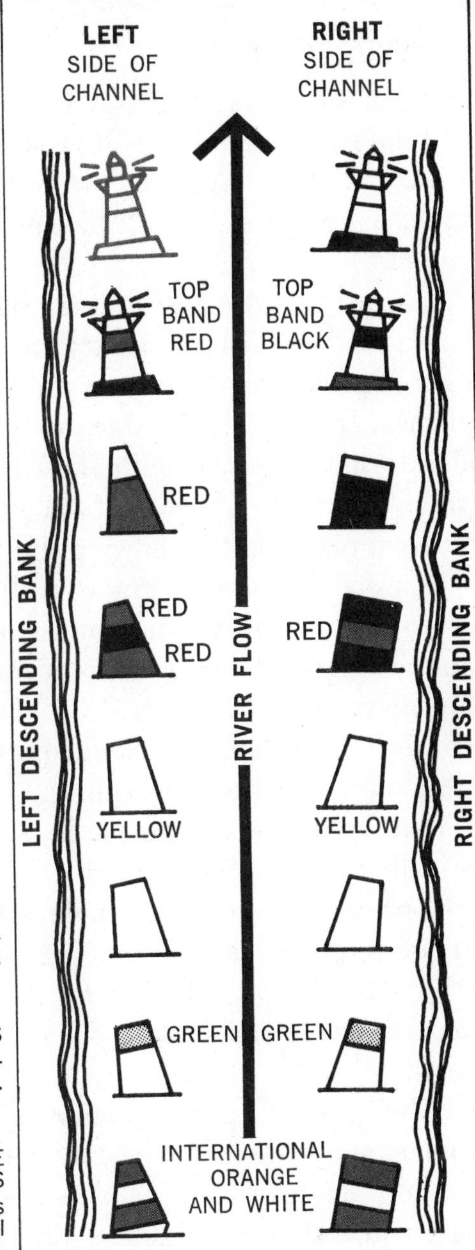

Note: In the Mississippi River System, the designations "left" and "right" used to denote the bank or side of channel are as observed looking downstream.

30° and 60°.

SECTION 12 ■ RIVER PILOTING

Since the days of Mark Twain, the challenge of piloting on the Mississippi and other Western Rivers has been legendary. Here the light list and the chart are the Alpha and Omega of safe navigation.

Before you take your first cruise, make sure you have all the charts necessary for the waters you plan to sail. Familiarize yourself with the meaning of chart symbols and be able to identify the various aids to navigation. Obtain the current and applicable Notices to Mariners from the Coast Guard.

Then observe the following suggestions:

• In unfamiliar waters, cruise upstream first. Your speed will be slower, your control of the boat surer and, if you do go aground, the current will help not hinder you.

• Learn as much as you can about the local waters from more experienced boatmen.

• Take frequent soundings. In shallow water, a lead line may be supplanted by a boat hook, fish pole or oar. A long, sturdy pole is useful for pushing off in case of light grounding.

• Note the course followed by other vessels, particularly commercial craft. Their captains are experts.

• If you ground, reverse promptly, but do not race your engine. In shallow water, the mud and sand you stir up may clog your cooling system, overheat and stall your engine. Shift passengers from the bow or grounded side to the stern or buoyant side.

• Constantly observe the surface of the water before

WHERE TO OBTAIN LOCAL CHARTS

UNITED STATES COASTAL WATERS
Environmental Science Services Administration
National Oceanographic and Atmospheric Administration
Washington, D.C. 20025

GREAT LAKES
U.S. Army Engineer District
Lake Survey, Corps of Engineers
630 Federal Building
Detroit, Michigan 48226

FOREIGN WATERS
Oceanographic Distribution Office
U.S. Naval Supply Depot
Philadelphia, Pennsylvania 19120

ILLINOIS WATERWAY (LAKE MICHIGAN TO MISSISSIPPI RIVER)
MISSISSIPPI RIVER (CAIRO, ILLINOIS TO MINNEAPOLIS, MINNESOTA)
U.S. Army Engineer District, Chicago
Corps of Engineers
219 Dearborn Street
Chicago, Illinois 60604

MISSISSIPPI (CAIRO, ILLINOIS TO GULF OF MEXICO)
U.S. Army Engineer
Corps of Engineers
P.O. Box 60
Vicksburg, Mississippi 39181

OHIO RIVER AND TRIBUTARIES
Corps of Engineers
P.O. Box 1159
Cincinnati, Ohio 45201

TENNESSEE VALLEY AUTHORITY RESERVOIRS
TENNESSEE RIVER AND TRIBUTARIES
Tennessee Valley Authority
Maps and Enginneering Section
Knoxville, Tennessee 37900

TOPOGRAPHIC MAPS OF THE UNITED STATES
U.S. Geological Survey
Washington, D.C. 20025

you. Eddies, ripples and swirls all have meaning. Even the character of your wake changes as you enter shallower water.

• Remember that you, as skipper, are responsible for the safety of your boat and those aboard. Lend your ears and your voice to your company but keep your eyes for the river and the boat.

AIDS TO NAVIGATION ■ SECTION 13

In 1915, the Lifesaving Service and the Revenue Cutter Service were combined to form the Coast Guard. In 1939, the Lighthouse Service was added. Since that time, the Coast Guard has been respon-

AIDS TO NAVIGATION ON NAVIGABLE WATER

LATERAL SYSTEM AS SEEN ENTERING FROM SEAWARD

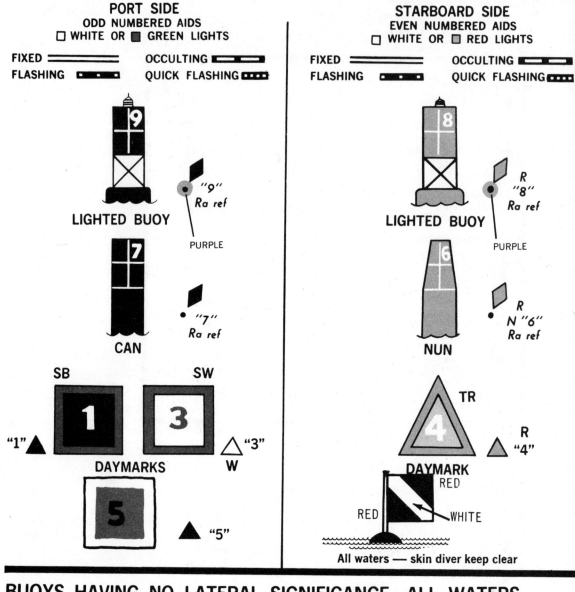

PORT SIDE

ODD NUMBERED AIDS

☐ WHITE OR ■ GREEN LIGHTS

FIXED ══════ OCCULTING

FLASHING QUICK FLASHING

9
"9"
Ra ref
LIGHTED BUOY
PURPLE
7
"7"
Ra ref
CAN
SB
SW
1
3
"1"
"3"
W
DAYMARKS
5
"5"

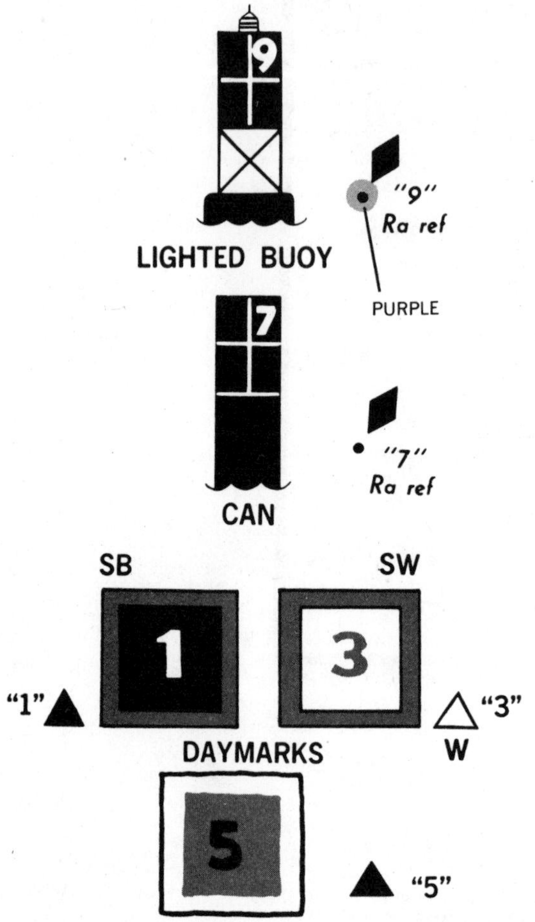

STARBOARD SIDE

EVEN NUMBERED AIDS

☐ WHITE OR ■ RED LIGHTS

FIXED ══════ OCCULTING

FLASHING QUICK FLASHING

8
R
"8"
Ra ref
LIGHTED BUOY
PURPLE
6
R
N "6"
Ra ref
NUN
TR
4
R
"4"
DAYMARK
RED
RED
WHITE

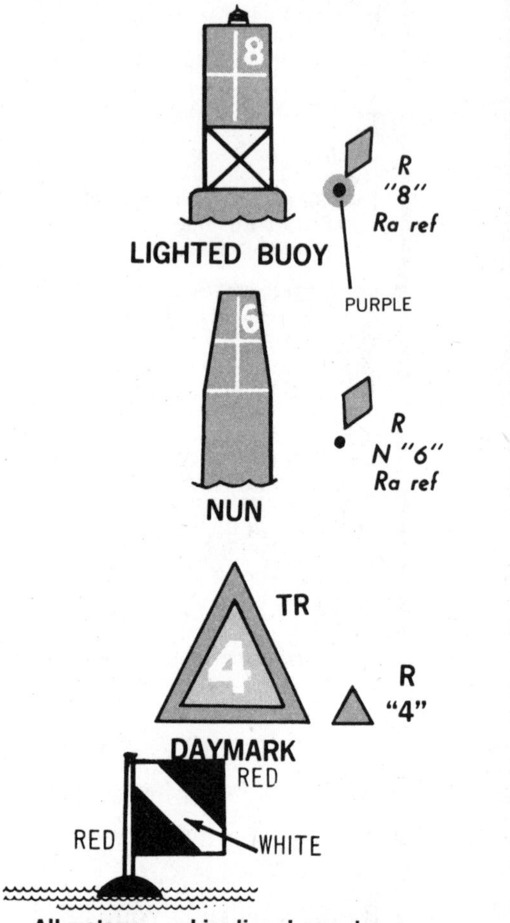

All waters — skin diver keep clear

BUOYS HAVING NO LATERAL SIGNIFICANCE—ALL WATERS

SHAPE HAS NO SIGNIFICANCE
NO NUMBERS—MAY BE LETTERED
MAY BE LIGHTED

ANY COLOR LIGHT EXCEPT
RED OR GREEN

FIXED
FLASHING
OCCULTING

BROWN
WOr
C Ra ref
SPECIAL PURPOSE
YELLOW
Y
C Ra ref
QUARANTINE ANCHORAGE
N
W
C "N"
Ra ref
ANCHORAGE
BW
C
Ra ref
FISH NET AREA
GW
C
Ra ref
DREDGING

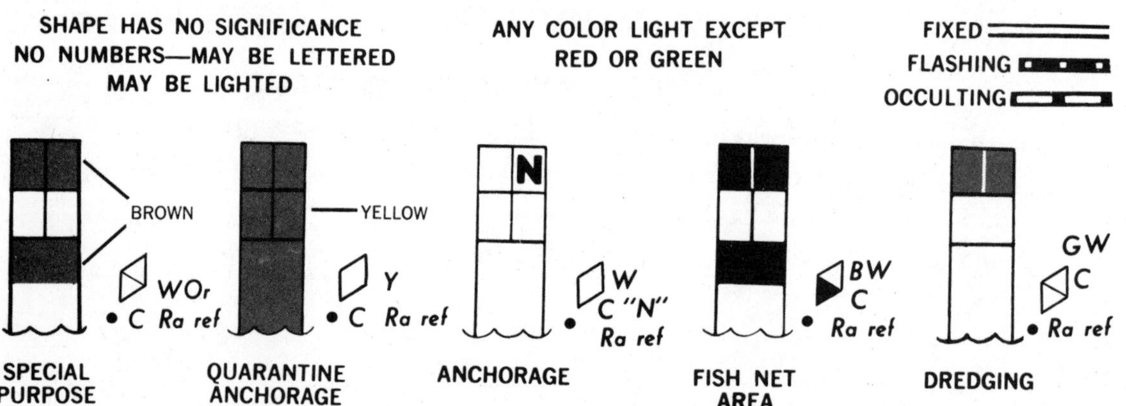

xcept Western Rivers and Intracoastal Waterway

MID CHANNEL

NO NUMBERS—MAY BE LETTERED
☐ WHITE LIGHT ONLY

MORSE CODE

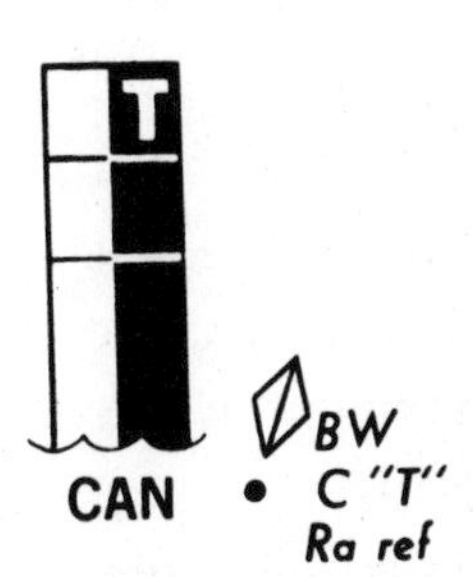

CAN

BW
C "T"
Ra ref

LIGHTED

BW
MoA
"N"
Ra ref

MB

DAYMARK

NUN

BW
N "B"
Ra ref

JUNCTION

MARK JUNCTIONS AND OBSTRUCTIONS
NO NUMBERS—MAY BE LETTERED
INTERRUPTED QUICK FLASHING

☐ WHITE OR ■ GREEN
☐ WHITE OR ■ RED

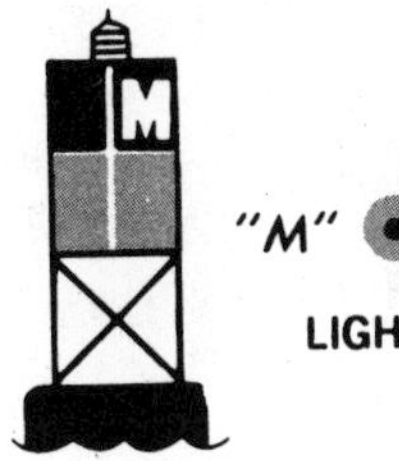

"M" RB "D"
Ra ref
LIGHTED

CAN

PREFERRED CHANNEL TO STARBOARD

TOPMOST BAND BLACK

RB
C "N"
Ra ref

NUN

PREFERRED CHANNEL TO PORT

TOPMOST BAND RED

RB
N "L"
Ra ref

JB

"L"
RB

JR

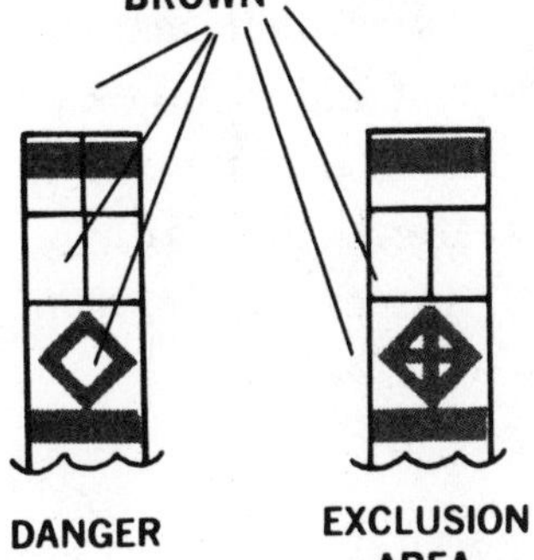

DANGER

EXCLUSION AREA

DAYMARKS HAVING NO LATERAL SIGNIFICANCE

MAY BE LETTERED

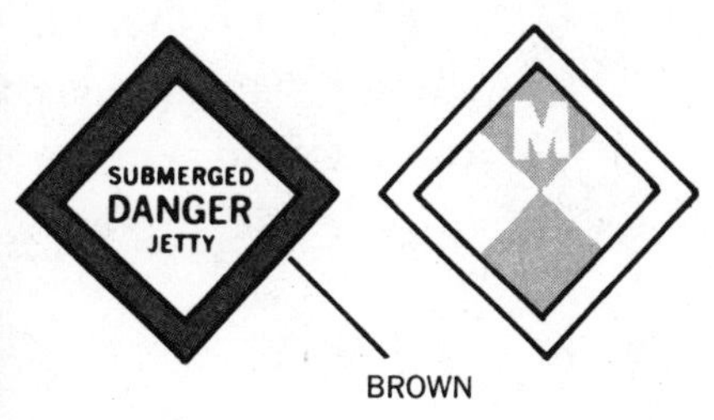

NW

NR

NB

sible for the standardization and improvement of the buoyage system in American waters.

Aids to Navigation form a carefully devised system of shapes and colors, sounds, numbers, and light characteristics which inform the experienced mariner at a glance where he may safely proceed and where hazards exist by day or night, in clear weather or fog—and often by electronic means when the mark can neither be seen nor heard.

The numbering system always progresses from seaward upstream. Along the coasts, the numbering system progresses in a clockwise direction around the country.

On the Western Rivers, the numbering progresses upstream, and on the Great Lakes, to the north and west, except in entering local harbors.

The vast majority of buoys are either red or black. On entering a harbor or heading up-channel, ***red*** buoys are to ***starboard*** and ***black*** to ***port.***

All odd-numbered buoys are black, all even numbers red.

Here are two simple memory-aids:

R-R-R—Red Right Returning
B-P-O-E—Black Port Odd Entering.

The Coast & Geodetic Survey and Lakes Survey charts, as well as government river charts, indicate precisely where lights and buoys are positioned. Symbols on the charts describe in detail the color, number, shape, light and sound (if any).

Red and black ***horizontally-striped*** buoys mark obstructions to navigation which may be passed on either side at a respectable distance. If the top band is black, the preferred channel leaves the buoy to port, going upstream. If the top band is red, the preferred channel leaves the buoy to starboard heading inland. When proceeding downstream, always consult the chart on approaching a horizontally striped red and black buoy.

Black and white ***vertically-striped*** buoys mark a mid-channel or fairway and can be passed close aboard on either side. Shape is of no significance.

Among other buoys, cylindrically-shaped or ***can*** buoys are ***black*** and conically-shaped or ***nun*** buoys are ***red.*** When horizontally banded, a can shape is used if the top band is black, and a nun shape if the top band is red. Cans and nuns are usually numbered.

Spar buoys are shaped like long, rounded timbers and may be used as either cans or nuns, or to mark special areas used for anchorage, quarantine, dredging and so on.

Buoys in important locations are lighted for night navigation. ***Green*** lights are used on black buoys, ***red*** lights on red buoys. White lights may be used on either type or color of buoy.

For ready identification at night, lights on buoys are adjusted to flash at varying intervals. The sequence of flashes is indicated in the light list. ***Quick-flashing*** lights (over 60 flashes per minute) are indicators of special dangers and should be approached and identified with caution. Interrupted quick flashing lights, with dark intervals of

CHART SYMBOLS FOR LIGHTS

F.	– Fixed	**W.**	– White
Fl.	– Flashing	**R.**	– Red
Gp.	– Group	**G.**	– Green
Occ.	– Occulting	**vis.**	– visible
Qk.	– Quick	**ev.**	– every
Alt.	– Alternating	**sec.**	– seconds
S-L	– Short-long	**SEC.**	– sector

An **occulting** light is on but flashes off briefly.
A **flashing** light is off but flashes on briefly.

about four seconds between groups, are placed only on horizontally striped lighted buoys.

A typical grouping of the above symbols describes the characteristics of Great Captain Island light:

FW Alt Gp FL R (2) ev 10 sec 73 ft vis 14 m

This signifies: a fixed white light alternating with two red flashes every ten seconds. The light is 73 feet above sea level and is visible 14 miles.

To provide ships with navigational references during times of poor visibility, important buoys are equipped with sound apparatus. Such buoys are bells, gongs, whistles or horns.

Bells have four clappers suspended above the bell; the rocking of the buoy in the sea activates the clappers.

Gongs have three or four gongs of different tones which sound in random sequence. They are readily distinguishable from bells.

Whistles are activated by the compression of air in the buoy as it rises and falls in the sea. They are usually found in open areas where a ground swell can activate them even when the sea is calm.

A ***horn*** buoy gives a trumpet-like sound at regular intervals by mechanical means.

A ***station*** buoy is an unnumbered can or nun stationed near a lighted or sound buoy of corresponding color. It indicates the direction of rocks or shoals and does emergency duty if the larger buoy gets off position.

Day beacons are shore structures of wood or masonry painted for maximum visibility. When used to mark the side of a channel, they follow the regular buoyage coloring and numbering system.

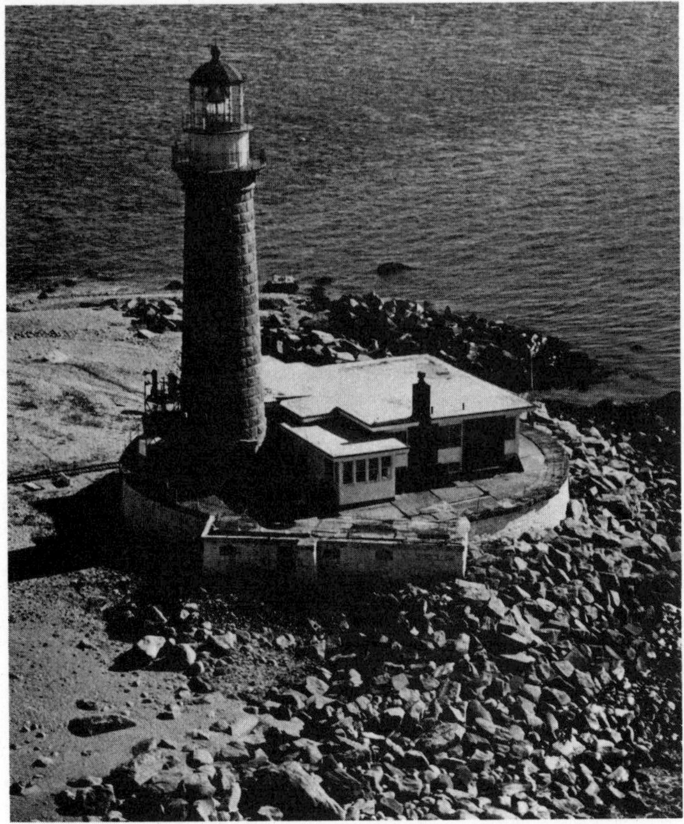
Little Gull Island Light. Note fog signals near base of tower.

They are frequently equipped with reflectors so that they can be picked up at night with a searchlight.

On the Western Rivers, they are referred to as ***day marks.***

The Intracoastal Waterway along the Atlantic and Gulf coasts from Manasquan, N. J. to Mexico has a special, distinctive system of buoys and markers. Skippers planning a trip on this waterway should obtain and study a chart of these aids.

Lighthouses are identifiable by day by the color and shape of the structure, and at night by the color or colors of the light and its characteristics.

A lighthouse may display a fixed white, green or red light or combinations of colors. The light may also be flashing or occulting, as described above. The distance a light is visible depends on its height, its power and the height of the observer.

LIGHTHOUSE WARNING PATTERN

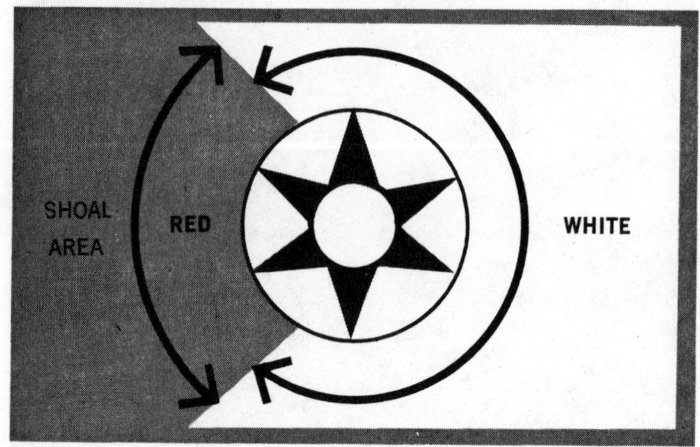

Height is an important factor because the curvature of the earth causes the light to disappear below the horizon at a distance.

A lighthouse adjoining rocks or shoals may show ***red*** over a part of its arc. When the skipper sees the color of the light shifting from its normal characteristic to red, he knows he is entering dangerous waters and should immediately take action to get out of the red sector.

Lighthouses may also be equipped with fog signals such as horns, sirens, or the two-toned diaphone. The light list describes the character and frequency of the fog signal.

Prior to World War II, the radio beacon system had already been brought to a high level of reliability. Vessels with ***radio direction finders*** tune in on radio beacons with easily recognizable signals. The loop antenna is rotated until a null is reached and a bearing taken. A ship's position may be determined through cross bearings on several radio beacons.

Even more accurate and sophisticated systems

of position-finding now include ***Loran C*** for navigation virtually world-wide and ***Omega,*** an automated system, suitable for larger yachts. Yacht-type ***Radar*** is now extensively used on larger boats for navigating in fog or at night.

Western Rivers Aids to Navigation

The Mississippi River and all of its tributaries are grouped together for navigating purposes and known as the Western Rivers. The river yachtsman will be guided in his piloting by the following aids:

lighted buoys
unlighted buoys
shore lights
day beacons
river gauges
lights on bridges and locks

River charts and light lists for the rivers may be ordered from the sources indicated at the end of this section. Safety harbor markers and safety landing markers, as well as direction boards and other indicators, will be found in certain of the rivers that feed into the main waterways.

On entering the Mississippi from the sea, the ***red*** buoys are found to the ***right.*** This system is followed uniformly through every branch and tributary: when proceeding upstream, the red buoys are to the right, the ***black*** buoys to the ***left.*** The direction of the current is the sole governing factor, not the entering or leaving of any port or harbor.

Buoys on the Western Rivers follow the lateral system as to shape and color, with certain simple exceptions. Unlighted red and black buoys have white tops to increase their visibility. They are also equipped with reflectors to increase their visibility at night. Red nun buoys have red reflectors; black can buoys have white reflectors.

The red and black horizontally-striped obstruction buoys, marking river junctions, wrecks or other dangers, do not have white tops. Special-purpose buoys in orange and white, and quarantine, anchorage and dredging buoys follow the standard lateral system. Unlighted buoys are not numbered. The numbers on lighted buoys are not sequential; they indicate the mileage to a given point. The reference point is readily determined from the chart or light list.

Lighted channel buoys painted black, or with black top band, show two-second flashing white or flashing green, i.e., 1.8 sec. dark, .2 sec. flash.

Lighted channel buoys painted red, or with red top band, show four-second group flashing white or group flashing red, i.e., 3 sec. dark, .2, .6, .2 sec. flashes.

Channel marker shore lights are wooden structures on shore, painted white. A wooden ladder leads to a small platform on which the light is mounted. An identifying number and a target appear behind the light.

Most of the self-contained shore lights show characteristics like the buoys, as indicated above. However, some which operate on commercial power will show fixed lights or occulting lights.

In general, each channel light is visible from the one preceding it. This means that they may be well apart on straight stretches and close together where the channel is narrow and twisting. As long as the helmsman holds to the straight line between the marker ahead and the marker behind, he is on a safe course. It is well to have a lookout with binoculars spotting the buoys for the helmsman.

Since the water levels in the Western Rivers may vary by reason of flood, drought or storm, it is impossible to indicate fixed depths on the charts. It is possible, however, to indicate relative depths based upon a reference number oriented to various points along the river. These variable numbers are known as river gauges. Locations are indicated on the river charts. The experienced skipper can determine the depth of the water in which he is traveling by referring the depth indicated on the chart

CHART SOURCES

PUBLICATION	SOURCE
Catalogue of Nautical Charts (Free) Number 1, Atlantic; Number 2, Pacific	National Ocean Survey Riverdale, Maryland 20840
Catalogue of the Great Lakes & Connecting Waters (Free)	U.S. Army Engineers Lake Survey Office 630 Federal Bldg. Detroit, Michigan 48226
Charts of U.S. Coastal Waters; Hudson River to Troy; Atlantic and Gulf Intercoastal Waterways	U.S. Coast & Geodetic Survey National Ocean Survey Riverdale, Maryland 20840
Charts of Great Lakes and Connecting Waters, Lake Champlain, Lake of the Woods, Rainy Lake and N.Y. State Canals	U.S. Army Engineers Lake Survey Office 630 Federal Bldg. Detroit, Michigan 48226
Mississippi River and Tributaries	U.S. Army Engineers 2195 Dearborn Street Chicago, Illinois 60604
Tide Tables Current Tables Tidal Current Charts Coast Pilots	National Ocean Survey Department of Commerce Riverdale, Maryland 20840
Light Lists Navigation Rules Nautical Almanac	U.S. Coast Guard Washington, D.C. 20590
Notice to Mariners World Charts Sailing Directions (foreign waters)	Naval Oceanographic Office Chart Sales Desk Suitland, Maryland 20390

to the variable river gauge number.

In passing through the many river locks, as well as in passing under bridges, the yachtsman will be guided by the colored lights which are indicated on the charts and which clearly mark the safe courses and channels.

River charts and light lists should both be kept aboard and should be used in conjunction with each other. They may be obtained from the sources shown in the accompanying table.

SECTION 14 ■ TIDE AND CURRENT

Tide is the vertical movement of the sea—the rise and fall of the waters under the influence of sun and moon.

Current is the horizontal movement of the sea—the actual movement of the water in known directions at known speeds. In rivers, the current is occasioned by the downhill flow of waters from interior areas to lakes or oceans.

Flood is the inward or rising movement of the water. ***Ebb*** is the outward or falling movement. ***Slack*** is the period of balance before the flow reverses. ***Set*** is the direction of current; ***drift*** is the velocity of this set.

In most seacoast areas, there are two high tides and two low tides a day. Tides are caused by the pull of the moon on the earth's waters. Tides are low when the moon is at either horizon, and high when the moon is overhead or at the other side of the earth. Because the moon does not quite make a complete revolution around the earth each day, the lunar day is almost an hour longer than the solar day. Thus there is a difference of 6 hours, 13 minutes, or 1/4 of a lunar day, between tides.

Because of its greater distance, the sun exerts a pull on the earth's waters only 2/5 as strong as the moon. At the time of the new moon and the full moon, the sun and moon both pull in the same direction. Therefore the high tides are higher and the lows lower. These are called ***spring*** tides. When the moon is at first and third quarter, the pull of sun and moon is opposite. During these ***neap*** tides, the highs are lower and the lows are higher.

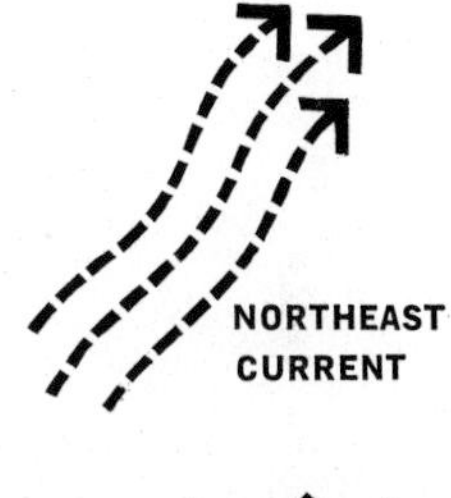

Tides are carefully tabulated for a full year in advance by the government Tide Tables. These can be bought wherever charts are sold. To determine local tides, look up the closest reference point to your location in the Tide Table. Then add or subtract the indicated time difference to the nearest high or low tide. All times indicated are Standard, not Daylight.

Current is the result of tide. Direction of current set is the direction toward which the current moves —unlike wind direction. In waters where the skipper is likely to encounter variable currents—that is to say, in most coastal waters—the Current Table and the Tidal Current Chart should be part of navigating equipment. These publications are inexpensive and invaluable for accurate navigation.

The change of current set or direction does not necessarily coincide with the change in the rise or fall of tide. Sometimes the current change follows the tide change by several hours. Remember, too—direction of current at ebb and flood is not necessarily opposite. Ebb currents and flood currents may be at right angles or even in the same direction.

Current is strongest in deep water and weakest in shoal. Anyone who has navigated a river knows that the current always flows strongest at the outside of a bend where the depth is greatest. Current is weakest on the inside of the bend where the water is usually shallower.

• Useful Tip: When navigating against a strong current, stay inshore near shallower water. A longer course may often be traversed more quickly.

• Useful Tip: You can usually judge current set and velocity by observing the eddies and swirls around buoys and fixed objects in the water. (Watch the water, not just the slant, since wind may tilt a buoy.)

• Useful Tip: In planning a day's run, consult the Tide and Current Tables. Plan your departure time to get the most benefit and least hindrance from the currents.

The skipper must distinguish between the course he sails or steers and the course he actually makes good. The boat may be making ten knots through the water, but with a four-knot current against it, will be making good only six knots over the bottom. Conversely, with a four-knot favorable current, it will make good fourteen knots over the bottom. A beam wind will cause a boat to make ***leeway.*** Leeway is the drift sidewise to leeward caused by wind or tide from one side or the other. ***Course made good*** is the actual path of the boat over the bottom.

In plotting a course, the skipper should know how to adjust for the influence of the current and calculate the course to steer which will allow him to make good over the bottom his corrected compass course. The accompanying diagram is a simple visual representation of how and what to allow for current influence.

In this case we assume that the skipper has plotted a due east course, 090°, at a speed of ten knots. Along his course line, between departure point (dp) and destination (D), he marks off ten units of distance. These may be miles, tenths, or quarter-miles—any fixed unit. Consulting his Current Table, he discovers the current along his course sets NE at three knots during the period he is sailing this course. He now runs a line three units in length back along the current direction. The

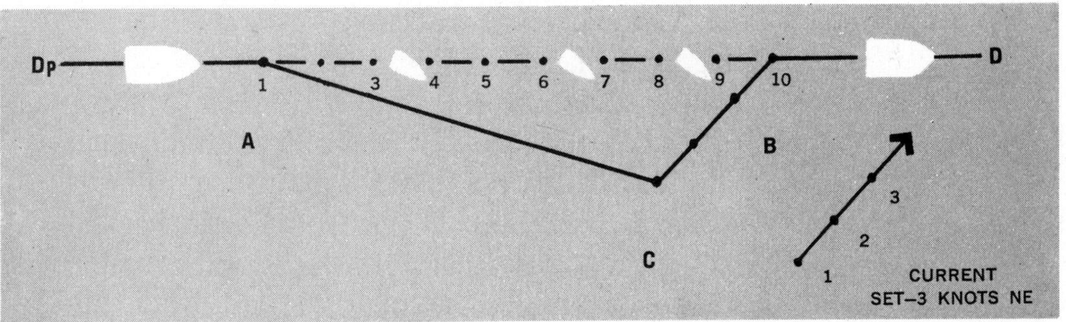

new line drawn from A to C will be the course to steer to make good the planned course from A to B. Note: The actual heading of the vessel as it proceeds along course line AB is the adjusted course heading, AC.

In case of doubt, just remember that you want to steer to the right of your compass course if the current is on that side, and to the left if the current is from the left.

• Useful Tip: To check the course your boat is making good over the bottom, take a bearing on the direction of your wake. The reciprocal of this bearing will show clearly whether the course you are steering is the course you are making good toward your destination.

SAFETY TIPS

• No matter how small your boat, if you plan to leave your harbor carry a compass on board. A sudden squall or fog can put you in a dangerous position if you lose direction.

• If you carry a portable compass, be sure that it is well secured on board so that a sudden roll won't smash it or send it over the side. Be sure that the lubber's line is squarely fore and aft when steering a course.

• Always mark your course on your chart. You can erase it. In any case, new charts are less expensive than new boats.

• Don't use old charts. The buoy that has been changed or replaced may be the one you're looking for.

• Keep a log book on board. In case of storm or fog, you may find the record vital on this trip.

• Don't let your charts, light list, or navigating equipment get wet. Wrap them in acetate sheets or plastic bags. Plastic chart covers are available to hold and protect your chart.

• Keep your chart weighted down or clipped when it is on deck. Good trips are spoiled when charts blow overboard.

• Don't ruin your chart by folding it up like an auto road map. If you haven't full size chart-table stowage, roll it up and secure it in the overhead between carlins. Otherwise fold it to a quarter, stow it flat.

• Practice making corrections from compass to True and from True to compass until you can make the proper additions and subtractions almost by instinct.

• Don't turn your head to talk to passengers when you're at the helm. Another craft suddenly cutting across your bow, a swimmer in the water, a half-submerged timber, all spell danger if your look-out is relaxed for an instant.

• Don't assume that buoys are infallible. They can be rammed or cut adrift. Lights can be off, sound signals inaudible because of calm sea.

• If in doubt about your position in a fog—anchor! Sound signals can be better heard with the engine off.

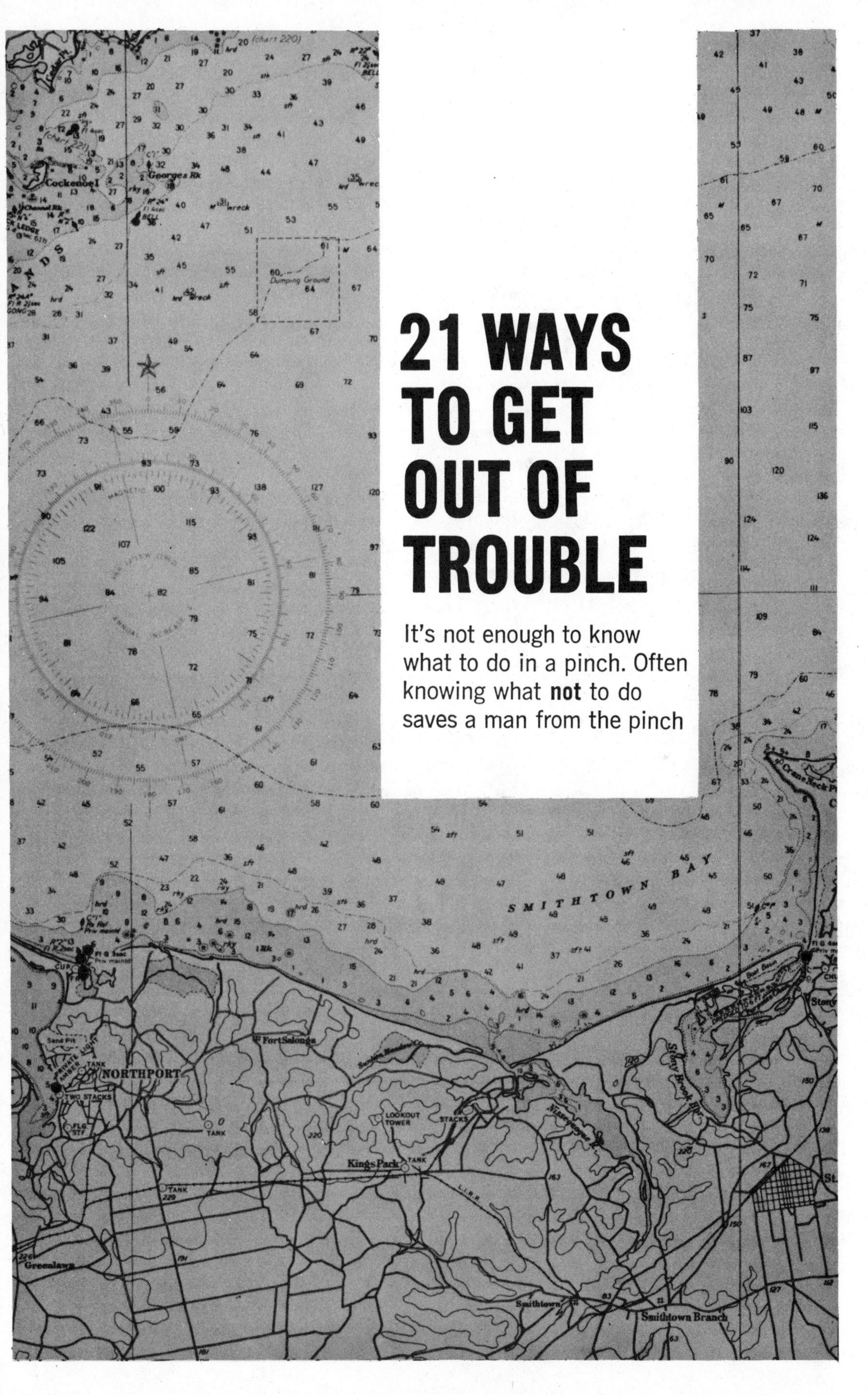

21 WAYS TO GET OUT OF TROUBLE

It's not enough to know what to do in a pinch. Often knowing what **not** to do saves a man from the pinch

OUT OF GAS

Anchor. Borrow gas from a passing boat. Ask for a tow. Row ashore in dinghy. Get a lift to shore in passing outboard or motorboat. In a small craft, paddle.

AGROUND

Check tide at once. If rising, wait for tide. Otherwise shift passengers and weight to heel boat and try reversing engine. Use boat hook to help push off. Carry anchor out in dinghy to deeper water and try to kedge off with anchor winch. If no dinghy, get passing boat to carry anchor out. Pass tow line to another boat for help in pulling off. If all efforts fail, get help from Coast Guard.

ENGINE FAILURE

Check Fuel System for: clogged air vent, clogged filter, clogged or damaged fuel line, needle valve stuck, choke stuck, out of gas. Check Ignition System for: fouled or cracked plugs or loose plug wires, shorting ignition wires, cracked distributor cap, bad points, bad rotor, loose plug, worn coil. (Keep spare plugs, points, rotor, coil and distributor cap on board for replacements.)

MAN OVERBOARD

Heave ring buoys and floating seat cushions promptly. (If at night, have electronic flare on one buoy.) Throw near, not at, man in water. Station one member of crew to keep unswerving eye on man in water. Tear pages from book or magazine to make trail in water. If a sailboat, lower jib and jibe around. If a power boat, turn in even circle. Approach man from leeward so he is carried toward ship rather than ship running him down. If anyone on board dives in, he must be wearing life jacket and be attached to boat by line. If there is time, rig boarding ladder or launch dinghy to get man out of water. If pet overboard, he may be retrieved by boat-hook. (Pets must wear harness on boats.) Rehearse procedures mentally. See page 248 for information on hypothermia.

TAKING WATER

Pump promptly and search for leak. If a break in hull, drive rags in with wood wedges. If leaking seacock or adjacent pipe, wind with rubber tape. If seam has opened, drive in oakum or twisted small stuff. If a large hole, cover from outside with canvas, or canvas and plastic seat cushion, tacking canvas snugly to hull. If hole is at waterline, trim boat to other side so damage rides out of water.

LOST IN FOG

At first sign of fog, take bearings, mark position on chart and commence keeping a log of courses and speeds. Start to blow fog signals (see page 51). Slow down. Station lookout forward. Stop engines from time to time and listen for lighthouse fog signals. Take bearings on them. Check bearings with direction-finder if you have one. If not, take a chain of soundings with lead line and match up with soundings on chart. When heading in to harbor, head in upwind of harbor and run down to it along the shore line. If in any doubt, anchor. And continue sounding fog signals.

STORM

Watch horizon for approach of storm. Turn on radio for weather information. Stow all loose gear below and lash any gear on deck. Close ports and hatches and secure them. As seas build, slow down. Require crew and passengers on deck to don life jackets. Run out drogue or sea anchor to keep stern or bow into seas. If seas are breaking, attach oil bag to drogue to provide oil slick to weather of vessel. If no drogue aboard, use canvas bucket on line or even drag cabin table or locker door. Maneuver to stay well off lee shore in case of engine failure. Use just enough power to maintain steerageway. Most boats ride best heading into seas. Experiment. Choose heading that is most easy riding.

SEASICKNESS

Stay topside. Avoid fatty foods, sweets and liquids,

including liquor. Eat solid, especially salty, foods. Don't take orange juice or carbonated beverages. Do take salt crackers. Wear sun glasses. Don't read or use binoculars. Avoid inhaling odors and fumes, including tobacco smoke. Take anti-motion pills containing such drugs as Bonine, Marezine and Phenergan.

FOULED PROPELLER

At first indication of fouled prop, disengage clutch or stop engine. Try reversing cautiously. Anchor. Put swimming ladder over and let strongest swimmer on board don goggles, take a sharp knife with a cord secured to it and cut foul line free. If line is dinghy painter, make sure dinghy is otherwise secured before it is cut loose.

RUDDER FAILURE

Check rudder cable and all its fittings. See if action of wheel is being transmitted to quadrant and thence to rudder stock. If cable is broken, try repairing with wire section and u-bolts. If rudder is broken or lost, twin-engine vessels still steer by altering port and starboard screw speeds. Single-engine craft and sailboats steer by holding paddle, board or bucket over side toward which turn is wanted. Sailboats steer by altering sail trim.

TORN SAILS

Lower sail promptly to prevent spread of rip. Use palm and waxed cotton thread. On heavy sails, use baseball stitch. Light sails may be sewn by roll-stitching rip and covering with pressure tape or adhesive tape. Very light sails can be mended with tape alone. If mainsail torn beyond salvage, try reefing above torn place. In storm, set heavy jib on main halyard and lash to boom and mast.

JURY RIGS

Masts usually go at spreaders, leaving stumps for jury rigs. If the whole mast is lost, a spinnaker pole, boom, club, or even a boat hook may be rigged as mast. Use rope as shrouds and stays. Remember that eight or ten feet of mainsail will still give a boat steerageway and keep it hove to or headed toward help.

FIRE ON BOARD

Work fast. For oil or grease fires, use extinguisher aimed at base of flame. Attack wood or cloth fires with water. Throw burning mattresses or bedding overboard. If in machinery compartment, cut fuel supply promptly. If in confined space, close hatches, ports, etc. to reduce oxygen, and use extinguisher. Reduce wind effect by stopping boat. If fire is forward, head stern into wind; if aft, head bow into the wind. Put all hands in life jackets. If fire is severe, make distress signal and call for help on radio. *Work fast!*

DISTRESS SIGNALS

Know what distress signals you have on board. Best is a radio telephone. Official distress frequency is Ch. 16 (156.8 MHz or 2182 kc), but use any frequency in an emergency. Newest emergency signal for small craft is the 3 foot by 3 foot orange distress flag with black square and ball. Hoist or wave flag. Shoot red flares. Use orange smoke distress signals. Shoot parachute, red flare, or rocket. (You must carry at least three devices.) All boats must carry automatic electric distress light except pleasure craft under 16 feet and open sailboats without motor under 26 feet. In voice radio, "Mayday, Mayday" is signal. In code, SOS is signal (• • • — — — • • •).

TOWING

Send over light messenger line and use it to carry towing line on board. Make tow line fast to forward cleat or bitts of towed boat and after cleat of towing boat, being sure deck is clear so that anchors, stanchions or other gear on deck will not be swept away in event of yawing. Use long, fresh line. Take out all kinks. Be able to cast off tow line fast in emergency. Keep all hands well clear of tow line in case it snaps. Take up strain slowly and evenly. Adjust length of line to keep boats in phase on waves. Towed boat keeps weight aft. Use minimum steering on towed boat. Arrange signals beforehand.

FIRST AID

Have first aid kit on board. Examine and renew contents regularly. Basic necessities include bandages (gauze), adhesive tape, antiseptic, tourniquet, ammonia inhalant, Band-aids, burn ointment, aspirin, swabs, eye dressing, and scissors. Stop arterial bleeding promptly and administer resuscitation promptly. Otherwise work slowly and don't move victim. Have Red Cross or Coast Guard Auxiliary Basic First Aid Manual on board.

PLUGGED HEAD

Apply suction with plumber's helper (rubber plunger). Probe and twist with wire coat hanger. Work vent lever slowly. Shut off incoming water. Remove blockage (usually wadded paper) in pieces. Bail head with tin and bucket to facilitate working. If no other remedy, disassemble valve and clear, making sure vent seacock is shut off to prevent entry of water.

SWAMPING AND CAPSIZING

Swamping arises from water through hull or over sides. If through hull, try to stuff up leak with rags, twisted rope strands or wooden plugs hammered into hole. Keep pumping and bailing while making repairs. If water comes over sides, retrim weight and change course to minimize effect of seas. In event of capsizing, get all hands into life jackets. Then try to right craft by having crew stand on keel and pull gunwale over. Lower sails before righting. Keep floating gear together. In any case, stay with vessel as long as it is afloat rather than swimming to shore. If you remain with the boat, rescue is much more probable and less hazardous.

DINGHY LOST

If dinghy is lost under way, check wind and action of seas. Drop over a board or cushion and note direction of its drift. Retrace dinghy's probable drifting course, note course you have made good. Report to Coast Guard and local police.

COLLISION

In event of serious collision, check gravity of damage before separating vessels. Stand by to help other craft unless your vessel or passengers in danger. If other bow has penetrated your craft be prepared to plug the fracture immediately on separation of boats. Nail canvas patch over serious break with wood strips. Trim weight to get hole out of water during repairs. Shore up mattresses against break on inside. If vessel in sinking condition, get all hands in life jackets. If other vessel sinking, you must stand by and give aid, no matter how serious your damage.

LOST

Try to reconstruct dead reckoning position on chart by recalling courses, speeds, and times. Follow a straight course and take a chain of soundings at intervals. Try to fit these onto your chart. Head inshore and, when in sight of land, follow coastline (taking soundings) until landmark is sighted. Watch for distant steamers and estimate your distance from steamer lanes. Direction of major city can often be determined with transistor radio by rotating toward loudest signal (usually at right angles to face of set). Avoid wasting distress signals if no other vessel is in sight. Do not wander aimlessly but pursue direct course toward probable landmark. Vary course sharply when you turn. Keep record of course, speed and time. Don't panic. Patience is your best hope.

5

THE OUTBOARD BOAT AND MOTOR

The outboard motor has done more to revolutionize boating than any invention since the oar. Not too many years ago, it served mainly to get the rowboat fisherman to his favorite fishing grounds. But today the outboard has become the great equalizer. Just as the old tin Lizzie put the poor man on wheels, so the outboard has made yachting the sport of millions rather than of a few.

The development of the outboard motor from one or two h.p. to throbbing V4's or straight 6's has been one of the more exciting pages of boating history. The outboard enthusiast can now rival the fixed-engine man in both speed and comfort. The light weight and flexibility of the outboard boat have opened up thousands of new boating areas in previously inaccessible waters, through the use of the trailer. Docks and moorings cease to be a problem when the vessel slides almost effortlessly out of the water and up onto its own rolling cradle.

SECTION 15 ■ HANDLING THE MOTOR

Unlike other types of boat in which the designer may specify a certain type or types of engine with the builder making the original installation, outboard motors and boats are usually matched up at the discretion of the owner. Too often in the past the decision was simply a matter of putting on the most powerful motor the boat could hold.

Today, a national organization, the Outboard Boating Club, has joined with the Coast Guard Auxiliary and the Power Squadrons to promote safety afloat. It has enlisted outboard manufacturers and dealers in setting up safety standards for both boats and engines.

Where outboard boating was once confined to rowboats and runabouts, today it is possible to buy a full-sized cruiser or houseboat with sleeping and galley accommodations for a family, powered by one or two large outboard motors. Each new year sees more refined, more powerful engines.

As the boatman knows, buying an outboard is like buying a house—the best choice must be the one that best fits the buyer's needs. From previous chapters in this book and from Coast Guard Auxiliary and Power Squadrons boating courses, which all yachtsmen are urged to take, the boatman will learn something of safe boat handling. Let us now consider the special problems which he (or the owner of a larger craft with an outboard-operated dinghy) will face.

Outboard motors differ from other engines, in general, in the following ways: the outboard motor fires on every revolution; the outboard operates at a higher rate of revolutions per minute than do other types of motor; many outboards are lubricated by oil mixed with the fuel in the tank.

Because of these factors, the outboard motor needs greater attention to its spark plug or plugs and a uniformly high grade of fuel and oil. In general, the mixing ratio of oil to gasoline is a half pint to a gallon, though somewhat higher with high horsepower and multicylinder motors. Fuel and oil should be precisely mixed before placing the mixture in the gas tank. If the engine has been standing for a long period, by all means empty the old mixture from the tank before starting. If the fuel has been standing in a gasoline can, be sure to use a funnel with a fine wire mesh strainer when pouring into the tank. Outboard motors often stall because of water which has condensed in the fuel.

If you find your motor running hot, it may be from too little oil.

If the exhaust is emitting blue smoke and the spark plugs foul excessively, you are using too much oil.

For long periods of operation at low speeds, such as when trolling, a spark plug with a "hotter" heat range should be installed. This is preferable to reducing the oil in the mixture.

When mounting the outboard, never step from the dock to the boat while carrying the engine. Climb into the boat with the motor still on the dock. Then, if you must mount the motor by yourself, carefully steady yourself in the center of the boat and slowly, gently take the engine aboard. Much better, have somebody on the dock hand it down to you. If two of you install the motor, one should remain on the dock, the other in the boat.

Place the outboard squarely in the center of the transom and securely fasten the bracket screws on the stern. Don't underestimate the power of vibration to loosen the clamps. Play it safe and fasten the engine to the boat with a chain or piece of line to avoid danger of losing it somewhere offshore.

If you're alone in the boat, cast off all lines before starting the engine. Then, from a sitting position squarely in the center of the boat, line up the motor fore and aft, face forward and give a stout, smooth pull on the starter cord.

If you have a passenger or passengers, see that they are properly seated and the boat evenly trimmed before starting. Then you can either cast off completely, or leave a line looped loosely around a cleat on the dock with both ends in the hands of one of your crew for quick casting off. If possible, avoid having your crew stand up to clear the dock lines.

If you have a motor with an electric starter, place the gear shift in neutral, square the engine fore and aft, advance the throttle and then press the starter button. You will then cast off your dock lines after the engine is warmed up and running smoothly.

Most outboard boats are of the displacement type, such as the rowboat and utility boat which

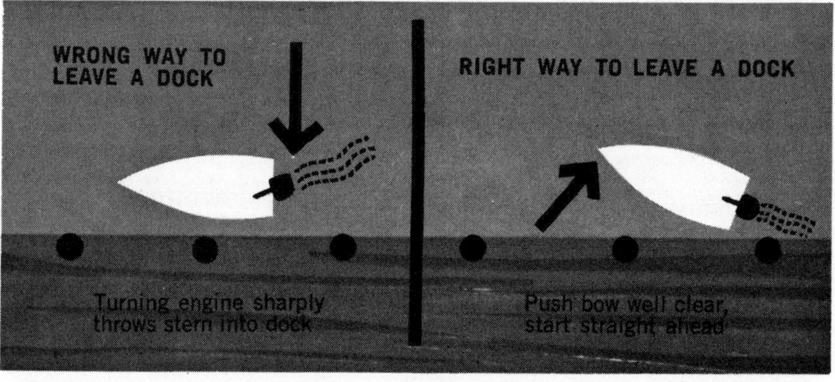
WRONG WAY TO
LEAVE A DOCK
RIGHT WAY TO LEAVE A DOCK
Turning engine sharply
throws stern into dock
Push bow well clear,
start straight ahead

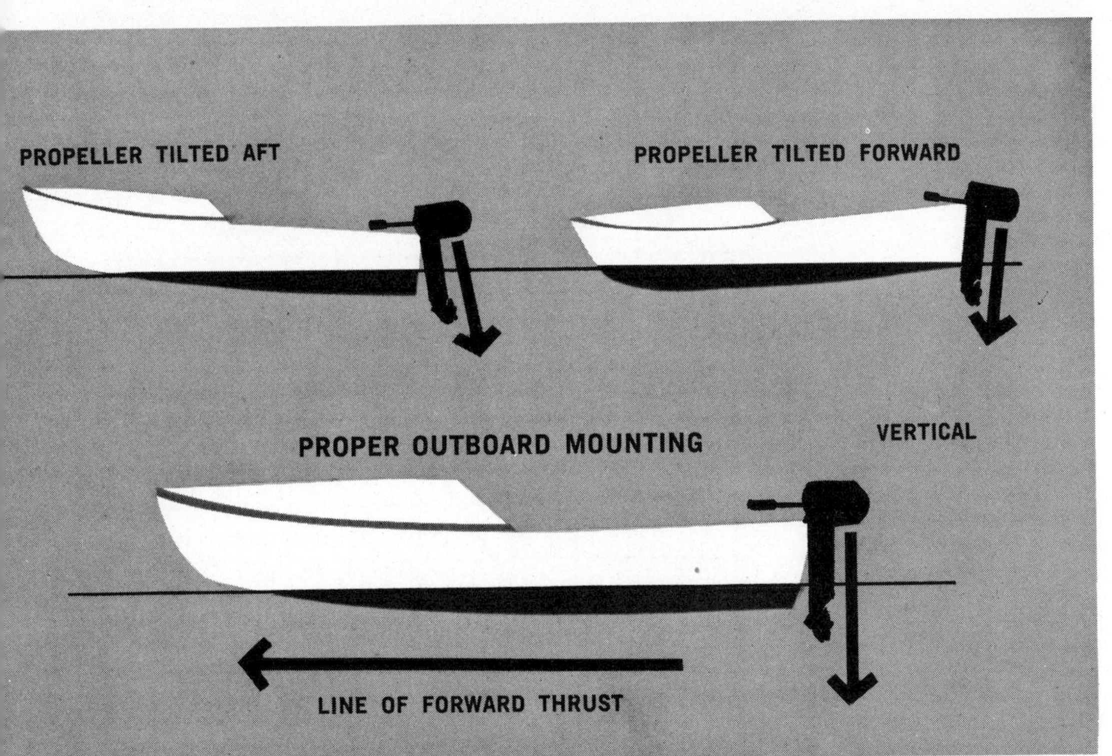

push the water aside as they force their way through it, the semi-planing type, or the planing type such as the average runabout which rides on the flat area near the stern and surges over the water when at planing speed. Each individual hull, including the semi-planing type, has a trim at which it operates best. To put all the weight in a rowboat aft and point the bow up in the air does not make a planing hull of the craft. Overloading is primarily dangerous because it makes a small boat subject to swamping, even on a calm day when the wake of a larger or faster boat can create a single wave large enough to come aboard and fill a crowded outboard sitting low in the water.

But also important is the fact that such a boat—even one only moderately overloaded—does not operate at its designed efficiency. A boat's capacity is by no means equal to the number of people it can seat. A rowboat may have enough places for eight simply to allow for combinations of seating for the

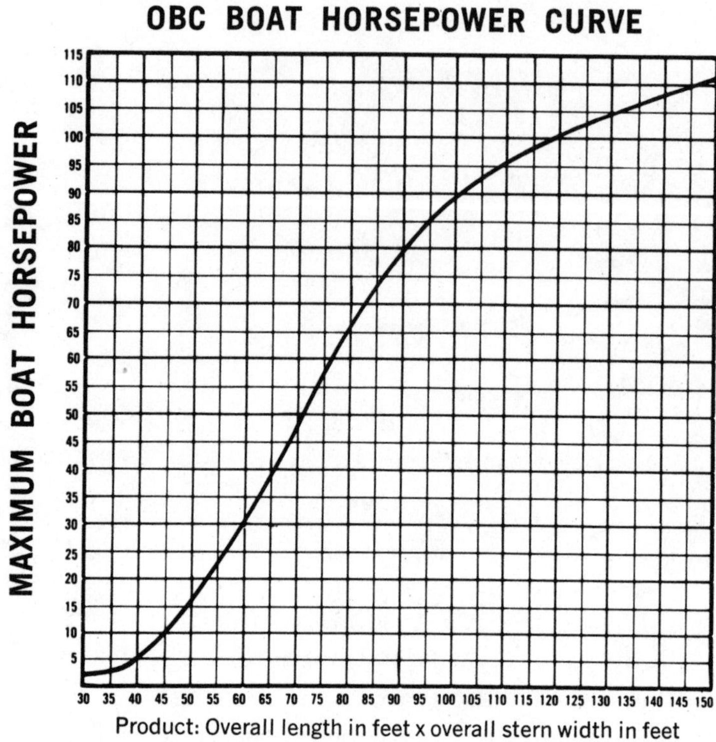

five it may be designed to hold safely.

Distribute your passengers so the boat neither lists nor is bow- or stern-heavy. Now adjust the motor angle on the transom so that the engine will be straight up and down when the boat is at operating speed. If the propeller is canted away from the stern, the bow will ride high. If the propeller is canted forward, the bow will dig in, reducing speed and impairing steering.

The Outboard Boating Club adopted a certain number of recommended standards for transoms and motor mountings, some of which are summarized in the accompanying table.

When the forward section of the motor cutout (S) is formed by the back of a seat and, in the event of a sudden tilt-up, it is possible for a passenger's arm to be caught, 3 inches should be added to B.

Over a period of years, the Outboard Boating Club conducted a series of experiments in the interests of safe family boating to determine a formula for the maximum horsepower engine to be used with a boat of given length and beam. The accompanying table shows boat horsepower capacity as recommended by their Boat Test Committee.

Figures at the base of the chart represent centerline length multiplied by the width at the stern, not counting fins. Remember that the chart represents maximum horsepower, not necessarily recommended horsepower.

Although in general an outboard handles much the same as any other boat, it is easily the most maneuverable of water craft. It does not depend upon water pressure against a rudder or rudders, but answers promptly and effectively to the direction of propeller thrust as the motor is rotated. Since, on some installations, the motor can be turned completely through an arc of 360 degrees, this means that the angle of bow-swing may be quite narrow and the angle of stern-swing wide and sweeping. In maneuvering to and from a dock, for instance, there is greater danger of banging the after part of the boat against obstacles than the forward part. In leaving a dock with an outboard, it is best to let the bow swing out, or else push the boat away from the dock so as to avoid risk of swinging the stern into pilings in getting away from the dockside.

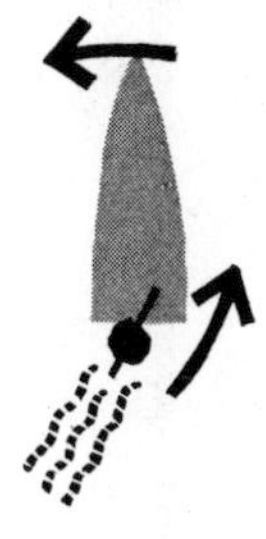

Today, more and more of the larger outboard craft are fitted with twin motors. Twin engines will cost more and be more expensive to operate than a

MOTOR HORSEPOWER	TRANSOM THICKNESS	TRANSOM HEIGHT	CUTOUT WIDTH			CUTOUT LENGTH		
			X	Y	Z	X	Y	Z
UNDER 12 H.P.	1⅜″-1¾″	15½″ OR 20½″	21″	23″	27″	21″	21″	21″
12-40 H.P.	1⅜″-2″	15½″ OR 20½″	28″	34″	34″	21″	21″	21″
OVER 40 H.P.	1⅝″-2¼″	20½″	28″	35″	36″	26½″	29″	29″

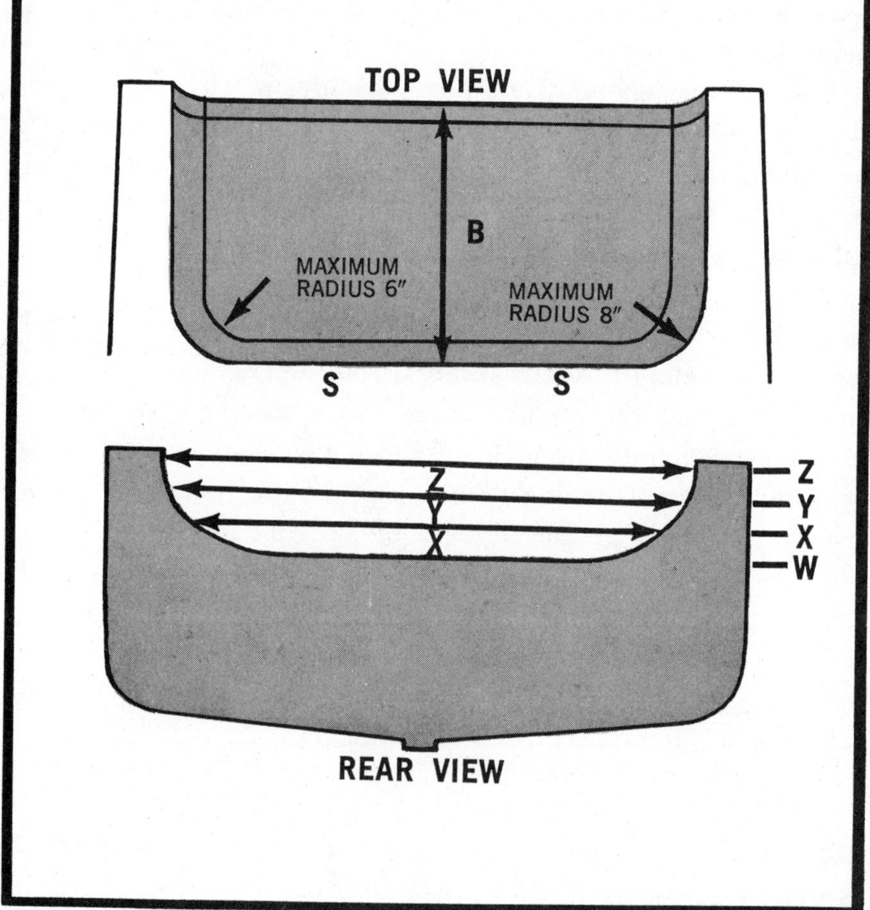

single engine of equal horsepower, but they have the advantage of added safety if one conks out. Also, steadiness and steering are improved with counter-rotating propellers. It should be noted, however, that although doubling engines will double horsepower, it will also double gasoline consumption and will add only fractionally to speed.

One may assume that, by the time the boatowner is ready to consider twin outboards, he is a fairly knowledgeable skipper. We shall therefore not take up the question of inboard vs. outboard power. Each has advantages, but the needs and pocketbook of the owner will determine the final answer.

Trouble Shooting

Every outboard boat owner faces the possibility that there may be a day when he will have trouble getting the motor started or restarted. The great majority of all engine troubles occur in the following categories: ignition, fuel, compression, cooling.

We shall refer to these as we consider the normal categories of engine trouble in the accompanying table.

Every outboard operator should be equipped with an adequate tool kit and an owner's manual describing the operation of the motor on his boat. Even if your motor is second hand, the manual can almost certainly be obtained from the manufacturer. A minimum tool kit should contain:

pliers	*spare plugs*
wrenches	*spare shear pin*
file	*cotter pins*
hammer	*spare wire*
screwdriver	*electrical tape*
plug wrench	*sandpaper*

ENGINE TROUBLESHOOTING

ENGINE WON'T START	**IGNITION** Loose battery connections Loose spark plug wires Short or break in ignition wiring Cracked plug Fouled plug **FUEL** Out of fuel Air vent clogged up Fuel line damaged or disconnected Choke stuck open or closed Dirt or water in carburetor or gas line	Needle valve stuck or incorrectly adjusted Strainer clogged Too much oil in fuel **COMPRESSION** New piston rings needed Loose spark plug
ENGINE STARTS AND STOPS	**IGNITION** Ignition wires shorting Spark plug fouling Magneto or distributor contact points fouled or worn High tension leads cracked **FUEL** Fuel low or out Stale gasoline Filler cap vent valve clogged Choke sticking Needle valve improperly adjusted	Carburetor float valve sticking Improper oil and fuel mixture Water in carburetor bowl due to condensation Carburetor strainer clogged **COOLING** Clogged intake Water pump not working Clogged outlet
ENGINE MISSING OR SPUTTERING	**IGNITION** High tension wires worn or loose Spark plug too hot or too cold Spark plug needs cleaning **FUEL** Choke needs adjusting Improper oil and fuel mixture Filler cap vent valve partly clogged Dirty carburetor filter Needle valve needs adjusting	**COOLING** Partly clogged intake or outlet Inadequate water pump pressure **COMPRESSION** Worn piston ring Spark plug not fully tightened

Never before in the history of yachting have boat owners had the mobility that they now have with outboard craft and boat trailers. Skippers a hundred miles from lake or river enjoy happy weekends afloat. Boat owners who were once limited to the neighborhood streams and ponds find boating pleasure in widely separated bays, rivers, lakes and inlets. And equally important, boating areas with underdeveloped harbor or marina facilities can accommodate scores of additional boats parked on trailers in parking lots. These same trailers, jacked up on wooden blocks, serve admirably as cradles for winter storage, often in the owner's back yard.

The single most important word in trailer boating is "caution." Caution begins with making sure that the car you own can pull the trailer and boat you plan to buy. A small, light car should obviously not be expected to pull a heavy trailer-boat combination. The strain on the car's transmission becomes too great and question arises as to whether the light car's brakes will hold the added weight.

Between boat and trailer there can be no compromise at all. The boat's transom should not extend out beyond the rear of the trailer, and the boat should so balance as to offer a weight of about 50-75 pounds at the coupler end. If either of these principles is ignored, serious whip or drag may result.

Trailers, under SAE recommendations, are divided into three classes: Class A—gross weight of up to 2,000 lbs.; Class B—gross weight of 2,000-5,000 lbs.; Class C—gross weight of 5,000-10,000 lbs. In all cases, the gross weight is that of boat, load including gear, and trailer. Weight limits on

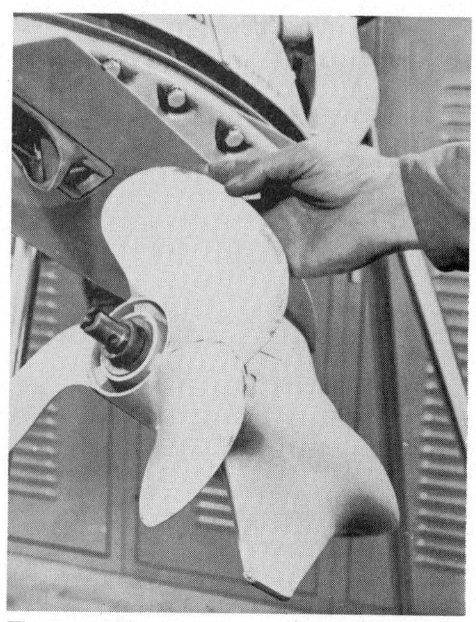

The propeller should be checked regularly for nicks and fouling which can seriously reduce your motor's operating efficiency

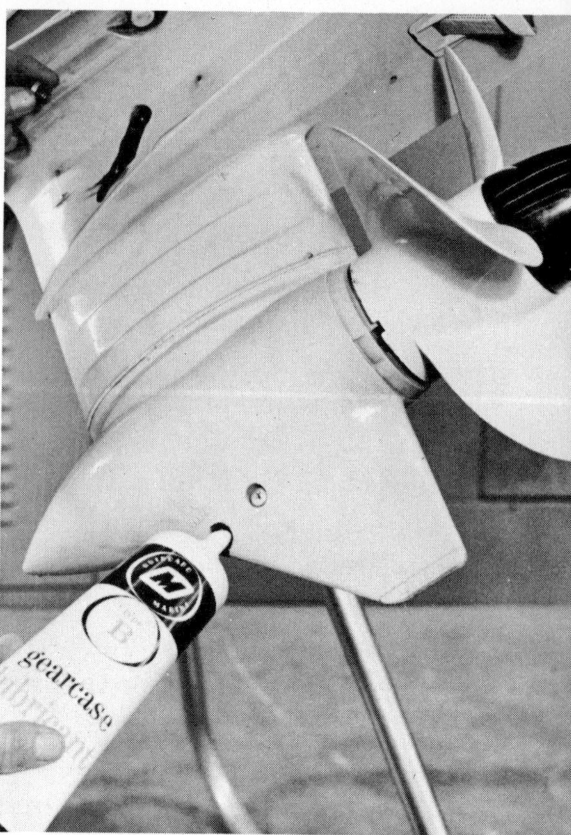

Fill gearcase through the lower hole until lubricant appears at upper hole. Replace upper plug before removing grease tube

roads and bridges are almost always in terms of gross weight.

Hitching a trailer onto the rear of your car subjects you to varying laws in the various states. These legal requirements will need to be checked into and carefully observed. Some states require brakes and chains. Most require special trailer lights.

If you've never driven with a trailer, you will want to experiment and practice before making your first trip with your boat. A quiet road will give you a chance to practice making turns and sudden stops, and controlling the trailer when backing. Since you will need to back the trailer onto the launching ramp in order to float the boat, diagrams

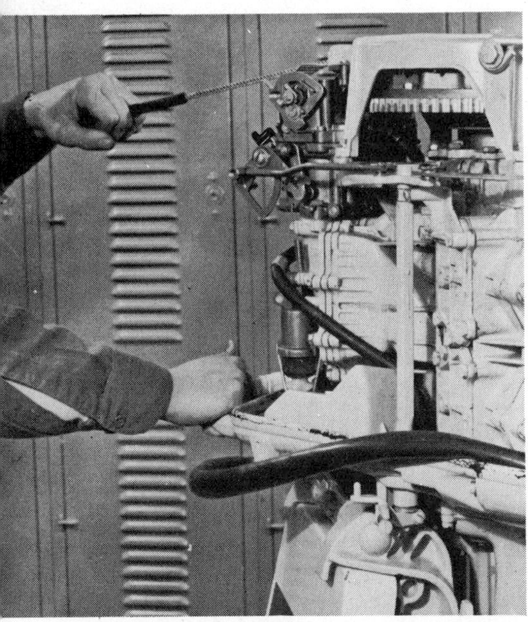

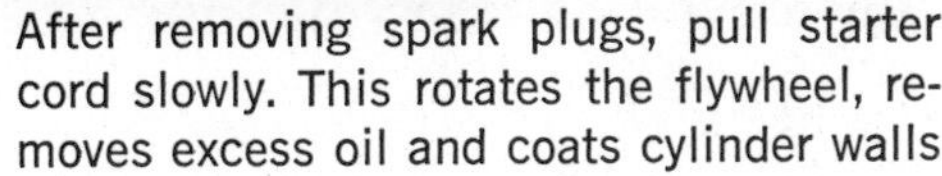
After removing spark plugs, pull starter cord slowly. This rotates the flywheel, removes excess oil and coats cylinder walls

To insure proper fitting of new spark plugs have mechanic check plugs with torque wrench before you try running your motor

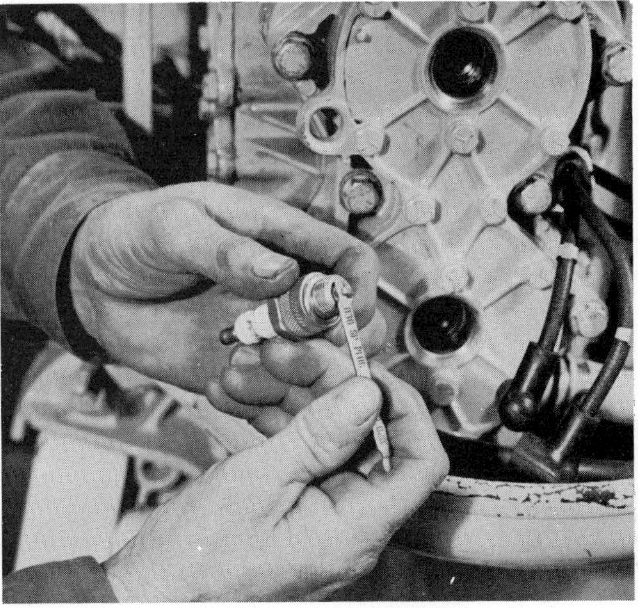

Before installing new spark plugs, check gap with feeler gauge that comes with motor's tool kit. Make sure gap is right size

Be sure to lubricate your engine at all the grease fittings recommended by the manufacturer. Always use prescribed lubricant

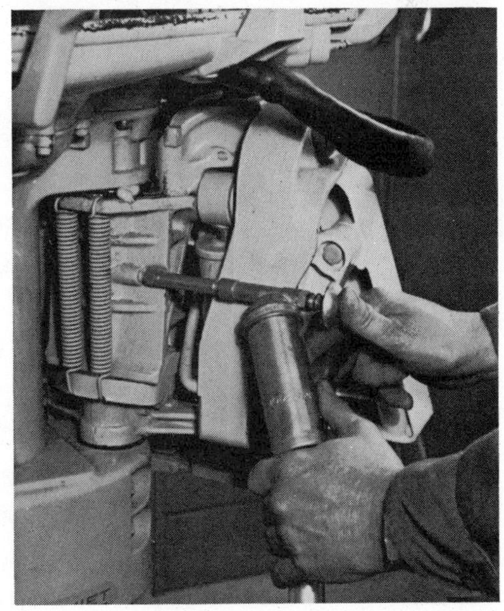

indicating the principles of maneuvering backwards may be helpful.

Be careful to give clear hand signals when making turns. Your car will need an outside rear-view mirror, since the usual windshield mirror will have the back view obscured by the boat. Make wide turns around corners, especially where curbs are high. When passing, swing wide and make sure that there is plenty of clearance in the road ahead. Slow down early and brake to a steady, smooth stop.

Before setting out on your first trip, make sure that the route you plan to follow permits trailering. Some throughways and parkways will not allow passage of any trailer vehicles.

The Boat Trailer Engineering Committee of the Outboard Boating Club has set up the following recommendations.

When you first fit boat to trailer:

- Are rollers, bolsters and other contact points adjusted to boat contour?
- When turned to maximum limit, is any part of the boat or trailer in contact with the towing vehicle?
- Is there proper slack in safety chains to allow maximum turns?
- Do lights, brakes, license, etc. meet the state legal requirements?

Every time you set out on a trip:

- Are all parts, nuts and bolts tight?
- Are all moving parts lubricated and operating properly?
- Are all tires inflated to correct pressure?
- Are all boat tie-downs properly secured?
- Are all lights operating properly?
- Is trailer hitch tight? Safety chains secure?

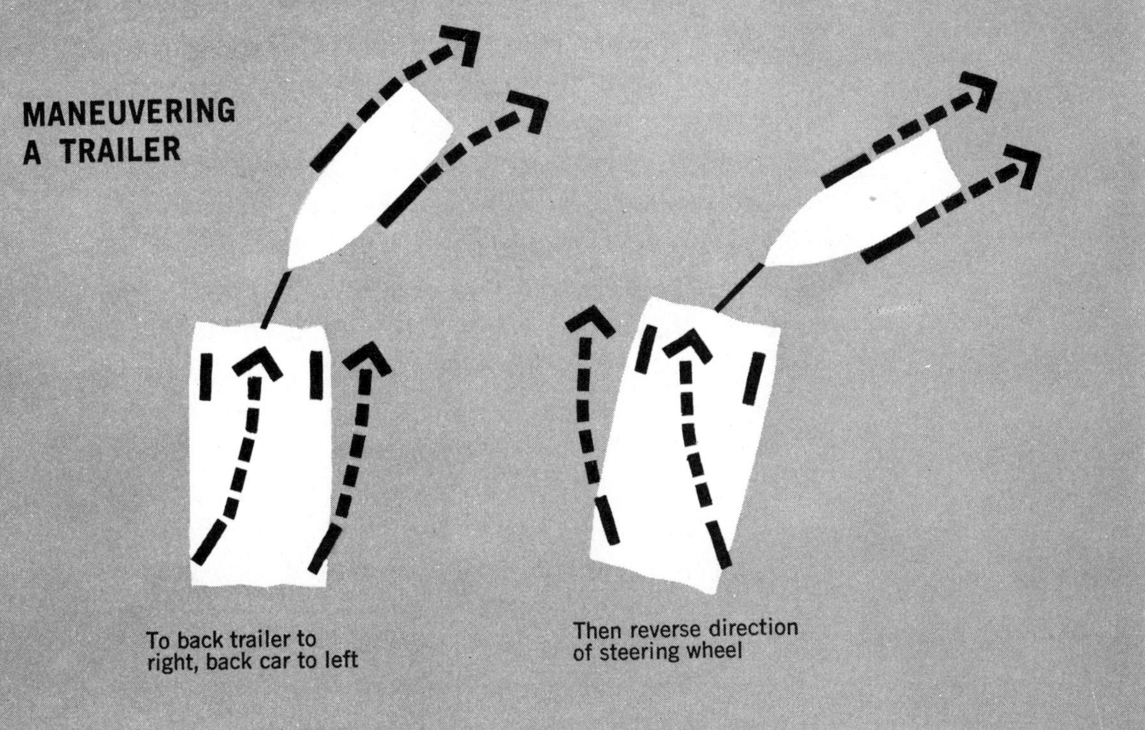
MANEUVERING
A TRAILER
To back trailer to
right, back car to left
Then reverse direction
of steering wheel

- Are brakes operating properly?
- Is motor tight on transom and locked or secured in position?
- Are locks on winch, bunk or tilt-mechanisms in proper position?
- If baggage or equipment is carried in the boat, is the load evenly distributed and secured?
- Are wheel bearings properly lubricated?
- Are boat gas tanks tightly closed? (It is recommended that tanks be left empty on long trips and filled upon arrival at destination.)

During the trip:

Always check the above safety items regularly while en route. Remember to check the wheel hub with your hand. Excessive heat indicates inadequate lubrication and possible bearing damage.

Launching on Arrival

Launching is a two-man job. The driver of the

car needs an alert guide with good judgment calling signals as the trailer is backed toward the launching ramp or the water's edge, as the case may be. If you're on a launching ramp, maneuver the trailer into position at the top of the ramp, ready to roll straight back into the water. If you're launching from a beach, try to pick a gradually sloping area. Now unlock the bow windlass or winch and make it ready, keeping the boat snubbed tight. Tilt your outboard up and remove the rear tie-downs.

If the ground is soft or sandy, you may find it useful to deflate the tires slightly to get firmer traction. Now back down until the trailer wheels are in the water to about the rim. (Never let the bearings get into the water.) Set the emergency on the car, turn off the engine and either block the car wheels or shift into low gear.

Have your assistant hold the bow line to the boat as you give the craft a firm push down the trailer. Now unfasten the launching cable and reel it in until the boat is afloat and held only by the bow

Launching and hauling out your boat are easy if you follow all the directions. Notice that car is on firm ground, trailer not too deep, and engine tilted up

line. Park your car and trailer, mindful of inconveniences to other boatmen (and possible rising tide), and you're ready for your day's outing.

Hauling Out for Re-Trailering

When the time comes to haul out again, place the trailer in position as before, with the car braked and in gear. Bring the bow of the boat to the trailer and let the winch do the actual job of pulling the boat up. Secure the tie-downs, lock the winch, stow the gear evenly and lock the motor on the transom. If you've deflated your tires at all, remember to reinflate them before getting onto the highway. If you have been cruising in salt water, it will be a good idea to hose down both boat and trailer on your arrival home.

WATER SKIING ■ SECTION 17

Water skiing originated in France over fifty years ago and was imported to this country in the mid-twenties. Although not exclusively an outboard sport by any means, it is certain that more water skiers are towed by outboard boats than by any other type. Water skiing is easy to learn and safe to engage in, providing reasonable safety rules are observed.

The American Water Ski Association was founded in 1939 and has established reasonable safety standards, signals and rules for competition. Safe skiing requires at least three people: the boat operator, the skier, and a man on board the boat to watch the skier so that the operator can keep his attention focussed on the water ahead.

Most skiers like a shallow-water start in about $2\frac{1}{2}$ to 3 feet of water. From a crouching start with

WATER SKIING HAND SIGNALS

TURN
Palm vertical, describe curving motion with hand in direction desired.

WHIP OFF
Point to direction and then give quick circular motions with hand.

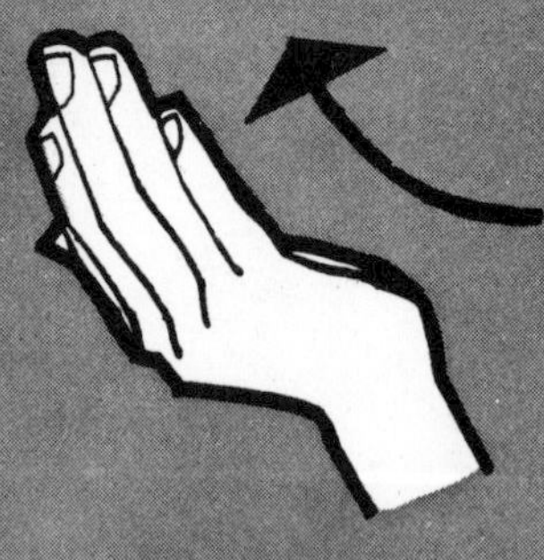

FASTER
Palm up—motion upwards, or nod head if both hands are in use.

BACK TO DOCK
Extend arm—and bend elbow so as to point downward with the forefinger.

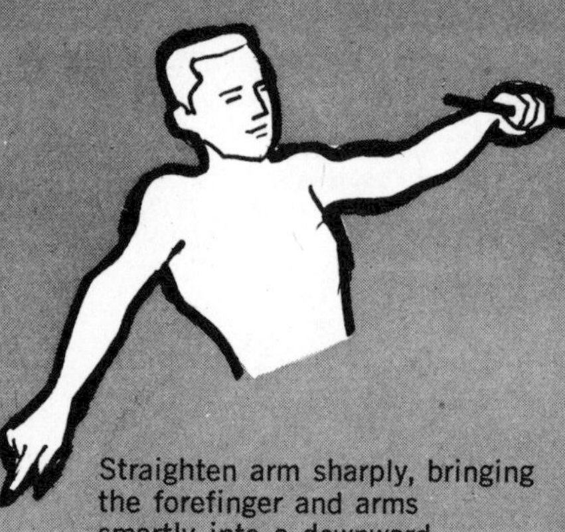

Straighten arm sharply, bringing the forefinger and arms smartly into a downward pointing position as above.

knees against the chest, with the skis well forward, arms straight, the skier gives the operator the "hit it" signal, sits back on the skis to point the tips up. With the legs bent, he gradually comes to a standing position as the boat accelerates. The skier must not lean forward, but keep his weight behind his feet. Turns are made by leaning inward, as with a bicycle turn, keeping the knees slightly bent.

In landing, the skier comes in parallel to the shore at slow speed, drops the tow bar, and coasts in to the point where he loses momentum and sinks

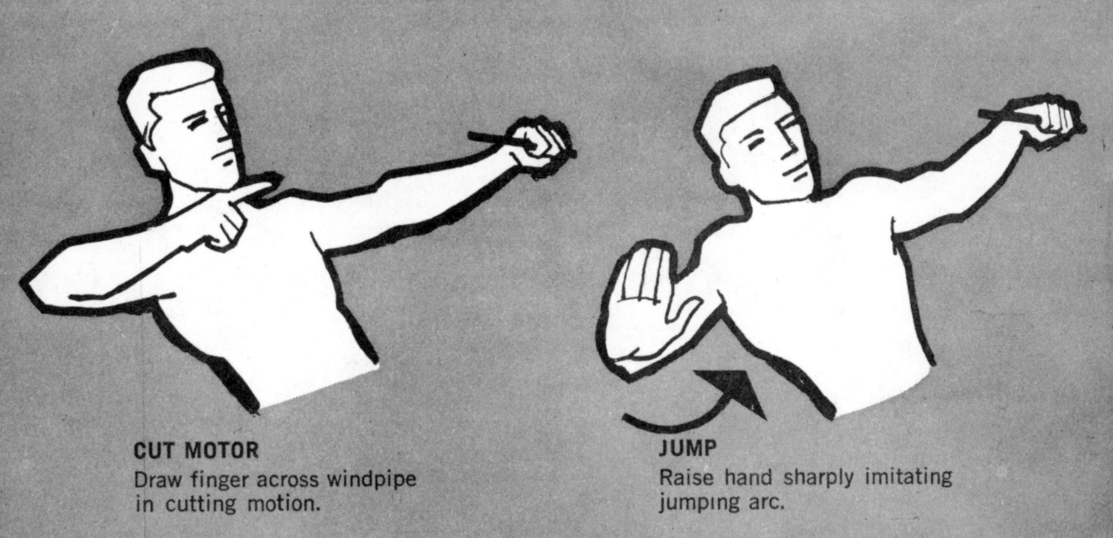
CUT MOTOR
Draw finger across windpipe in cutting motion.

JUMP
Raise hand sharply imitating jumping arc.

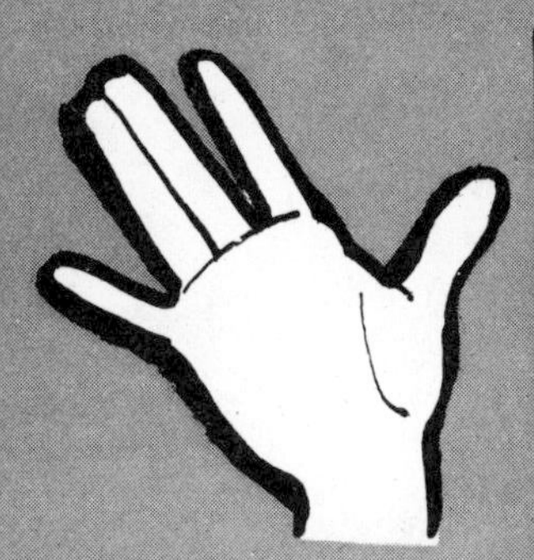
STOP
Hand up, fingers outstretched —policeman style.

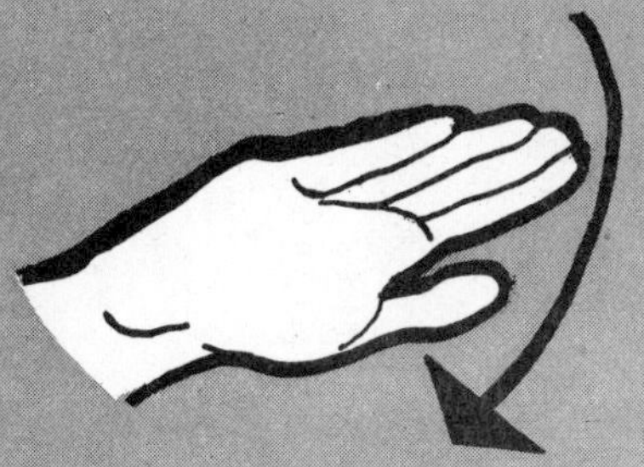
SLOWER
Palm down—motion downward, or shake head if both hands are in use.

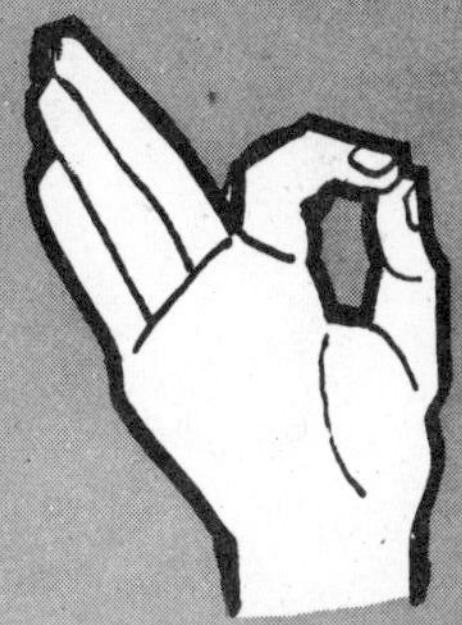
SPEED OKAY
The okay signal, with thumb and forefinger making an "O." No motion of head if both hands are in use.

to the bottom. Getting in too close will result in a bad fall if the skis ground while the skier is still moving forward.

Under no circumstances should the beginning water skier slip his arm, leg or any part of the body through the bridle. Spills under way are to be expected and, when they happen, the skier should raise an arm or a ski as soon as possible to indicate to the boat that he is all right. All water skiers should be strong swimmers, and all must wear a life jacket or belt.

Water skiing is said to be America's fastest growing sport. But it has dangers. Well-rehearsed signals and a look-out in the boat are crucial safety elements Skier at left is at fault; he is not wearing PFD (Personal Flotation Device).

The boat operator's chief concern is to keep the boat away from swimmers and bathers and congested waters so that the skier will have open water for maneuvering. The operator must remember not to make a sharp turn when the skier is already inside the turn since the strain on the side of the boat at a sharp angle can readily capsize the craft. Likewise, the skiing tow-line should not be made fast to the lifting handles at the transom, since the strain will be unbalanced.

Other rules well worth remembering are: make wide turns; keep the motor running at a steady speed; if the skier falls, the lookout should keep his eyes fixed on him for a prompt return; if the skier is to be taken aboard, the motor should be stopped when the boat comes alongside and the skier helped in over the transom or, preferably, by means of a boarding ladder; if the skier wants to continue skiing after a fall, the operator should circle slowly and come up to him cautiously so that he can take hold of the line a good distance from the tow bar. The skier allows the rope to run slowly through his hands until he can grasp the tow bar. The operator then speeds up gradually and smoothly.

Skier, operator and lookout should all study the accompanying illustrations of signals before setting out. These signals are standard and, once mastered, may be used with any operator and any skier.

PLANNING A CRUISE ■ SECTION 18

Unhappy is the boat-owning family today without plans for at least one or more summer cruises.

In times gone by, cruising was restricted to our ocean coast lines and to the Great Lakes areas. Only the owners of stately cabin cruisers with full accommodations for living aboard had the temerity to embark on long trips.

Today, the owners of the luxurious cabin cruisers still make their annual cruises. But they are often accompanied by owners of outboard cruisers, by owners of outdrives and even by owners of runabouts and utility craft who carry their tents and camping equipment and sleep ashore.

The owners of the smaller cruising craft can trailer their boats to cruising waters never before available to yachtsmen. In addition, the dredging program of the U.S. Corps of Engineers is constantly opening rivers and channels for yachting providing access to new, often fascinating waters.

The planning of a cruise is entirely dependent upon the amount of time available. Once you know the exact number of days and the itinerary you propose to follow, it is well to spend a number of evenings with your charts, working out each day's travel and probable layover spots. Be sure to file a float plan before departure. Be guided by the following common-sense principles:

• Don't plan to cover so much mileage that you may have to push to make it good. Since you're to be on vacation, a relaxed schedule is your aim. Starting early and running until sundown every day is more fatiguing than it is refreshing. Plan to be moored with plenty of time for a swim and a cocktail or soft drink before dinner time. Neglect of this will result in your getting poor moorings in a crowded harbor, in arriving at about the same time as the sundown mosquitoes or gnats, and in sitting around in a wet, cold bathing suit after dark.

• Plan your stops where fuel and water will be available. Anyone who has ever tried to hitch rides or tramp down a hot road with a gasoline can, knows the tax it is on energy and patience. Even the forehanded skipper who carries a safety can with extra gas on board has been known to face this embarrassment.

• Plan regular stops close enough to shopping centers so that you can replenish your groceries, milk, butter and soft drinks without having to take taxis or trek cross-country to a distant store.

• Plan occasional stops at motels, boatels or hotels. Your wife will be grateful for the surcease from cooking and the whole family will enjoy a good shower, a night between clean, dry sheets and an evening of entertainment in town.

SAFETY TIPS

• There are three sure signs of the beginner in outboarding: running through harbors at excessive speeds; buzzing docks and swimmers; discomfiting other boats with boat's wake. Avoid these errors. Teach youngsters to avoid them. They can subject you to state or federal fines.

• Always watch your wake when passing near other boats or in a crowded harbor. Remember that you are legally responsible for any damage done by your wake.

• When testing your outboard engine in a barrel, be sure you have adequate ventilation. Gas fumes in an enclosed garage or basement can be silent assassins.

• Extra gasoline aboard should be carried only in an approved container and stowed in a safe location.

• Motor should be turned off when fuel is being added.

• Tanks should be removed from the boat for filling. Tank should be resting on a level surface, preferably a dock, away from any flame or spark in the event of spillage.

• Batteries should be protected by a plastic top or cage to prevent accidental shorting.

• Don't jump into your boat. When boarding from a dock, step gently into the center, steadying yourself on the dock.

• Ski hitches, in attaching the line to the boat, should hold the line above the motor or to the transom in such a way that a slack line will not foul either the motor or the propeller.

• A good speed for water skiing is 12-15 miles per hour. Anything over 22 should be tried only by experts.

• Don't turn or circle around a fallen skier or you may wrap the tow line around his body. Don't get close while your propeller is turning. Cuts from even a slowly-turning prop are dangerous. Don't put skier in a position where he will swing into bank or fixed object.

• Don't take up water-skiing — in fact, don't even buy an outboard — unless you are fully prepared to obey the basic rules of courtesy and safety afloat.

6

OUTFITTING AND UPKEEP

Almost no other possession a man has is a clearer expression of his personality than his boat. A man who might be embarrassed at being complimented for an extremely stylish suit will beam with pride when an admiring stranger looks over his craft and says, "She looks beautiful!"

But to the non-millionaire, this admiration is only earned through hours of sanding, painting, varnishing and polishing. This chapter sets forth the basic, accepted methods of keeping a smart ship.

The sound yachtsman, however, is interested in more than the superficial appearance of his boat. To him the matter of upkeep centers around proper maintenance of his equipment. The outward symbol of this good maintenance is the display of the prized Coast Guard Auxiliary Courtesy Examination seal.

Of all the sources of pride a man may have, few are more justifiable than a beautifully-kept, well-handled and well-equipped ship.

SECTION 19 ■ OUTFITTING

Buying equipment for a boat is like furnishing a house: it is a continuing process that starts with necessities and continues toward a goal which is limited only by the bank account of the owner. For useful reference, we are subdividing items of equipment into four classes: legally required equipment, essential equipment, desirable equipment, and useful luxuries.

By Act of Congress, the government has established certain minimum requirements for motor boats. Enforcement of the Act is delegated to the Coast Guard, and offenders may be punished by court action. Sailboats without engines must carry lights in accordance with the Pilot rules. Rowboats and small sailboats (up to 18 feet in length), which are regarded as rowboats under sail, are often required to show only a white light at night unless in exceptionally crowded harbors.

Motorboats are divided into four classes, according to size. Outboard boats are included but are exempted from certain requirements as to engine ventilation.

All power craft with engines of over 10 horsepower and all motor craft in some states must have numbers. In most areas, numbering is under state supervision, as indicated in subsequent tables. In other areas, apply to local Post Office.

The table on pages 166-7 gives a summary of required equipment. The skipper should examine the table carefully to make certain that his boat conforms in all respects to the requirements.

To be accepted as Coast Guard-approved equipment, life preservers, ring buoys, buoyant vests, flame arrestors, and fire extinguishers must meet

Coast Guard specifications and be clearly marked with approval number and inspector's stamp or with a model number recorded by the United States Coast Guard.

When purchasing approved equipment, the buyer is urged to insist on a sales slip describing the article as Coast Guard-approved.

As of January 1, 1962, carbon-tetrachloride extinguishers and those of the chlorobromethane types were no longer approved because of the toxic vapors released in enclosed spaces.

In selecting extinguishers, reference should be made to the accompanying table.

FIRE EXTINGUISHER CLASSIFICATION

Class	Foam	Carbon dioxide	Dry chemical	Freon
size	gallons	pounds	pounds	pounds
B-1	1¼	4	2	2½
B-11	2½	15	10	–
B-111	12	35	20	–

The laws governing the showing of running lights were revised in accordance with the table shown on page 168. In this table, Class A and Class 1 are grouped together and Classes 2 and 3 are also grouped together.

It should be noted that Option 1 lights are limited to the Inland Waters, Great Lakes, and Western Rivers. These cannot be used on the high seas. However, the Option 2 lights may be used on either the high seas or Inland Waters, Great Lakes, and Western Rivers.

Essential Equipment

Certain items of equipment on board are not required by law but are universally recognized by good yachtsmen to be essential to boating safety. Most of these items are also recommended by the Coast Guard Auxiliary and the Power Squadrons in their seamanship and safe boating instruction. Let us enumerate them alphabetically:

Anchor(s)—A second anchor on board is a must, one light, one heavy.

Anchor rode—An ample length of fresh, sturdy line or chain.

Bilge pump—Large-volume, galvanized type is recommended. If your boat has an engine-operated bilge pump, keep a manual pump as a spare.

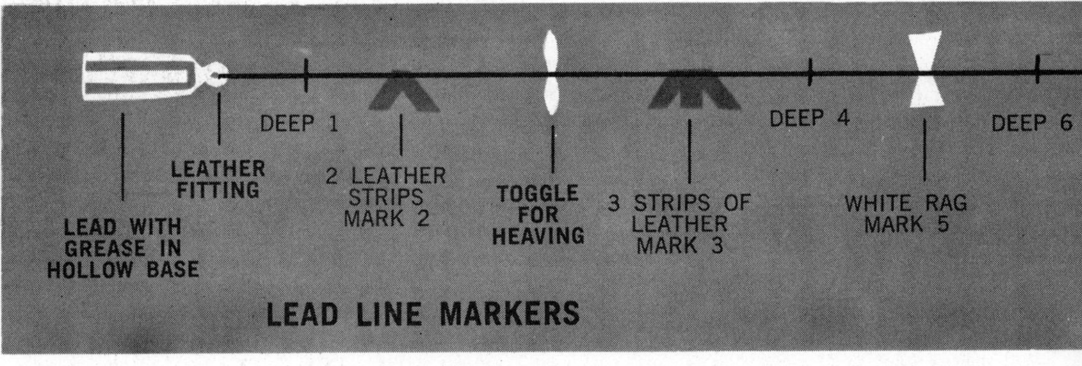

LEAD LINE MARKERS

Boat hook—Keep it easily accessible on cabin top or deck.

Clock—An electric or an eight-day clock is needed.

Compass—If you plan to be more than a mile from your mooring, have one on board for fog, bad weather, or unexpected travel after dark.

Charts—Use official up-dated National Ocean Survey Charts or area equivalent. Have a chart for every area in which you may conceivably be traveling.

Current and Tide tables—Invaluable in unexpected emergencies.
Deviation table—One belongs with every compass.
Distress signals—Always carry flares, water dye marker, smoke material, signalling mirror, and flashlight. New shark repellent is also reassuring to have on board in coastal waters.
Dividers—Necessary for chart work. Better yet, have a standard navigator's kit and keep it with your charts.
Fenders—Should be standard equipment.
First aid kit and manual—A must.
Flashlight or electric lanterns—Always carry extra batteries.

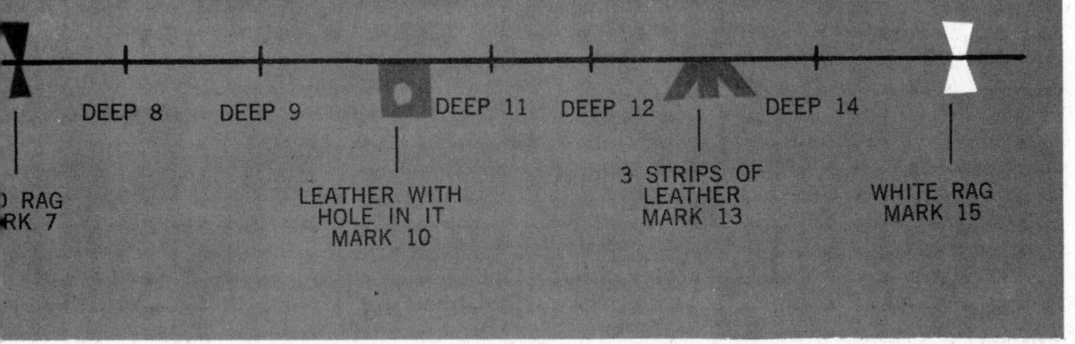

Food and water—Always carry emergency supplies.
Lead line—Can be bought measured and marked.
Light list—Buy it when you buy your charts.
Mooring lines—Carry in sufficient number and strength to hold your boat securely in a blow or for use as a tow line.
Motor oil and grease—Lay in an adequate extra supply.

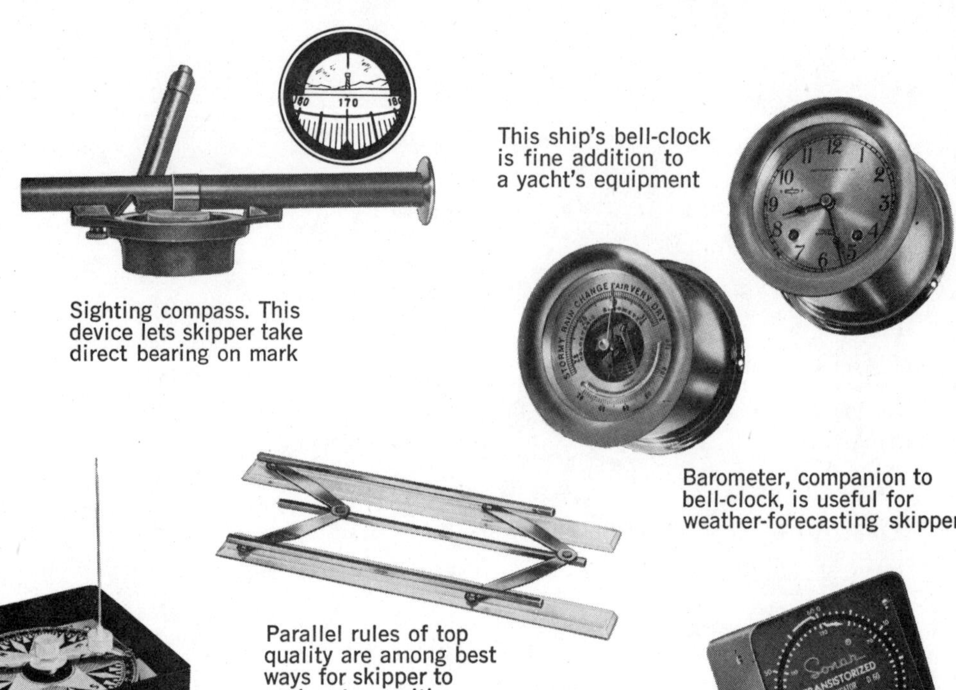

Sighting compass. This device lets skipper take direct bearing on mark

This ship's bell-clock is fine addition to a yacht's equipment

Barometer, companion to bell-clock, is useful for weather-forecasting skipper

Parallel rules of top quality are among best ways for skipper to work out a position

Pelorus may be used with compass card. It is accurate when lined up with lubber's line

Fathometer—a useful "luxury". Transistorized device gives reasonably accurate depth readings

Paddle or oar—This is an ancient and essential form of emergency power.

Pail or bucket—To be used for emergency bailing or as a sea anchor.

Parallel rules or protractor—Needed for charting courses.

Radio set—Tune in regularly for weather forecasts.

RPM table—Make it yourself with form included in this chapter.

Ring buoys—On all but very small craft, have two on board for assistance to man overboard. Length of good nylon or manila line should be attached to one. Many boatmen prefer Horseshoe buoys.

Spare parts—Carry spark plugs, gaskets or gasket material, coil, condenser, wire, distributor head,

Yacht compass is compact and easily-read. Dashboard compass is to be installed on bulkhead —card is magnified

This pelorus-compass lights electrically and magnifies reading under the bearing vane

Radio direction finder receives both broadcast and marine frequencies

Good binoculars are essential aboard. Many yachtsmen prefer 6 x 30 for daylight and 7 x 50 for use at night

rotor and points, fuses, fuel pump, repair kit, and spare bulbs. (For outboards, no spare part is more vital than a supply of extra shear pins.)

Sewing kit—You will need a ditty bag with needles, palm, sail twine, wax, marlin and knife.

Tool kit — It should contain wrenches, screw drivers, hammer, chisel, drill, pliers, wire clippers, files, saw, awl, mallet, electrical tape, wire, sand paper and crocus cloth.

Miscellaneous—A well-found yacht will always have an assortment of screws (brass, Everdur, stainless), nuts and bolts, cotter pins, shackles of various sizes, spare blocks and light lines, glue, penetrating oil, and other items proved necessary by personal experience, including seasick and sunburn remedies.

Coast Guard approved type of fire extinguisher has Underwriters' approval

Flares and smoke signals are waterproof, come in accessible container

Called a loud hailer, this hand-held electronic voice amplifier can be heard on shore as well as by other boats

A megaphone is a must in case loud hailer's power fails or on boats that do not have one

Desirable Equipment

The following equipment is more desirable on cruising yachts than on small craft. Some of it is expensive and will be beyond the means of many boat owners their first few years of yachting. Most of it is standard equipment on boats intended for off-shore cruising or racing:

Barometer—Purchase a good aneroid "glass" with legible figures.

Binoculars—These are vital at night or for identifying landmarks, other vessels and buoys.

Boarding ladder—Use for swimmers and for boarding from a dinghy.

CB radio—Useful in emergencies but not as reliable as Marine Radiotelephone.

Deck shoes—Buy the non-skid type.

Depth finder—The double-range transistorized type is excellent.

Drogue—A well-made sea anchor is invaluable in a storm; use it with an oil bag to keep seas from breaking to windward. The drogue, shaped somewhat like a wind sock, though larger, and made of stout canvas, holds the bow into the wind and seas. The oil bag may be rigged on a line and small block, so that it can be refilled from time to time and hauled out to the drogue. The oil film resulting

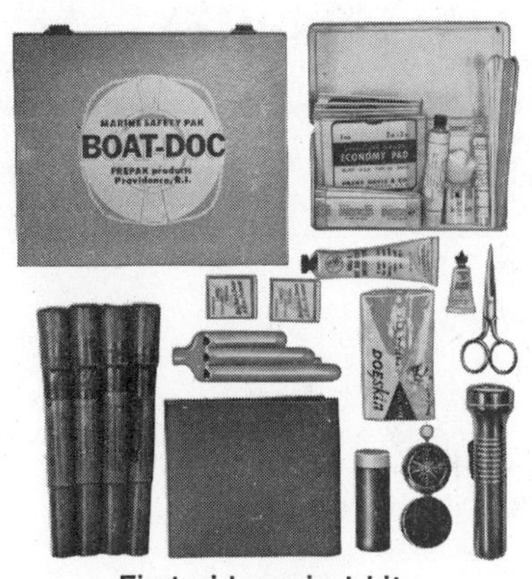

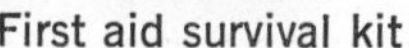
First aid survival kit

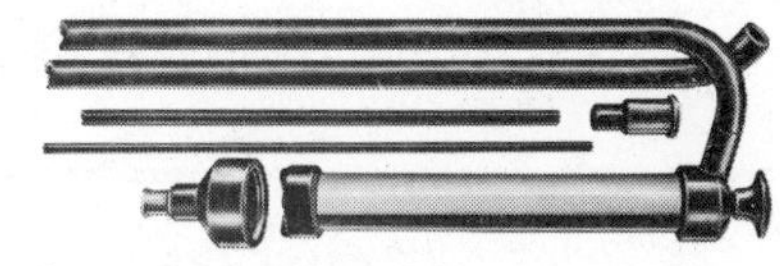
The essential bilge pump must be highly durable, resistant to rust

Distance ray has narrow but very powerful beam

from seepage through the bag spreads over a wide area and keeps seas from breaking over the ship.

Lantern—Have one (electric or kerosene) that is self-contained, in case of electrical failure.

Flags—A highly desirable flag for any yacht is the Coast Guard Auxiliary flag or the Power Squadrons flag, or both. Earning the right to fly them is your best assurance of becoming a safe boat handler.

Foul weather gear—Storm suits are desirable for all on board.

Galley seat—This is a stool for the cook, preferably one that is rigged to fold out of the way.

Heaving line—Use as a messenger to carry heavier line to shore or to another vessel.

Insecticide, insect repellent—Do not count on guests bringing their own.

Marine radiotelephone—Operates on VHF/FM frequencies. Channel 16 used as "hot line" to Coast Guard Search and Rescue units.

Megaphone—Useful for hailing other vessels and people on dock.

Motor crank handle—Used for cranking engine.

Patent or taffrail log—This is used for measuring the distance travelled.

Pelorus or hand-bearing compass—Devices used for sighting.

Pilot rules—Keep at least one copy handy.

Radio direction finder—A device to which you

(continued on page 170)

LEGALLY REQUIRED SAFETY EQUIPMENT

	FIRE EXTINGUISHERS	VENTILATION	FLAME ARRESTER
CLASS A Less than 16 feet	At least 1 hand portable fire extinguisher of type classified as B-I.	Two or more ventilators with cowls or equivalent capable of removing gases from bilges in engine and fuel tank compartments. (For boats built between April 25, 1940 and August 1, 1980)	Carburetors must be fitted with approved device for arresting back fire.
OUTBOARDS	Not required if boat is of open construction.	Not required.	
CLASS 1 16 feet to 26 feet	As Above.	As Above.	As Above.
OUTBOARDS	As Above.	As Above.	
CLASS 2 26 feet to 40 feet	At least 2* Class B-I hand portable fire extinguishers or 1 in addition to a fixed fire extinguishing system in machinery space.	As Above.	As Above.
OUTBOARDS	As Above.		
CLASS 3 40 feet to 65 feet	At least 3* B-I hand portable fire extinguishers or 2 in addition to a fixed fire extinguishing system in the machinery space.	As Above.	As Above.

*One Class B-II may be substituted for 2 Class B-I.

PERSONAL FLOTATION DEVICES (PFD's)	HORN OR WHISTLE	BELL	LIGHTS
›ne Coast-Guard approved fe preserver, buoyant vest, ing buoy or buoyant cushion 1 good and serviceable con- ition for each person board.	Not required by Motor Boat Act of 1940. However, 72 COLREGS require **all** vessels to carry means of making "an efficient sound signal." Rowboats are not exempt.		See Lights Chart.
›ne wearable approved per- onal flotation device for each erson aboard plus one cush- ›n or ring buoy.			
›s Above.	Hand, mouth or power-operated horn or whistle capable of producing a prolonged blast (at least 4 seconds' duration) audible for at least .5 mile.		See Lights Chart.
.s Above.	As Above.		
›s Above.	One hand or power-operated whistle or horn capable of producing a blast (at least 4 seconds' duration), audible 1 mile.	One which when struck produces a clear bell-like tone of full, round characteristics.	See Lights Chart.
›s Above.	As Above.	As Above.	
As Above.	As above but only power-operated equipment is acceptable.	As Above.	See Lights Chart.

Note: MSD's (Marine Sanitation Devices) are now required on all vessels built since January 1975. Older boats which had already installed Type I devices as of January 30, 1978 may continue using them. Otherwise, Type II or Type III devices will need to be installed. See your dealer or write Coast Guard for CG 485 for further details.

LEGALLY REQUIRED LIGHTS Classes A, 1 – Under 26 feet

POWER ALONE Inboard, Outboard, or Auxiliary

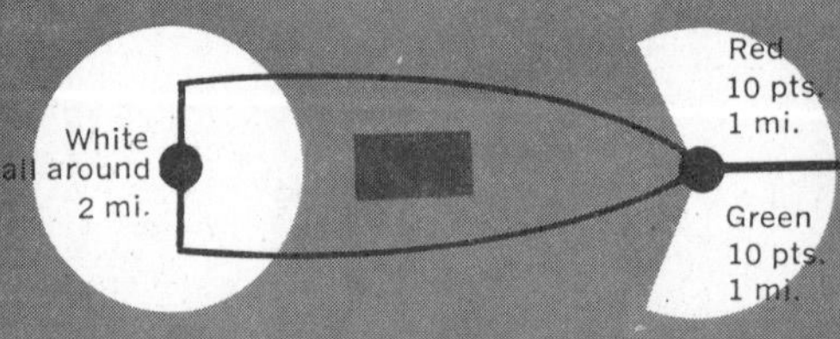

White
12 pts.
2 mi.

(on mast)

White
20 pts.
3 mi.

Must be 3 ft.
above colored
lights

Red
10 pts.
1 mi.

Green
10 pts.
1 mi.

INLAND RULES
inland waters, western
rivers, Great Lakes only

INTERNATIONAL RULES
required on high seas,
may be used inland

SAIL AND POWER Auxiliary

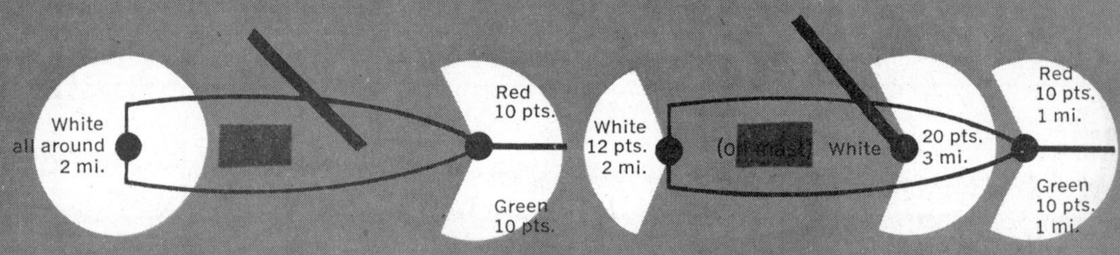

INLAND RULES
inland waters, western
rivers, Great Lakes only

INTERNATIONAL RULES
required on high seas,
may be used inland

SAIL ALONE

Sternlight not required for vessels under sail alone on Great Lakes

Red over Green
20 pt. 2 mi.
near masthead
optional for
all sailboats

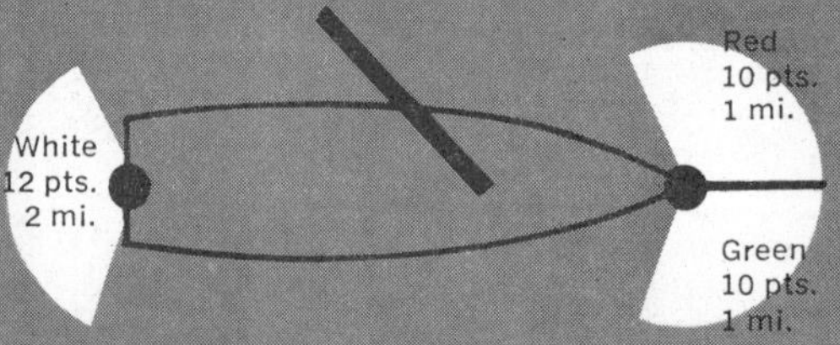

INLAND RULES
inland waters, western
rivers, Great Lakes only

Manually propelled vessels shall have a white light ready to be temporarily exhibited in time to avoid collision

Sailboats: separate side lights and 12 pt. white sternlight. Only International Rules will accept either a combination lantern or side lights on sailboats of less than 20 tons

EGALLY REQUIRED LIGHTS Classes 2, 3 – 26 through 65 feet

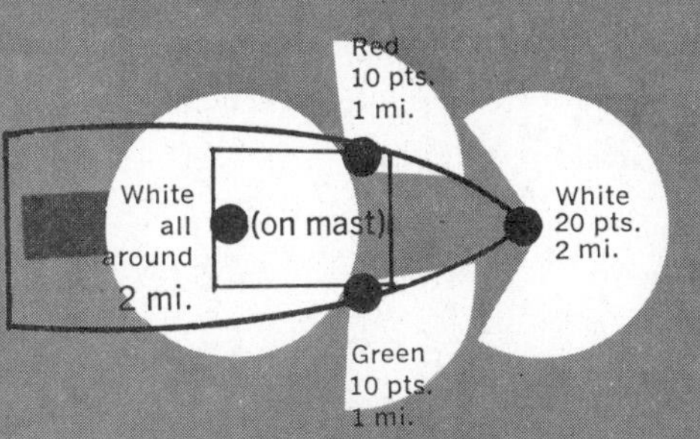

INLAND RULES
inland waters, western rivers, Great Lakes only

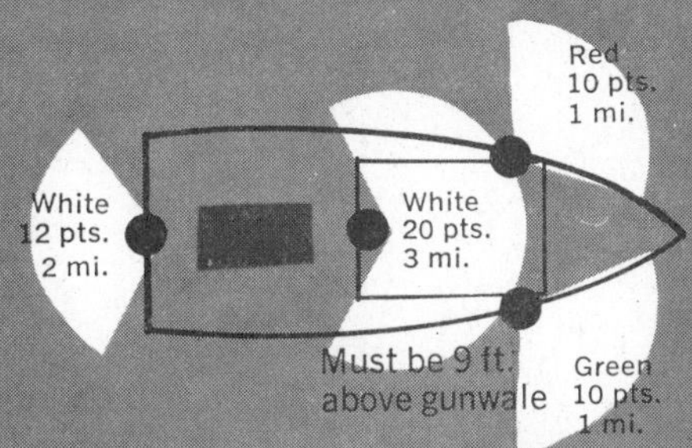

INTERNATIONAL RULES
required on high seas, may be used inland

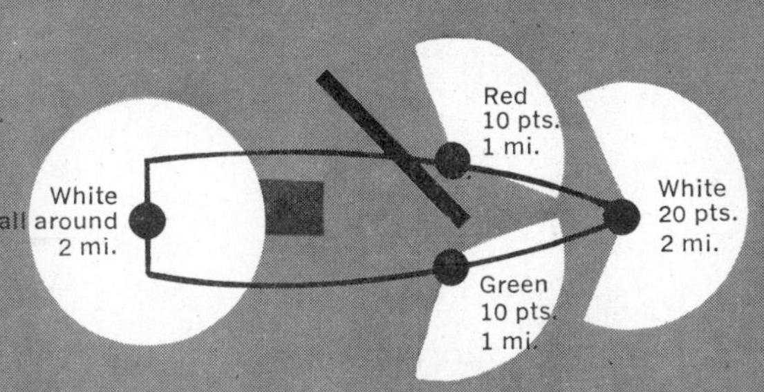

INLAND RULES
inland waters, western rivers, Great Lakes only

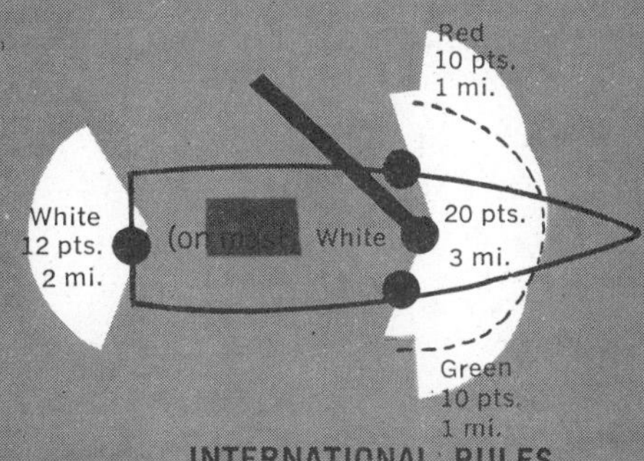

INTERNATIONAL RULES
required on high seas, may be used inland

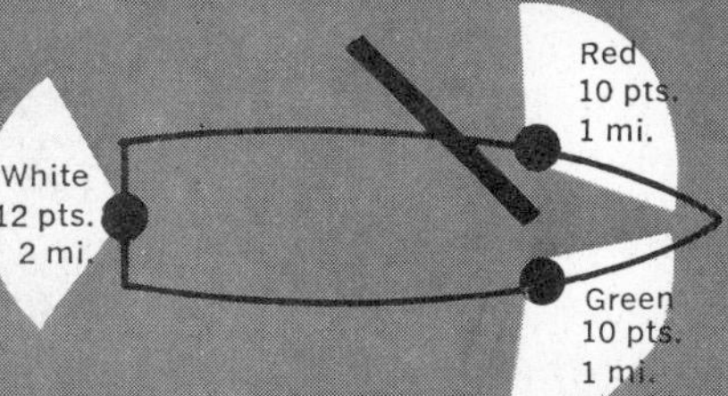

INLAND RULES
inland waters, western rivers, Great Lakes only

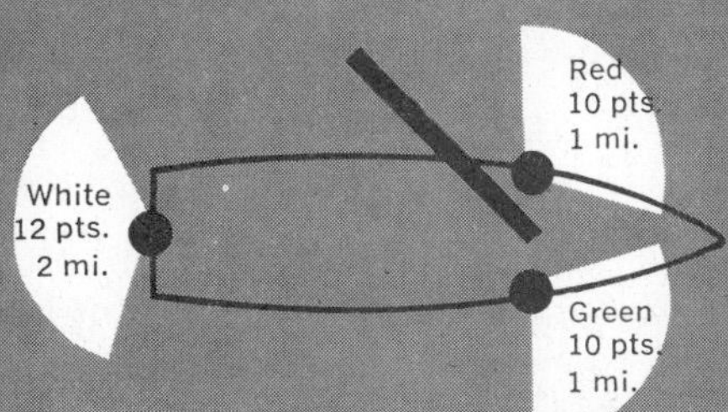

INTERNATIONAL RULES
required on high seas, may be used inland

will refer for getting your bearings.
Rigging knife—For splicing, serving and so on.
Searchlight—You may have either a permanent installation or the half-mile beam type.
Ship's log—Entries should be scrupulously kept when you are navigating by dead reckoning or during sustained piloting.
Spare battery—This should include a hydrometer and distilled water in a plastic bottle.
Sun glasses—Include suntan oil and sunburn lotion.
Stop watch—One is vital for timing lights and fog signals to insure accurate identification.
Swab or soojee—Needed for cleaning cabin and decks.
Water pump—It is wise to carry a spare.

Useful Luxury Equipment

This is virtually an endless category and includes items all yachtsmen would like to have but often have to defer acquiring until more urgent items are purchased. They make excellent gifts for the skipper, however, from friends and relatives:
Cordless electric drill—This runs on batteries and may be used anywhere.
Cordless electric razor—Ditto.
Electric flare—Attach it to a ring or horseshoe buoy; it lights when it hits the water and burns for hours.
Electronic anchor light—It turns itself on at dusk and off at dawn.
EPIRB— Electronic Position Indicating Radio Beacon will send out an automatic distress signal on 2182 kc, international distress frequency; it enables a rescue ship or aircraft to track a distressed

yacht, dinghy, or man overboard by a continuing transmission.

Horseshoe life ring—This comes in bright yellow or crimson, and should be kept, in its stainless holder, quickly available for heaving to a man overboard. Its color makes it readily spotted in heavy seas.

Loran C and Omega—Electronic position finders.

Plastic chart cover—Keeps charts fresh and dry.

Plastic-insulated glasses—Since ice is often in short supply, these drinking glasses keep drinks cold with less ice.

Power megaphone or loud hailer—Amplifies the voice and projects it electronically.

Radar—Suitable for large yachts only.

Signal flags—Most skippers would like to have a complete alphabet set, numerals and repeaters, as well as their yacht club burgee, owner's pennant, guest and absent flags, and even a cocktail flag.

Speedometer—A must for the racing skipper, and a useful source of information when cruising.

Ship-to-shore radio—Many skippers regard this as essential nowadays. When you're in serious trouble, you can call the Coast Guard or another vessel.

Yacht ensign—Legally, only documented vessels are permitted to fly this. Other craft may fly the American flag. Fly it only at anchor between dawn and dusk unless you know complete etiquette for its use.

VERY pistol or flare launcher—For firing signal flares high into air in an emergency.

In surveying the several lists above, it is obvious that the requirements of a 16-foot outboard and a 55-foot racing yawl differ widely. In normal practice, however, yachtsmen work their way from

CONVERSION TABLE—RPM TO KNOTS AND MPH

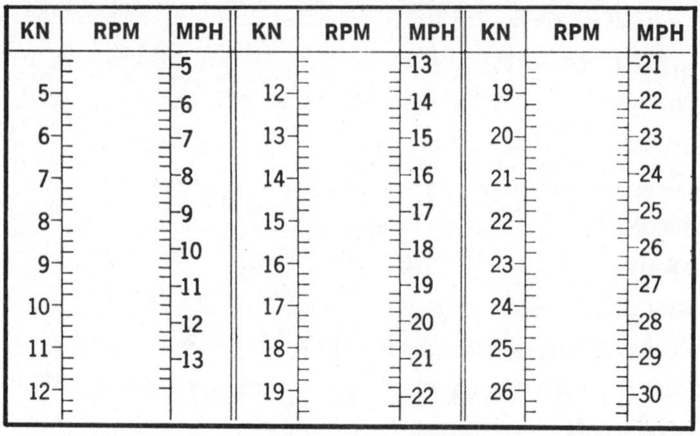

KN	RPM	MPH	KN	RPM	MPH	KN	RPM	MPH
		5			13			21
5		6	12		14	19		22
6		7	13		15	20		23
7		8	14		16	21		24
8		9	15		17	22		25
9		10	16		18	23		26
10		11	17		19	24		27
		12			20			28
11		13	18		21	25		29
12			19		22	26		30

smaller to larger craft and the above lists should prove useful guides to the skipper who aspires to rise steadily up the scale of performance in either sail or power boats.

Listed among the "essential" items was an RPM conversion table. The accompanying card may be copied and affixed with rubber cement close by the throttle for ready reference.

Directions for Calibrating: Find a measured mile with beacon indicators on the chart or, if none is nearby, measure off a mile on the chart between buoys or landmarks on which bearings may be readily taken. Run the mile at even speed on a constant heading. Then reverse course and repeat run in opposite direction, again maintaining the same RPMs. Average the two to obtain speed in still water. Divide 3600 by elapsed time in seconds. Speed obtained is in knots, if nautical mile was run or in miles per hour, if statute mile was run. Plot the throttle setting in RPM against the average speed obtained. Repeat the process for as many RPM readings as convenient, and plot them on the chart. Intermediate readings may then be interpolated.

SCRAPING, SANDING AND VARNISHING ■ SECTION 20

Spring commissioning actually begins in the fall. The skipper who is already enjoying life afloat in April and May is usually the skipper who started work on his boat at decommissioning time in late October or November. Laying out the work to be done will depend much on whether the boat is to be stored inside or outside, or kept in wet storage. How much the owner will have done by the yard is another factor. Some boatyards require that a stipulated minimum amount of work be done by yard labor.

Before hauling out, the boat should be thoroughly washed down. Equipment kept on board should be safely stowed for the winter in the yacht locker or in the owner's basement. Items to be cleaned should be taken care of now and stored, well-wrapped or covered, so as to be fresh for use in spring.

Once the clothing, linens, pillows, cushions and miscellaneous gear have been removed, the boat should be brought alongside the dock where a hose and running water are available. A good going over with standard liquid and powder cleansers and a brisk scrubbing brush and sponge will remove the spots, stains and grime, as well as the heavy salt coating on boats kept in coastal waters. A heavy, grease-cutting detergent should be used to freshen up the bilges. When the boat has been pumped dry, leave everything open that can admit air and sunlight to give the craft a thorough ventilating.

On hauling out, the yard will normally rough-clean the bottom. Re-check to make sure that all barnacles and marine growth have been removed. Scrub brush, wire brush and scraper will do for this job. In the case of sailboats, spars, standing rigging, running rigging, and blocks should be washed clean of salt and tagged before the mast is removed to insure quick and accurate reinstallation in the spring. Lines should be carefully coiled and hung in a dry place. Dirty line can be cleaned in a tumbler type washer. All wire rigging should be lashed to the spars so that it does not drag on the ground. All spars should be tagged with the name of the ship before being committed to the spar shed.

As much preliminary sanding on bottom and topsides as there is time for should be done in the fall. Any bare or rusting metal should be given a cleaning and a coat of anti-corrosive paint. Once the bottom is clean, a fresh coat of anti-fouling bottom paint will help stop rot or rust as well as the cracking and flaking that means so much extra scraping, sanding and filling in the spring.

In lining up your work projects, remember that, if the cabin has a good coat of durable interior paint every three or four years, the only work that needs to be done below on a yearly basis is freshening up of the varnish. Varnished items like blocks, drawers, locker doors and ladders can be taken into the club or home to the basement to be worked on over the winter.

Having drained the water tanks and bilges, you should pour anti-freeze into the basins and heads to make sure that any residual water will not freeze. Normally, the water pipes will have a drain at the lowest point in the system. Follow the pipes from tanks to all faucets or pumps to be sure that the drain actually is at the lowest point.

Consult the maker of your engine for instructions on laying it up, or check with the yard mechanic. Normally, water and fuel are carefully drained and a spoonful or two of oil placed in each cylinder through the spark plug aperture. Crank-turn the engine to distribute the oil. The battery must be taken off and kept on trickle or occasional charge and, of course, all electronic equipment should be stored indoors in a dry location.

Whether you set up the frames and lash down the winter cover yourself or have the yard do it for you, make certain that your boat's name is stencilled on it so that, in the haste and pressure of getting her over in the spring, your framing and tarp don't end up in an anonymous heap.

As much varnishing as can be accomplished should be done in the fall when the weather is usually crisp and clear as against the frequently showery, humid weather of spring. Ideally, varnishing should be done twice a year—in the fall and in mid-summer. No more varnish should ever be applied than is absolutely necessary. Remember, every coat that builds up will eventually have to be taken down.

During the winter, the equipment that has been taken home should be cleaned up and overhauled. Any sails that need repairing should be left with the sailmaker during the slack season to get the best work at lowest cost. And if the engine needs an overhaul, don't wait for the hectic, delay-fraught weeks of spring. The same is true for repairs on electronic equipment. No matter how standard an engine or radio may be, inexplicable delays seem to happen when you are in a hurry for a spare part.

Spring. The frames and cover have come off. You have visited your paint supply store and fortified yourself with scrapers, light, medium and heavy sandpaper, turpentine, remover, wire brushes, gloves, caps, brushes, and pigments. In your permanent collection you will want to have dust goggles, a dust mask, extra lengths of heavy electric cord and an electric sander, and a combination drill-sanding-polishing outfit.

If your fall de-commissioning work was not as thorough as it might have been, rudder, rudderpost, skeg, keel, keelson, stem and centerboard will need to be freed of flaking or crumbling paint and buffed clean of rust. A coat of paint that looks sound should be tested with a good going over with sandpaper. A loose, powdery or flaky coat will quickly reveal itself. On Fiberglas, use a solvent wash to remove mold-release agents.

If the bottom is just too patchy to save, you will want to take it down to the bare surface with paint remover (non-inflammable type), scraper, wire brush, and sand paper. Steel-hulled boats should be given a priming coat of anti-corrosive paint. A wood-hulled craft should have her seams well cleaned out of old seam compound with a sharp tool such as a beer can opener. Now a good sanding with a belt or vibrating electric sander will smooth out any rough spots on the surface and get you ready for the priming coat.

On wood hulls, new seam compound should go in after the priming coat, and the seams should be grooved a little after filling so that when the planking expands, the compound won't be squeezed out into ridges. Nicks, dents and scratches can be filled in next with trowel cement or seam compound mixed with anti-fouling paint. A second coat of anti-fouling paint should now be applied. Some owners prefer not to put on the final coat of bottom paint until just before the boat is launched, since some paints are more effective if not allowed to dry out before going in. Check your own paint dealer on this. Bottom paints of various manufacturers have varying qualities. Never use copper bottom on an aluminum boat.

If you wood either the bottom or topsides, take care not to leave the bare wood exposed for more than a day or two. Unprotected planking dries out rapidly and your seams will open if you let this happen.

If the topsides are to be scraped, obviously this should be done before the bottom is worked on since paint remover has a nasty habit of running down the sides. In general, in all kinds of painting aboard ship, you should paint from the top down. If the removing is confined to a small area with danger of spoiling good paint below or beside, use a cream remover which will not run. In any case, be sure to rub down the area removed with soap and water or with a rag thoroughly wetted with turpentine or paint thinner. The wax in the remover can spoil your paint or varnish coat if left on the wood.

Any time you expose bare wood or bare metal in scraping, use it as an opportunity to spot-check the condition of the hull. Dry rot, causing the wood to become soft and pulpy, is the worst danger. In smoothing down your finishes, scrupulously avoid the use of steel wool. Small fragments are bound to break off and cause rust stains the rest of the season anywhere they lodge. A good bronze wool will give no such trouble. Neither will the Fiberglas scraping pads now available.

In the case of Fiberglas hulls, the topsides may be treated almost as one would keep up an auto finish. A good cleaning with a detergent should be followed by waxing and polishing. The bottom of

Have the yard check any sputtering, choking, slow starting, vibration. Be kind to your engine—it will return the favor

a boat used in coastal or brackish waters will want to have a coat of anti-fouling paint against barnacles and, in fresh water, against marine growth. A brisk sanding, careful cleaning, and painting with a good grade of anti-fouling bottom paint will do the job. Decks and topsides tend to fade after four or five seasons. Although regular topside and deck paints may be used, a good epoxy finish is more durable, adheres better and is easier to apply.

One coat of epoxy is usually all that is needed; it may be expected to stand up for several years. An occasional scrubbing with soap and the application of a coat of wax will keep the finish sparkling. If your sailboat has wire rope rigging, you can usually detect signs of wear by the tell-tale tiny wire splinters that nick you as you run your fingers along the stays. If you have rust but no splinters, a thorough cleaning and a coat of aluminum paint will keep the rigging in good condition. Replace any wire that has developed a kink. Turnbuckles should be freed up, oiled and, when set up, wired to prevent their loosening unnoticed. Sheaves in blocks need to be oiled and running freely as do swivels, snap shackles and other moving gear. The mast track should be thoroughly cleaned and adjoining sections carefully aligned to assure easy hoisting and quick dropping of canvas.

Some sailboat owners prefer to paint wood spars, others prefer varnish. The advantage of the latter is that it permits the skipper to detect cracks or checking before serious danger develops. On aluminum spars, use a medium grit emery cloth to brighten. Then clean with special thinner to remove residue. Apply a coat of special mast protective sealer.

There are scores of books and pamphlets on the techniques of painting and varnishing but the true professional touch comes only with experience. A few helpful tips follow:

• Don't paint from a stepladder. Set up a plank or trestle and adjust its height so that you paint only from shoulder level to waist level.

• Use only the very best of brushes. When you have finished painting, it is far better to hang the brush in a container of turpentine or solvent than to clean and dry it.

• Before you start to paint, be sure the paint is thoroughly mixed. If it is at all old, strain it through cheese cloth or plain window screen.

• Always keep a few jobs on hand to do below decks. Rare is the spring without a weekend or two of rain. No matter how damp or cool, you can always clean and sand. If you try to paint or varnish interiors in bad weather, however, you had better turn on the stove or heater (making sure to have proper ventilation).

• Bottom painting can be speeded up by using a roller.

• Don't pick out a color without consulting your wife

• Use masking tape to get a sharp boot-top.

• When edging varnish and paint, hold your last coat of paint until after your last coat of varnish. This will allow you to varnish across the intervening seam and seal up a boundary that is often subject to leakage.

SECTION 21 ■ THE ENGINE

The engine that has been giving trouble at the end of the season is best left to the yard mechanic before the beginning of the next season. However, if your engine has been purring smoothly and you have laid it up carefully, it is possible for you to get it in shape with a little care.

First remove the wires to the spark plugs and unscrew the plugs with a deep-socket wrench. Usually it is desirable to replace the plugs but, if you consider them in good condition, you may take them out, set the bottoms in a tray of non-toxic solvent and let them soak in it for several hours. Similarly, remove the distributor cap along with the wire that connects the distributor and coil. The whole assembly should then be washed thoroughly in cleaning fluid (always being sure to work only in the open or in a large well-ventilated area). If the insulation is broken, cracked or dried out in any places, replace the wiring.

Now carefully clean out the openings in the

cylinder head where the plugs fit, removing the dirt, not letting it drift into the cylinder. If there are plug gaskets, replace them before setting the plugs back in. If you know how to set the gap in the plug, fine. Otherwise, have your service station do it for you and watch the process carefully.

After reinstalling the wiring, but before putting the plugs back, connect your battery, making sure that terminals are clean, and wires firmly clamped on. Coat the terminals with grease or vaseline to slow corrosion. Then pour about a shot glass full of engine oil into the head of each cylinder and cover the openings with either lint-free rags or paper towels. Keep the ignition off and the plugs out and turn your engine over a few times with the starter or with the hand crank, if you prefer. Turn the engine over for about a minute in short spurts to get the cylinder walls nicely coated with oil. First, cover the spark plug openings or the oil will tend to spurt out and mess up your clean engine compartment.

It is now time to reconnect the plugs with their wiring, in proper sequence, of course. Fill all grease cups and bring the oil in the crankcase to the proper level. Fill the water cooling system, add enough gas for a brief run-in, and you are ready to check out the engine. As you run the engine to open the season, keep a steady check on your oil pressure gauge, engine temperature gauge, and ammeter. If the engine functions smoothly and quietly, you are ready for launching.

As an extra precaution, well worth the time, drain and flush the fuel tanks to remove sediment, sludge and condensation which cause engine stalling and sputtering.

Engine Care

The dangers and inconvenience of engine failure at sea need not be overdrawn, and the man who boasts that he scarcely knows what goes on under the hood of his car had best not carry this same attitude to sea. The marine engine is his friend but not necessarily his slave. In a word, it must be treated with attention and consideration.

Engine care begins with fitting out. If you are not an old hand at working on a gasoline engine, have the yard check any choking, sputtering, undue vibration or slow starting problems. Thereafter, be kind to your engine and it will return the favor.

• Before you cast off, warm up the engine well. Be sure that it is running smoothly and has reached average operating temperature.

• Check the oil pressure and water temperature gauges regularly after you get under way.

• When you anchor or tie up, warm up the engine each time. Never race or strain a cold engine.

• Remove and clean out your carburetor air intake regularly.

• Keep the engine clean. Keep all fittings and connections tight. Guard against chafing of the wires.

• Let your engine drop to idling speed before reversing.

• Don't let the engine idle for long periods of time.

• Clean the sediment bowl of your carburetor regularly.

• Check your bilges regularly to be sure that oil or gas is not collecting.

• Make permanent a temporary repair or connection as soon as possible, no matter how well the expedient may seem to be working.

• Most yachtsmen fill their fuel tanks in the morning before taking off on a day's run. You too will avoid potential trouble by filling at the beginning of the day, thus preventing possible condensation and formation of water in the tank during the cool hours of the night.

• Be certain that you only use white gas. This is all you will get at marinas and docks but don't make the mistake of assuming that, in a pinch, you can fill a jerry can at the corner service station and carry it aboard.

• Procure and keep an engine manual on board. Every manufacturer has certain checks which he recommends during each season such as carburetor adjustment, breaker point adjustment, point clearances, distributor breaker cam lubrication, cleaning of generator commutator, inspection of generator and starter brushes for wear, and adjustment of valve tappets. Distributor adjustment for maximum power and minimum fuel consumption is important. Learn how to do it with your engine.

LAUNCHING AND HAULING OUT ■ SECTION 22

Most of the details of launching in the spring can be safely left to the yard. The prudent skipper, however, will usually want to check for himself to be sure that the work boat or a friend already in the water will be able to tow him to his mooring. He will inspect his hull carefully to be sure that the drain plug has been replaced and that all seacocks are closed. Knowing that he has not been able to paint the bottom where the shorings have been supporting the sides of his boat, he will be prepared with a brush and some bottom paint to cover these exposed bare patches.

Meticulous yachtsmen will not connect the propeller coupling until the boat has been a few days in the water. Letting the planking soak up moisture and "settle" will cause very fine shifting of the vessel's lines which the boatman will want to allow for when connecting his propeller.

Careful attention to the mooring and mooring pennant goes without saying. Assuming that our skipper has taken this book's recommendation and changed his hawser in mid-season, he will have his last season's heavy line clean, covered with fresh chafing gear where it goes through his bow chock or hawse hole, and he will have his mooring and pick-up can freshly painted and marked with his boat's name. As important as anything else, he will put fresh chafing gear on the mooring can itself to protect the beautiful finish of his bow which has represented so many hours of assiduous (and possibly backache-making) labor. Everything from rubber tires to nylon-covered felt can be found in the average harbor but, in general, the most satisfactory protective padding is sponge rubber covered with a vinyl or plastic surface.

Turn your helm from side to side while someone on the ground observes the rudder. Then follow the steering cable back to the rudder quadrant and forward again, making certain that it is in good condition and connections are all tight.

Make a last check of pipe inlets and outlets to be certain they are clean and unclogged by paint or foreign matter. Check keel and rudder bolts to be sure they are tight. Tighten engine-lag bolts.

Now make a last check-over below and remove all the gear that goes in your locker or basement, especially paints, solvents and varnish. It's far easier to hand supplies over the side than to row them ashore. Vacuum the cabin thoroughly.

On sailboats where the mast is to be stepped after the vessel is in the water, be sure that the mast step is clean and ready to receive the spar. The knees and mast partners should be checked for any kind of give. Fastenings in this area should be set up. The mast collar should be in good condition, ready to secure to the mast. The preferred method is by lashing rather than tacking.

The boom, staysail club, spinnaker pole or other spars may be set on deck, but it is preferable to give the boat up to a week in the water (if of wood construction) to allow the planking to soak up moisture and expand to normal before placing strain on the chainplates through the rigging.

Be sure that you have your bilge pump in good working order. You may never need it more than the first day your boat is in the water.

Hauling Out

Fortunately, hauling out does not involve the same labor or solicitude that launching does. Even so, it should be prepared for with thoroughness.

Get a profile of your boat from the designer or builder. Your yard will be much better able to handle her on the ways if they know what her underbody looks like.

Choose your hauling-out time with an eye to launching in the spring. If you know you have a lot of work to do, try to be early hauling out both for your sake and the yard's. Try to keep your time flexible. Tides, wind, weather, and other work may keep the yard from adhering to a firm schedule.

If you're a sailboat man, you'll certainly want

to be there when the mast is unstepped so that you can carry it gently to the spar shed (with the help of several sturdy friends), make certain that it rests in a level, well-supported situation safe from sagging or warping, and that all of the running rigging and blocks are removed and the standing rigging gathered and lashed to the spar. Booms, clubs and poles should be properly tagged and stowed.

SECTION 23 ■ BUYING A USED BOAT

Luckily for the yachtsman, the life of a well-built boat is far greater than that of a car. Many boat owners have worked their way up from 15-footers to 45-footers without ever having taken a loss in the purchase and sale price of any craft they owned. From this, one may conclude that depreciation of a boat is closer to that of a house than to that of an automobile. (In point of fact, the big cost of boat-owning is in the upkeep.)

No matter how much any yachtsman loves his present boat, he is already dreaming and planning about his next boat. For this reason, virtually every craft afloat is for sale—at a price.

However, when you go to buy a used boat—particularly if it is to be your first boat—you are well advised to buy through an accredited yacht broker or an established yard. Having found what may or may not be the boat of your dreams, the next step is to hire an experienced marine surveyor and have him give the craft a thorough inspection. Boating friends are helpful but normally not as thorough as a marine surveyor.

In setting out to buy a boat, the first person to question is not the boat owner or the yard man. It is yourself. Ask yourself the following questions:

What do I want the boat for?

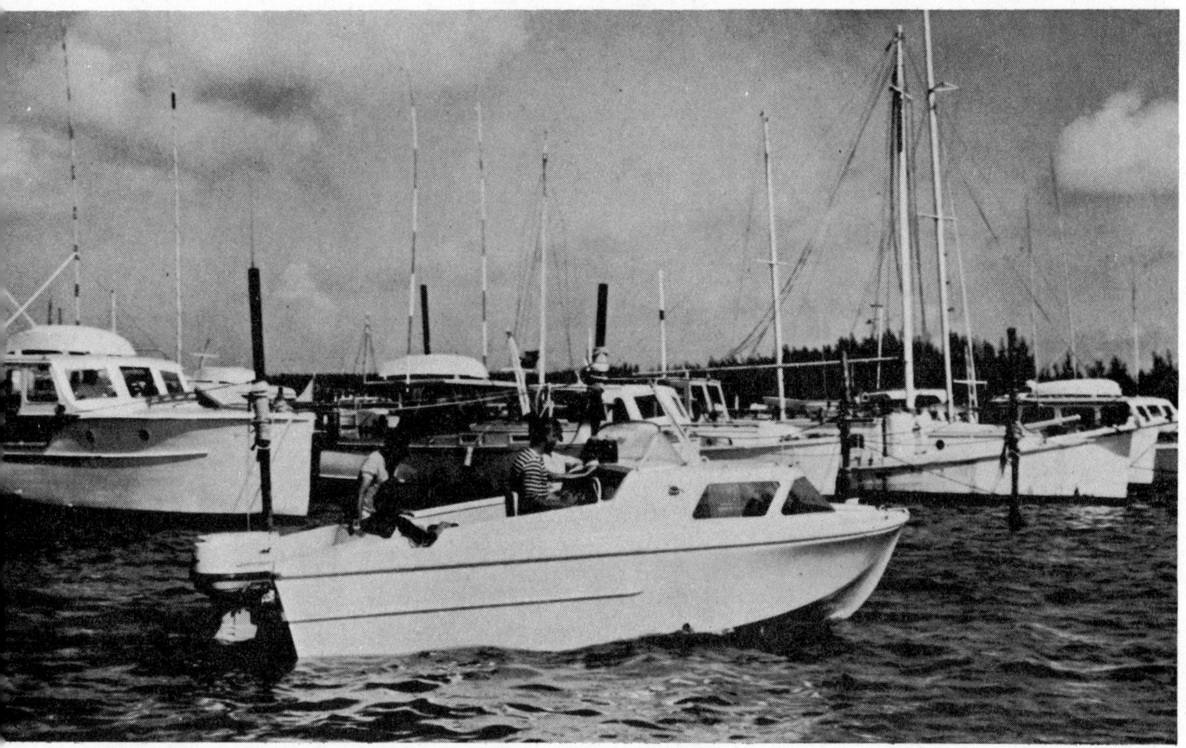

The skipper who is enjoying life afloat in May is the one who started work on his boat at decommissioning time in November

Fishing? Water skiing? Cruising? Day sailing? General family use? Transportation?

How much can I afford to spend?

Am I allowing enough to cover fitting-out and operating expenses? Will I want to have the purchase financed at the bank? What kinds of boat will the bank finance?

How big a craft do I need?

Do I realize that many of the costs of yachting are based on the boat's length? What is the maximum draft that will easily enter and leave the harbor where I plan to keep the boat and the areas where I propose to operate?

How powerful an engine do I need?

Do I realize that more people are annoyed by fast boats than are impressed by them? Do I realize that speed is the most expensive commodity in a boat?

How much work can I actually do on the boat?

If the salesman says, "She needs a little fixing that you can handle yourself," am I prepared to put in the time necessary? And do I have the know-how to do a satisfactory job?

Will I have patience enough to wait and try the boat out before I buy it?

Do I realize that most mistakes in boat-buying are made by people who buy in the yard without ever having gone out on the boat? (Almost as many mistakes are made by people who buy in the water without examining the boat on dry land.)

Am I reasonably familiar with the advantages and disadvantages of the various materials and types of construction?

Having asked yourself these seven questions, you will understand, of course, that you will not have perfect answers for them all, nor will you find the exact boat that fulfills both the requirements and your desires. There will be compromises. But let them be compromises in size, power and luxury, not in construction, condition and convenience.

If you are buying a wooden-hull vessel, see her out of water before you see her afloat. Go over the hull with a pen-knife or nail file, searching out soft spots. The usual spots where dry rot starts are in the deadwood, the transom, the stem, the cabin trunk and, in sailboats, at the partners where the mast fits through the deck. Look down in the bilges, checking for cracked ribs. If the vessel is afloat, check the bilges before you go out and again when you return to see how much water was taken.

Beware of the boat that has a fresh, heavy coat of paint over a bumpy, uneven surface.

Beware of any home-made boat.

Beware of the boat whose wiring system is

tangled, with brittle insulation.

Beware of the motor that seems to be leaking oil. Check the bilge of an inboard installation for signs of excessive oil drip, even if there isn't a visible leak, and check the propeller housing on an outboard for signs of grease leakage.

Wood:

In a wood boat, pay particular care to the fastenings. The most serious repair jobs on a boat are replacing the engine and having the hull refastened. Preferred fastenings are of copper, bronze and Everdur. Next is galvanized. Other metals suffer from corrosion and rust. Stains at fastening points are a bad sign. Excessive amounts of caulking in the hull often indicate that loose fastenings are causing the planking to work open in rough seas.

Check the hardware carefully. Rusty, pitted fittings indicate cheap materials, a poor chrome job, inadequate upkeep. Any fitting that is intended to take heavy strain such as a towing eye in the stem, a Samson post for securing the mooring line, or cleats fore or aft for securing mooring or towing lines, should be bolted through the deck. In Fiberglas boats the bolts should be reinforced, since a fracture will permit nut, bolt and fitting to pull out simultaneously. This danger is also present in aluminum boats where builders sometimes consider screws into the hull adequate to secure fittings. Don't be misled. Screws may hold the fittings perfectly for an entire summer and then, with the first autumn storm when you need them most, they may give way. The best method for securing fittings that could have to hold the boat is to use stainless steel bolts through the hull with a supporting member on the inside.

In buying a non-wood (aluminum or Fiberglas) boat or a plywood-veneer craft, you may feel reasonably safe if the vessel is four years old or less. Beyond that length of time pay particular attention to the following:

Aluminum:

Look for spots of corrosion. Be cautious of scars and bad scratches which may impair the anti-corrosive qualities of the finish. In salt water, inspect for pitting. Test the strength of the construction by pressing against the hull and bottom sections and deck. Areas that pop in and out indicate plating that is too thin or too scantily supported.

Fiberglas:

The surface should be smooth and polished on the outside. Many manufacturers purposely keep it rough or pebbled on the inner surface. Look for any severe cracking or chipping, especially at the ends. This is where delamination commences. In the case of a Fiberglas-covered wood boat, pay particular attention to areas in the bow, stern and bilge where lack of ventilation may cause dry rot to attack the wood inside the Fiberglas. Check for bubbling.

Plywood:

Check the entire planking to make sure that no delamination is setting in. Examine the joints to make certain that they are reinforced with blocks of solid hardwood or plywood. Check the fastenings for rusting, as noted above. Some woods with a great deal of grain, such as fir, must be thoroughly filled and smoothed when made into plywood or they will never present a polished surface. Rough-grained plywood surfaces are an open invitation to deterioration. Properly finished, however, Douglas fir is one of the best of the plywoods.

SAFETY TIPS

- Never keep paints and thinners on board during the season. Bottles break, cans rust and, in general, fire hazards are greatly multiplied by these highly inflammable liquids.
- Any liquids that must be kept on board, either in the galley or lockers, should be in metal or plastic containers.
- Bottom paint is generally highly toxic. Before you start work, check the directions on the can for proper antidotes, particularly if any paint splashes in the eyes.
- Polyester resins and epoxy paints are also exceedingly toxic. Use the same precautions with these paints as with the anti-fouling paints, being even more careful to keep them from the skin where they may produce burns.
- In removing bottom paint with a sander, always wear dust mask and goggles.
- Don't use a blow torch to burn off bottom paint. The torch may vaporize the toxic compounds and cause even greater injury than inhaling the dust.
- When working with carbon tet or naphtha, be sure you are in a well-ventilated, open space. Inhalation of the vapors of these and similar compounds can cause serious illness.
- Deck paints are now made with highly successful non-skid additives. If you have a painted deck, make it non-skid.
- Don't smoke while working with paints and solvents.
- If your boat carries a man-rail or life line, check the stanchion fittings during fitting out. Normally, they should be bolted through the covering board and should have no play.
- Life lines should be above knee height. Too low a line can prove to be tripping gear rather than life-saving equipment.
- Check the insulation and taped connections on all electric wires each spring. If dried or cracked, replace them.
- Soon after launching, have a courtesy inspection by the Coast Guard Auxiliary. If your boat fails, you'll get a safety warning. If it passes, you'll get a safety seal. Both are important to you.

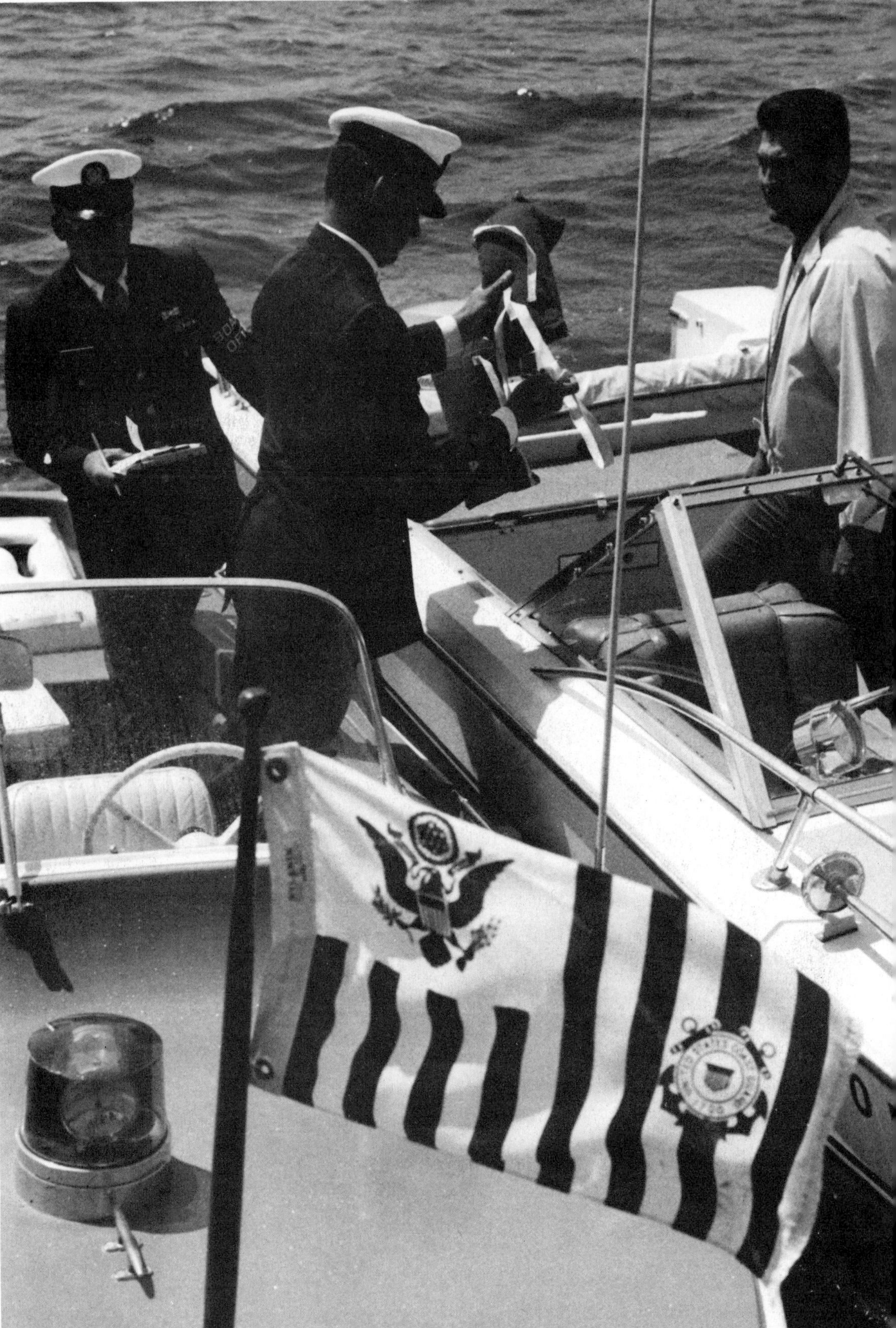

7

RIGHTS AND RESPONSIBILITIES

A few years ago, a popular television comedian decided to buy a yacht, or so the story goes. The day the boat was delivered, he went to an exclusive store and outfitted himself with a brass-buttoned jacket and a yachting cap with owner's insignia.

Bursting with pride, he jumped into his sports car, whirled across Hollywood to his mother's house, and shouted, "Look, Ma, I'm a captain!"

His mother studied his outfit thoughtfully for a while, nodded sagely, and said, "All right, son. On your boat, you're a captain. In this house, you're a captain. But tell me—among captains, are you a captain?"

The greatest satisfaction that a new yachtsman can have is to become a "captain among captains." This is a satisfaction earned only by a study of all the responsibilities of a skipper and by respect for all the rules governing the operation of his boat and the safety of his guests and crew.

SECTION 24 ■ NUMBERING AND REGISTERING

If you intend to drive a car or fly a plane, you know that you will have to pass an examination and get a license. Part of the study involved in obtaining a license is learning the laws about operating cars and planes. In return for obeying the laws, the license gives you certain rights and privileges that non-holders don't have.

Boats are required to be numbered for identification just as cars and aircraft are numbered. However, yachtsmen and yachting organizations have so far avoided the necessity for operators to be licensed, though most states have penalties for reckless operation of motorboats and the Coast Guard has authority to impose civil penalties. Such criminal offenses as reckless operation endangering life, limb or property, may draw a fine of up to $2,000 and imprisonment of up to one year.

A man in a boat often and rightly has a sense of extraordinary freedom of movement, freedom from constraint, freedom for self-expression. Yet this freedom never gives him the right to impair or impose on the freedom and rights of others. In this case, "others" include swimmers, divers, fishermen, other boatmen and even his own passengers.

In the naval services, rank confers both privileges and responsibilities on an officer. In the same way, the status of boat owner and/or boat skipper involves both rights and duties. Let us assume that you have just become a boat owner. The following questions and answers may clarify the responsibilities you face:

Do I need an operator's license?

As described above, no.

Will I have to get a number for my boat?

Yes, unless it is a vessel documented by the U.S. Bureau of Customs. In some states, boats of less than 10 horsepower are exempt.

Where do I put the number?

Numbers must be block numerals at least 3 inches high, spaced as in illustration on page 199, painted or fastened on each side of the bow.

If I use the boat in more than one state, in which do I apply?

Register for your number in the state where the boat spends most of its time.

How much does a number cost?

States may set their own fees. The Coast Guard charges $3 and issues numbers only through the U.S. Post Office. Renewal is $3.

For how long is the number good?

The state decides, but in any case not longer than 3 years before renewal. Coast Guard numbers are good for 3 years from the date of your next birthday after registration.

Is a number issued in one state good for use in other states?

Out-of-state and inter-state reciprocity exists where the states have a federally approved numbering system or where the number has been issued by the Post Office. Owners often ask if an outboard of 10 horsepower or less, not required to be numbered in its home state, may be operated in a state requiring numbering. The answer is generally no.

If I buy a second-hand boat, do I get the number with it?

The law says that within a reasonable time of sale (or change of address) owner is required to notify the agency which authorized the number. In case of sale, the new owner may apply for the

Where to Get Your Number

Under the Boating Act of August 1971, all undocumented pleasure boats propelled by machinery must be numbered.

ALABAMA
Water Safety Division
Department of Conservation
State Administrative Building
Montgomery, Alabama 36104
205-269-6325

ALASKA
Commission of Public Safety
Pouch "N"
Capitol Building
Juneau, Alaska 99801
907-586-5451

ARIZONA
Arizona Game and Fish Department
2222 W. Greenway Road
Phoenix, Arizona 85023
602-942-3000

ARKANSAS
Game & Fish Commission
Game & Fish Building
Little Rock, Arkansas 72201
501-376-1317

CALIFORNIA
Department of Navigation & Ocean Development
4616 Ninth Street
Sacramento, California 95814
916-445-2427, 2428

COLORADO
Game, Fish & Parks Department
6060 Broadway
Denver, Colorado 80216
303-825-1192

CONNECTICUT
Boating Commission
Department of Agriculture and Natural Resources
State Office Building
Hartford, Connecticut 06115
203-566-4409

DELAWARE
Division of Fish and Wildlife
Dover, Delaware 19901
302-678-4431

DISTRICT OF COLUMBIA
Metropolitan Police Department
Harbor Precinct
550 Main Avenue SE
Washington, D.C.
202-626-2401

FLORIDA
Bureau of Boating Registration and Licenses
Department of Natural Resources
Larson Building
Tallahassee, Florida 32304
904-224-7141

GEORGIA
Special Services
State Game & Fish Commission
Room 710
Trinity-Washington Building
Atlanta, Georgia 30334
404-656-3534

HAWAII
Boating Branch
Harbors Division
Box 397
Honolulu, Hawaii 96809
808-538-1365

IDAHO
Motor Vehicle Division
Department of Law Enforcement
P.O. Box 34
Boise, Idaho 83707
208-344-7471 Ext. 391

ILLINOIS
Boating Inspection
Conservation Department
400 South Spring Street
Springfield, Illinois 62706
217-525-2837

INDIANA
Enforcement Division
Department of Natural Resources
606 State Office Building
Indianapolis, Indiana 46209
317-633-5254

IOWA
Waters Section
State Conservation Commission
300 Fourth Street
Des Moines, Iowa 50319
515-281-5766

KANSAS
Forestry, Fish & Game Commission
Box 1028
Pratt, Kansas 67124
316-672-6473

KENTUCKY
Water Patrol
Department of Public Safety
New State Office Building
Frankfort, Kentucky 40601
502-564-3980

LOUISIANA
Revenue
Wildlife & Fisheries Commission
400 Royal Street
New Orleans, Louisiana 70130
504-527-5629

MAINE
Bureau of Watercraft Registration & Safety
State Office Building
Augusta, Maine 04330
207-289-2571

MARYLAND
Boating Division
Department of Chesapeake Bay Affairs
1825 Virginia Street
Annapolis, Maryland 21401
301-267-5933

MASSACHUSETTS
Division of Motorboats
100 Nashua Street
Boston, Massachusetts 02114
617-727-3900

MICHIGAN
Marine Safety Section
Boat & Water Safety Section
Stevens T. Mason Building
Lansing, Michigan 48926
517-373-1650

MINNESOTA
Outdoor Safety
Department of Conservation
625 North Robert Street
St. Paul, Minnesota 55101
612-221-3336, 3373, 2317

MISSISSIPPI
Law Enforcement
Boat & Water Safety Commission
Room 403
Robert E. Lee Building
Jackson, Mississippi 39201
601-354-7281

MISSOURI
Missouri Boat Commission
P.O. Box 603
Jefferson City, Missouri 65101
314-635-7261

MONTANA
Law Enforcement Division
State Fish & Game Department
Helena, Montana 59601
406-449-2453

NEBRASKA
State Game & Parks Commission
Capitol Building
Lincoln, Nebraska 68509
402-471-2571

NEVADA
Department of Enforcement
P.O. Box 10678
Reno, Nevada 89510
702-784-6214

NEW HAMPSHIRE
Division of Safety Services
85 Loudon Road
Concord, New Hampshire 03301
603-225-6611

NEW JERSEY
Motorboat Numbering
Department of Conservation and
Economic Development
Box 250
Trenton, New Jersey 08625
609-292-2466

NEW MEXICO
Boating
Park & Recreation Commission
P.O. Box 1147
Santa Fe, New Mexico 87501
505-827-2726

NEW YORK
Marine & Recreational Vehicles
1220 Washington Avenue
Albany, New York 12226
518-457-3790, 2121

NORTH CAROLINA
Motor Boats & Water Safety
Wildlife Resources Commission
Box 2919
Raleigh, North Carolina 27602
919-829-7191

NORTH DAKOTA
State Game & Fish Department
Bismarck, North Dakota 58501
201-223-8000

OHIO
Watercraft Division
1350 Holly Avenue
Columbus, Ohio 43212
614-469-3686

OKLAHOMA
Water Safety Division
Department of Public Safety
Box 11415
Oklahoma City, Oklahoma 73105
405-424-4011

OREGON
Oregon State Marine Board
109 Agriculture Building
Salem, Oregon 97310
503-378-3785

PENNSYLVANIA
Fish Commission
South Office Building
P.O. Box 1673
Harrisburg, Pennsylvania 17120
717-787-2192

PUERTO RICO
Marine Operations Department
Ports Authority
G.P.O. Box 2829
San Juan, Puerto Rico 00936
512-475-2087

RHODE ISLAND
Department of Natural Resources
Veterans' Memorial Building
83 Park Street
Providence, Rhode Island 02903
401-277-2284, 3070

SOUTH CAROLINA
Boating Division
Wildlife Resources Department
P.O. Box 167
Columbia, South Carolina 29202
803-723-7925

SOUTH DAKOTA
Department Game, Fish & Parks
State Office Building
Pierre, South Dakota 57501
605-224-3396

TENNESSEE
Game & Fish Commission
P.O. Box 9400
Nashville, Tennessee 37320
615-741-1431

TEXAS
Water Safety Services
Parks & Wildlife Department
John H. Reagan Building
Austin, Texas 78701
512-475-4751, 4293

UTAH
Division Parks & Recreation
1596 W. North Temple Street
Salt Lake City, Utah 84116
801-328-5881

VERMONT
Marine Division
Department Public Safety
Montpelier, Vermont 05602
802-223-5211

VIRGINIA
Game & Inland Fish Commission
P.O. Box 11104
Richmond, Virginia 23230
703-770-4974

VIRGIN ISLANDS
Department of Commerce &
Aviation Services
Ports Authority, Marine Division
Charlotte Amalie
St. Thomas Island, Virgin Islands

WASHINGTON
Parks & Recreation Commission
P.O. Box 1128
Olympia, Washington 98501
206-753-5757

WEST VIRGINIA
Law Enforcement Section
Department of Natural Resources
State Office Building
Charleston, West Virginia 25305
304-348-2754

WISCONSIN
Boating Activities
Bureau of Law Enforcement
P.O. Box 450
Madison, Wisconsin 53701
602-266-1369

WYOMING
Watercraft
Game & Fish Commission
P.O. Box 1589
Cheyenne, Wyoming 82001
307-777-7604

number already on the boat in his registration.

What is the certificate of number?

This is a small certificate (similar to an auto certificate of ownership). When you are using your boat, you must have it on board and present it for inspection if so required.

Where can I write for information about my state?

See the explanation and table on pp. 196-7.

Boat Numbering

Under the Federal Boating Act of 1958, motorboats of more than 10 horsepower and operated on the navigable waters of the United States must be numbered in the state of principal use. Motorboats documented by the Bureau of Customs are exempt.

Under the law come all vessels less than 65 feet in length which have permanent or detachable motors. A boat of five net tons or over which is used exclusively for pleasure may be documented as a yacht by the Bureau of Customs. A documented yacht must display her name and home port on some conspicuous part of the hull such as the stern, and her official number and net tonnage must be permanently inscribed on her main beam.

Since most pleasure craft are not documented, the owner must apply either to the State or the Post Office for an official number. This number must be painted on or attached to the forward part of the vessel on both sides. It must be of block letters not less than 3 inches high. The letters must contrast with the color of the background so as to be clearly visible.

Every undocumented boat regardless of size, which at any time carries a motor of 10 horsepower

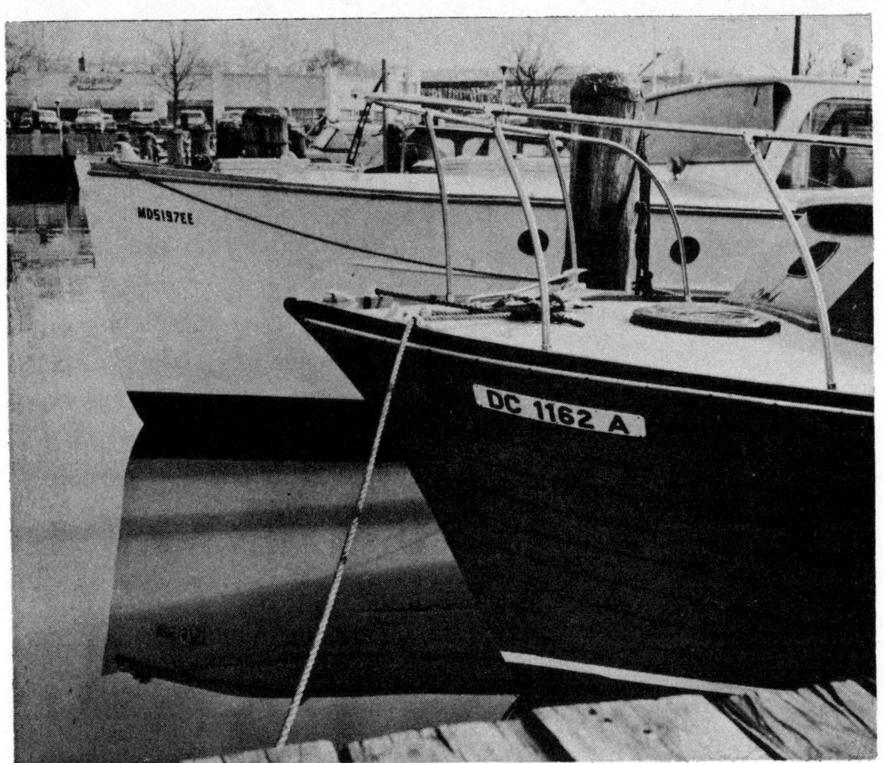

Numbers: boat in foreground shows correct size, grouping, and type of numbers. Rear boat numbers are wrongly grouped

or more, *must* be numbered. Numbers must be renewed every *three* years.

The granting of official number does not confer any privileges on the holder, but the law does require a boat operator to report accidents involving personal injury, or property damage in excess of $100, to stop and give aid if involved in any accident, and to carry the certificate on board at all times.

A vessel numbered by the Coast Guard or by a state having an "approved" numbering system may use the navigable waters of the United States within any of the 50 states for at least 90 days. After that, the owner must comply with the numbering requirements applicable in the new state of principal use.

The Coast Guard is numbering motorboats in the following states: Alaska, New Hampshire, Washington and the District of Columbia. Apply at the Post Office and buy a Federal Boating Stamp.

The cost of this Federal Boating Stamp is $3.

Motorboat numbering regulations state in part, "... the numbers shall read from left to right and shall be in block characters of good proportion, not less than three inches in height. The numbers shall be of a color which will contrast with the color of the background and so maintained as to be clearly visible and legible; i.e., dark numbers on a light background, or light numbers on a dark background."

The requirements of the laws and regulations as to size and style impose certain limitations on the individuality of numbers. However, there are no restrictions as to type of material used (e.g., "Scotchlite," plastic, metal, etc.) or as to the color, as long as the required contrast with the hull is adequate to furnish clear legibility for identification. It must be remembered that these numbers are placed on boats for identification and not for ornamentation, serving the same purpose as do license plates on an automobile.

The states listed in the accompanying table have their own (approved) numbering systems in accordance with the Federal Boating Act of 1958, and numbering is required on all waters of the state. Application should be filed with the state or local agency indicated.

SECTION 25 ■ LAWS FOR THE WATERS YOU SAIL

Once I have the number, what other laws must I observe?

Measure your boat from the foremost part of the deck at the bow to the aftermost part of the deck at the stern, parallel to the waterline. You must then check the required equipment for the class as described in the table on pages 166-167. Classes are defined as follows:

CLASS A	Under 16 feet in length
CLASS 1	16 to 26 feet in length
CLASS 2	26 to 40 feet in length
CLASS 3	40 to not more than 65 feet in length

The various states have recently enacted pollution laws. If your boat has a head, check the local laws regarding disposal of waste.

How can I be certain I have all proper equipment on board?

Contact your nearest Coast Guard Auxiliary Unit for a free courtesy examination. Shortcomings will be pointed out but you will not be reported. If you pass the examination, you will be awarded a decal shield with the Coast Guard Auxiliary emblem which insures that you will not need to be boarded and inspected by the regular Coast Guard boarding teams.

Are there any traffic regulations to observe?

Traffic regulations divide into the following:

Rules of the Road must be observed at all times. There are federal laws concerning reckless and negligent operation. Most states have laws forbidding operation of a boat while intoxicated or permitting your boat to be operated by one who is intoxicated. Many states forbid operation of a boat by the physically or mentally handicapped. Most states have speed limits in harbors, near shores and docks, and in restricted areas. In general, boats must be operated at speeds reasonable to their situation and must be under complete control at all times. Most states have laws prohibiting pollution of water, limiting speed near swimming beaches, etc.

What if I have an accident?

Federal law requires that, unless your own boat or its passengers are in danger, you must render "such assistance as may be practicable and necessary to other persons" affected by the accident in order to save them from danger. You must give your name, address, and the identification of your boat to any person injured and to the owner of any property damaged.

The law also says that if the collision, accident or casualty results in death or injury of any person, or damage to property exceeding $100, a full description of the accident must be reported to the state of number registration or to the Coast Guard, if it is the number-issuing authority.

Can a boat owner be fined for not observing the law?

Operating a boat without required number makes the owner liable to a penalty of $50.

Operating a boat without proper equipment makes the owner liable to a fine of $100.

Operating a boat in reckless or negligent manner may draw a penalty of up to $2,000. (Speeding through anchorages or in proximity to swimmers or while intoxicated are some examples of reckless operation.)

In print, the laws are imposing and may even seem restrictive of the boat-owner's freedom. But in practice, the good skipper will find that if he operates his boat safely and with due regard to the safety of others, he will always be operating legally, since the only purpose of the law is to prevent unsafe operation, and to protect the boat-owner, his family and guests, and other vacationers.

No boat owner likes to visualize his craft lying on the rocks, a total wreck. Yet storms happen, skippers make mistakes, fittings part, and boats suffer all kinds of damage.

For many such reasons, the wise boat owner will want to take out a full marine policy, covering the hull, machinery, and equipment against partial damage or total loss to the extent of the face value of the policy. The insurance covers the boat against the perils of the sea including such dangers as fire, collision, theft, lightning, grounding, windstorm, stranding and sinking.

The vessel is covered whether she is in port, at sea, on the ways, in dry dock, or stored for the season. The policy usually confines the coverage to certain specified waters in which the boat is normally at home or to limited cruises. Of course, broader coverage may be obtained for distant voyages. Policies usually cover the boat *in commission* from May 1 to November 1 and *laid up* the other six months. If you want to launch your boat earlier or haul out later, clear it with your insurance broker to be certain of uninterrupted coverage.

Loss or damage to spars or rigging while racing must be covered by special insurance. Damage or loss while in transit by truck or other means is covered only by special arrangement. Boats with certain types of built-in fire-extinguishing systems receive lower rates, as do boats with diesel engines.

A good friend to any boat owner is a knowledgeable insurance broker. Be guided by his advice and depend on him when you have trouble. Such a broker is a specialist—he will be able to recommend the policies best suited to your individual needs.

SECTION 27 ■ THE COAST GUARD AUXILIARY AND THE POWER SQUADRONS

The United States Coast Guard Auxiliary is a voluntary, national, non-military organization administered by the United States Coast Guard. There is no charge for membership nor is there any tuition charge for its courses in basic seamanship and safe boat handling, though in certain areas a charge for building services is made. Texts are bought by the individual.

The Coast Guard Auxiliary was authorized in 1939 by an Act of Congress to assist the Coast Guard in promoting safety afloat in the maintenance, operation and navigation of small craft. Membership is open to any citizen of the United States over the age of 17, male or female, who has not less than a 25% interest in a boat, plane or amateur radio station, and certain people with special qualifications as approved by the Commandant. A boat on which membership is based must be a motorboat of Class A, 14 feet or over, or of Class 1, 2 or 3, a sailboat 16 feet in length or over, or a pleasure boat over 65 feet long.

A plane-owning member must hold a private pilot's certificate or aircraft and engine license issued by the FAA. His plane must have a current FAA air-worthiness certificate.

A member basing his eligibility on radio must be a regularly licensed amateur or professional operator (any class) with a fixed radio station licensed by the FCC.

The basic unit of the Auxiliary is the Flotilla, consisting of ten or more boats, planes or radio stations. Five or more Flotillas become a division. The Divisions are organized geographically into

Classes afloat and ashore: the boatmen and women attending these Coast Guard Auxiliary classes in Florida are gaining priceless basic knowledge that will make them skilled and knowledgeable boat-handlers when they cruise the waterways

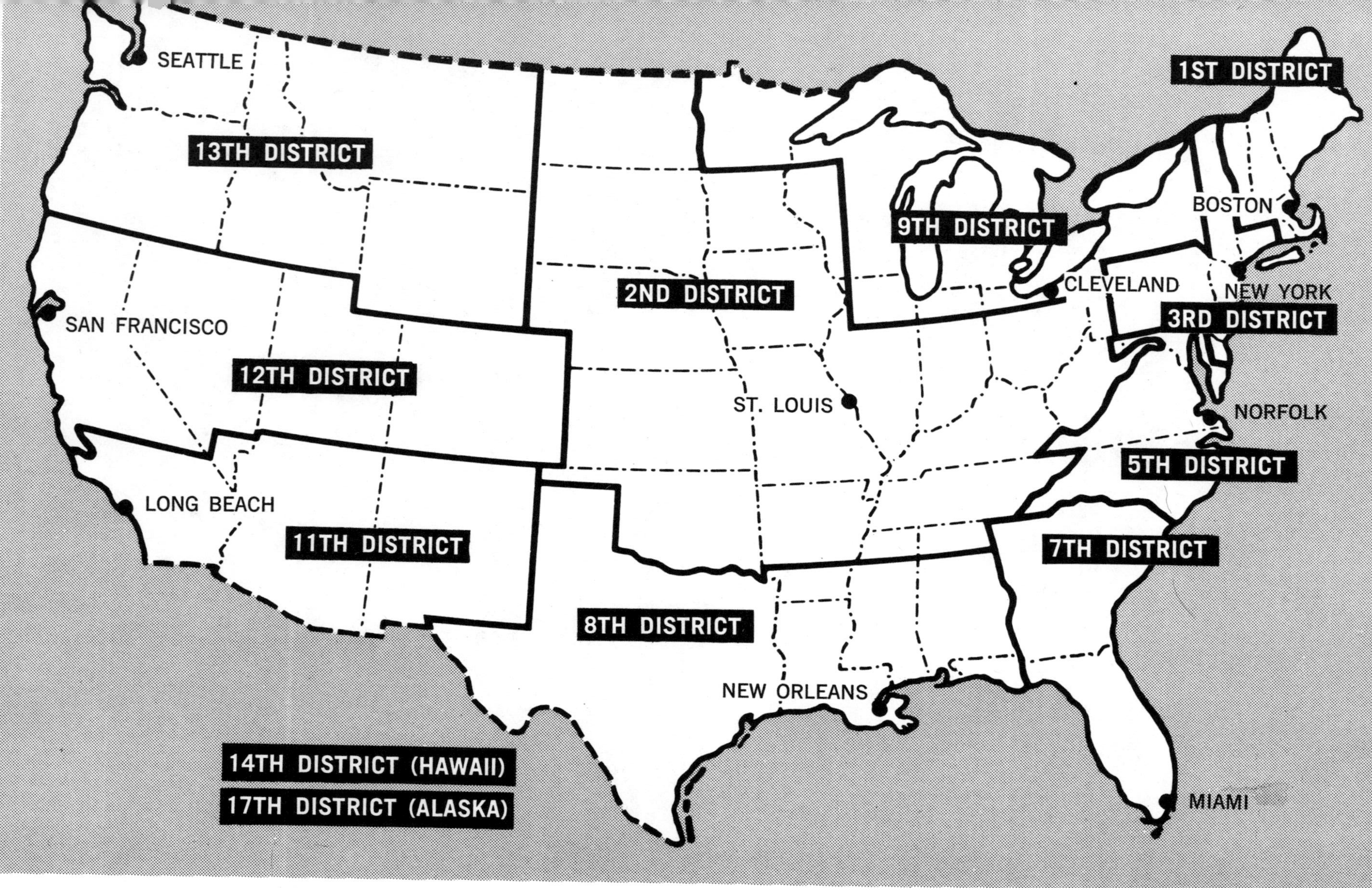
SEATTLE
1ST DISTRICT
13TH DISTRICT
BOSTON
9TH DISTRICT
2ND DISTRICT
CLEVELAND
NEW YORK
SAN FRANCISCO
3RD DISTRICT
12TH DISTRICT
ST. LOUIS
NORFOLK
5TH DISTRICT
LONG BEACH
11TH DISTRICT
7TH DISTRICT
8TH DISTRICT
NEW ORLEANS
14TH DISTRICT (HAWAII)
17TH DISTRICT (ALASKA)
MIAMI

COAST GUARD DISTRICT OFFICES

COMMANDER
1st Coast Guard District
150 Causeway St.
Boston, Mass. 02114

Rescue Coordination Center
223-3645

C.G. Marine Inspection Offices
447 Commercial St.
Boston, Mass. 02109
227-3710 ext. 261

76 Pearl St.
Portland, Maine 04112
775-3131

409 Federal Building
Providence, R.I. 02903
528-4338

COMMANDER
2d Coast Guard District
1430 Olive St.
St. Louis, Mo. 63103

Rescue Coordination Center
622-4604

C.G. Marine Inspection Offices
1520 Market St.
St. Louis, Mo. 63103
622-4657

425 New Post Office Bldg.
Cairo, Ill. 62914

301 Post Office & Courthouse Bldg.
Dubuque, Iowa
582-7225

550 Main St.
Cincinnati, Ohio 45202
684-3295

4th and Chestnut St.
Louisville, Ky. 40202
582-5194

167 N. Main St.
Memphis, Tenn. 38103
534-3556

801 Broadway
Nashville, Tenn. 37203
242-5421

1215 Park Building
Pittsburgh, Pa. 15222
644-5809

5th Avenue at Ninth St.
Huntington, W. Va. 25701
529-2524

COMMANDER
3rd Coast Guard District
Governors Island
New York, New York 10004

Rescue Coordination Center
422-5700

C.G. Marine Inspection Offices
Customhouse
New York, New York 10004
944-4676

313 Federal Building
Albany, New York 12207
472-2314

205 Federal Bldg.
Oswego, New York 13126
343-6581

424 Federal Bldg.
Detroit, Michigan 48226
226-7777

311 Federal Bldg.
Duluth, Minn. 55802
727-6286

312 Post Office Bldg.
New London, Conn. 06321
449-7203

2d at Chestnut St.
Philadelphia, Pa. 19106
597-4350

COMMANDER
5th Coast Guard District
431 Crawford St.
Portsmouth, Va. 23705

Rescue Coordination Center
393-6081

C.G. Marine Inspection Offices
431 Crawford St.
Portsmouth, Va. 23705
393-6312

Customhouse
Baltimore, Maryland 21233
752-2181

Customhouse
Wilmington, N.C.
763-9435

COMMANDER
7th Coast Guard District
51 S.W. First Avenue
Miami, Florida 33130

Rescue Coordination Center
350-5011

C.G. Marine Inspection Offices
51 S.W. First Avenue
Miami, Florida 33130
350-5691

316 Franklin St.
Tampa, Florida 33601
228-7143

210 Federal Bldg.
Jacksonville, Florida 32201
354-7555

625 Federal Bldg.
Charleston, S.C. 747-4171

1 East Bay St.
Savannah, Georgia 31402
232-4349

302 Federal Bldg.
San Juan, P.R. 00904
722-2697

COMMANDER
8th Coast Guard District
Federal Building
500 Camp St.

Rescue Coordination Center
527-6225

C.G. Marine Inspection Offices
423 Canal Street
New Orleans, La. 70130
527-6273

563 Federal Bldg.
Mobile, Alabama 36602
433-3421

1601 Proctor Street
Port Arthur, Texas 77641
983-7240

232 Customhouse
Galveston, Texas 77550
763-1335

101 Federal Bldg.
Corpus Christi, Texas 78401
883-5218

7300 Wingate St.
Houston, Texas 77011
228-4801

COMMANDER
9th Coast Guard District
1240 East 9th Street
Cleveland, Ohio 44199

Rescue Coordination Center
861-0400

C.G. Marine Inspection Offices
1055 East Ninth Street
Cleveland, Ohio 44114
861-0400 ext. 315

1212 Ellicott St.
Buffalo, N.Y. 14203
842-2000

423 Federal Bldg.
Toledo, Ohio 43604
248-7261

Municipal Bldg.
Saint Ignace, Michigan 49781
39

10101 S. Ewing Avenue
Chicago, Illinois 60617
721-3070

National Bank Bldg.
Ludington, Michigan 49431
843-9135

135 W. Wells Street
Milwaukee, Wisconsin 53203
272-3788

COMMANDER
11th Coast Guard District
Union Bank Building
400 Oceangate Blvd.
Long Beach, Calif. 90822

Rescue Coordination Center
437-2941

C.G. Marine Inspection Offices
750 N. Broad Avenue
Wilmington, Calif. 90744
831-9281

Broadway Pier
San Diego, Calif. 92101
293-5000

COMMANDER
12th Coast Guard District
630 Sansome Street
San Francisco, Calif. 94126

Rescue Coordination Center
556-9000

C.G. Marine Inspection Office
630 Sansome Street
San Francisco, Calif. 94126
556-5169

COMMANDER
13th Coast Guard District
Federal Building
915 Second Ave.
Seattle, Wash. 98174

Rescue Coordination Center
624-2902

C.G. Marine Inspection Offices
618 Second Avenue
Seattle, Wash. 98104
682-1375

208 S.W. Fifth Avenue
Portland, Oregon 97204
226-3802

COMMANDER
14th Coast Guard District
Prince Kalanianaole Federal Building
300 Ala Moana Blvd.
Honolulu, Hawaii 96850

Rescue Coordination Center
50-5888

C.G. Marine Inspection Office
610 Fort Street
Honolulu, Hawaii 96813
50-2466

COMMANDER
17th Coast Guard District
P.O. Box 3-5000
Juneau, Alaska 96802

Rescue Coordination Center
568-2680

C.G. Marine Inspection Offices
Third Street
Juneau, Alaska 99801
586-2680 ext. 20

P.O. Box 1286
Anchorage, Alaska 99501

Districts which are identical with the Coast Guard Districts as indicated in the accompanying chart.

Flotillas are administered by a Flotilla Commander, a Vice-Commander, and a Training Officer. Divisions elect a Division Captain, a Vice-Captain and a Training Officer. Districts elect a Commodore, Vice-Commodore and a Rear Commodore. A regular Coast Guard officer, the District Director, supervises the activities of the district auxiliary. All non-military officers are elected for one year.

As the Auxiliarist becomes more proficient in his boat handling skills, he may take an examination and become an AUXOPS member of the Coast Guard Auxiliary.

The Coast Guard Auxiliary is dedicated to four major activities:

Examination-Inspection. As a public service to boat owners, the Auxiliary carries out a safety program known as the Courtesy Motorboat Exam-

Coast Guard Auxiliary Courtesy Examination includes inspection of all life-saving gear

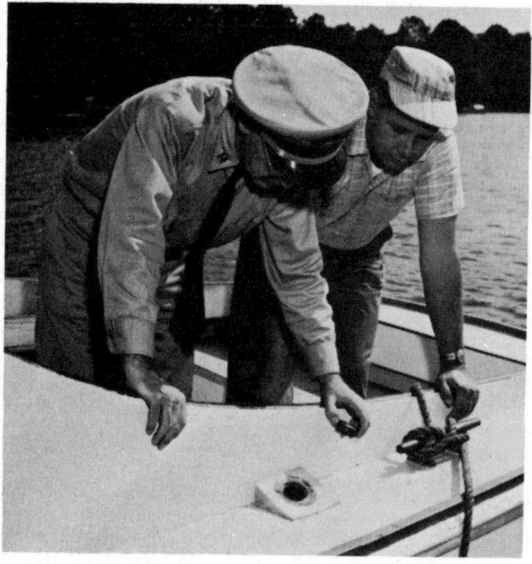

Auxiliarist checks gasoline filler pipes outside of coaming and down to bottom of tank

ination. Any boat owner may request that his boat be examined by a member of the Coast Guard Auxiliary who is especially trained to be a qualified courtesy examiner. If the vessel complies with all equipment requirements and is deemed safe to operate in all respects, it will be awarded, without charge, an Auxiliary decalcomania. Barring a noticeable violation, no further boarding will be made by the Coast Guard during the season of issue.

Instruction-Education. Auxiliary members undergo basic training in motorboat operation, seamanship, piloting, Rules of the Road, and boating laws. Members who qualify as instructors may then conduct courses of Public Instruction offered for non-members. Three separate Public Instruction Courses are conducted with training aids, films, lectures and texts used in the instruction, covering the field of boating.

Operations. Auxiliarists, with their boats, are

Fire extinguishers are examined to see if they meet requirements for type and number

Masthead light check. Courtesy Examination findings warn owners to meet legal minimum

trained to assist the regular Coast Guard in certain of its activities such as search and rescue, patrolling of regattas, safety patrols, and flood and hurricane relief.

Fellowship. Few sports make for a deeper and more lasting bond of common interest than boating. Activities and festivities of the Auxiliary give the boat owner a sense of self-improvement, useful public service, and good fellowship in the boating fraternity. As a member of a national organization, the Auxiliarist finds men of like-minded interests dedicated to the cause of safe boating in whatever area of the country he may cruise.

An organization of similar scope and appeal is the United States Power Squadrons composed of boat owners and others interested in the science of navigation. The Power Squadrons are divided into 15 districts and each district averages five or more Squadrons. The elected officers of a Squadron are Commander, Lieutenant Commander, Secretary, and Treasurer. There is also a local Board of Admission which is in charge of the Piloting Course and is appointed by the National Governing Board.

In charge of each district is a Rear Commander who is appointed by the Governing Board. Twice a year a District Conference is held, at which time Squadron work and instruction are reviewed, and resolutions voted upon and sent to the Governing Board for action.

At the national level, the top officer of the Power Squadrons is the Chief Commander, who is elected by the delegates from the local Squadrons each year at the Annual Meeting. The meeting also elects a Vice Commander, a Secretary and a Treasurer, along with the Governing Board, Chairmen of the Committee on Admission and Committee on Advanced Grades, as well as the Chairman and members of the Committee on Rules.

The Committee on Admission has charge of the Piloting Course, making up examinations and keeping the course up to date. This Committee also has general supervision over the local Boards of Admission.

The Committee on Advanced Grades has charge of all advanced navigational grades. It prepares rules and standards for instruction and examination in the grades of Advanced Piloting (AP), Junior Navigator (JN), and Navigator (N). It also exercises supervision over the local Boards of Advanced Grades.

The national Special Course Committee has charge of Motor Maintenance, Meteorology, Seamanship, and Signalling courses as well as supervision over the local Special Course Boards.

The national Committee on Rules is a sort of Supreme Court of the Power Squadrons, reviewing prospective changes in the constitution and by-laws.

The Coast Guard Auxiliary and the Power Squadrons have recently been joined by the Outboard Boating Club in providing free public instruction in safe boat handling. It should be noted that these organizations do not consider themselves rivals but co-operate closely and warmly in the single aim which they share — the promotion of safety afloat.

CHARTS, TABLES AND PAMPHLETS ■ SECTION 28

Charts and other publications of use and interest to the boat-owner are reasonable in cost and easily obtained. A complete library of charts, tide and current tables, cruising information, Coast Pilot, Notices to Mariners, Light Lists and, where appropriate, Great Lakes or Western Rivers Charts and Light Lists, is indispensable in the boating season and a source of instruction and interest out of season.

The table on page 119 indicates these important publications and where they may be obtained.

The National Ocean Survey maintains branches in the various Naval Districts, and many of the other publications listed can be obtained from private map firms and boating supply houses at government-established prices.

Government charts are usually priced at about the cost of paper and printing.

SECTION 29 ■ CLUBS, YARDS AND MARINAS

Unless you own an outboard with a trailer, you will face the problems of mooring, docking, hauling out and, coincidentally, joining a yacht club.

Even before buying the boat, it is well to decide what harbor is most convenient to you and then apply early for a slip or mooring. With the enormous growth of boating over the past years, good municipal facilities are at a premium and often involve a wait of a year or more. The next choice open to the boat owner is the marina or commercial installation. Many marinas provide launch service, gas and oil, restaurant and clubhouse facilities. Some even have flags similar to the flags of yacht clubs. If you have boating friends, talk to them about the service and conveniences offered at local marinas. Rentals at marinas may run from $1.25 to $6 and more per foot per month. These rental figures may include dockside electricity and the use

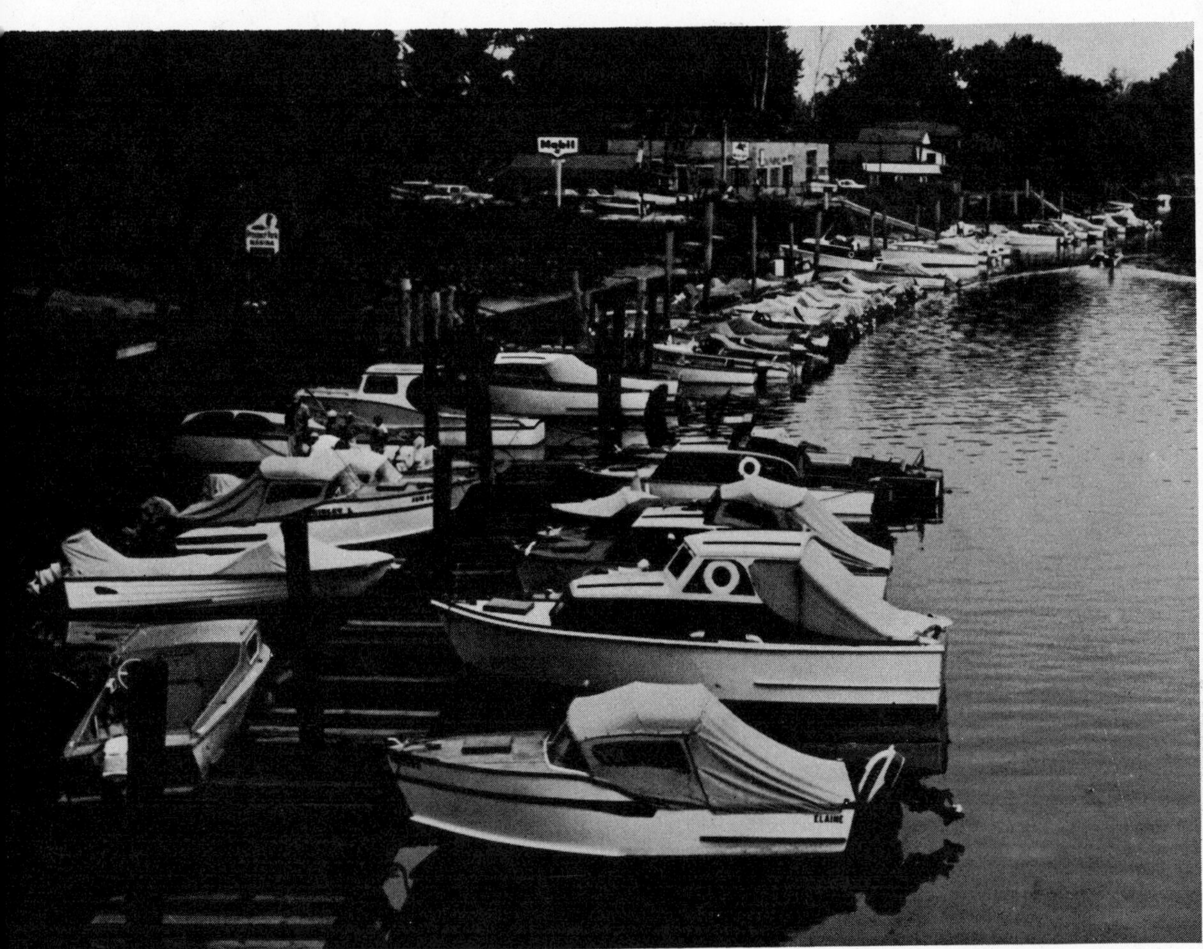

The ubiquitous marina, or mooring area, often offers the comforts and facilities of yacht clubs in addition to docking and mooring accommodations which are standard

of a fresh-water hose connection.

When you discuss the cost of slip or mooring, you should also check on hauling-out facilities.

Some marinas have boatyards and can provide either inside or outside storage over the winter. Some also require that all yard work done on the boat, such as sanding, painting and varnishing, be done by yard employees at yard prices.

Even marina prices may seem modest compared to what it may cost to belong to an elite yacht club with swimming-pool and tennis-court facilities. Such a club, of course, can take the place of a golf club and provide waterside and shoreside entertainment for the entire family all season.

Ideally, for the average boat owner a well-equipped yacht club with reasonable initiation fee and dues is the best solution. Without the frills of luxurious grounds and an elegant clubhouse, he will have the use of mooring facilities, club launch, locker facilities, fresh water at the dock, showers, restaurant, bar and, quite possibly, use of the club yard for hauling out and doing his own work.

Membership in a yacht club entitles the boat owner to wear the club insignia in his cap device, to carry the club burgee on his mast, to engage in inter-club races and cruises and, among clubs that have reciprocity arrangements, to use their facilities too when cruising in strange ports.

Whatever your choice, make your plans early—before the season opens—and you'll have an easier time getting to and from your boat all season long.

Accompanying are reproductions of typical insignia which the boat-owner will want to recognize. It might profit a boat-owner to keep reproductions of these insignia near his binnacle.

SECTION 30 ■ ETIQUETTE AFLOAT

Any human activity that survives through centuries develops customs and amenities which become traditional. Often the original reason for the custom is forgotten but the visible symbol survives. In marriage, for example, the reasons for a band of gold on the fourth finger, for the husband to carry his bride across the threshold, or for the bride to wear "something borrowed and something blue" are revered because we have an affectionate respect for our hereditary habits and ancestral symbols, though their origins belong to a distant past.

Boating is one of mankind's oldest activities,

Boating is one of man's oldest livelihoods and sports. Above is a luxury cruiser available for charter to fishing parties

livelihoods and sports. Boat races date back to the times of the Phoenicians, who were the great sailors of the ancient world. It is natural that, through the centuries, yachting customs have grown up and been preserved. Today, the man who knows and respects the traditions and etiquette of the sea is not paying tribute to a vain or idle fetish but to a proud, historic way of life, handed down from generation to generation of sailing men.

Much of this symbolism is embodied in the flying of flags. A 26-foot sloop making a transatlantic passage flies the American ensign with as much pride as an ocean liner, and a 40-foot two-masted motor sailer has as much right to fly the union jack at its jack staff as a battleship.

Yachting etiquette requires, for instance, that a dinghy or tender bring owner and passengers aboard on the starboard side, if possible, and that, when flown at the mooring, the yacht ensign be raised only between 8 A.M. and sunset. Most yacht clubs sound a "sunset gun" to mark the lowering of the flag at the clubhouse. A simple table of

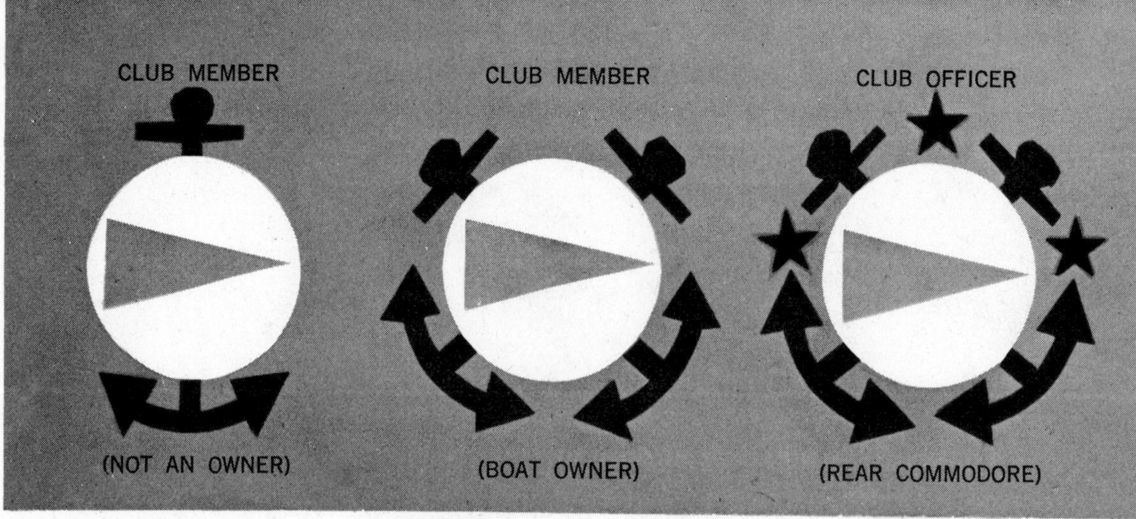

etiquette for the carrying of flags is shown.

The yacht ensign and the U.S. ensign (or familiar American flag) are used according to the owner's preference on yachts, except that documented vessels should carry the yacht ensign. The latter is similar to the American flag but, instead of the familiar blue field studded with stars, the blue field has a circle of 13 stars surrounding an anchor.

The Coast Guard Auxiliary flag is solid blue with white Auxiliary insignia in the center. The flag of the Power Squadrons consists of seven blue and six white vertical stripes with a red field containing 13 stars surrounding an anchor. When carried, the flag of the Power Squadrons may be flown in place of the U.S. or yacht ensign aft, or at the starboard main spreader.

Club burgees are usually either triangular or swallow-tail in shape. Owners' flags may be square or swallow-tail. The Union Jack is the blue field with white stars of the U.S. flag carried as a full-sized emblem.

Other flags which may be seen on yachts include the owner's absent pennant which is carried on the starboard spreader or yardarm to indicate the owner's absence. Normally this flag is flown only when

YACHT CLUB
BURGEE

AUXILIARY FLAG

POWER SQUADRON
FLAG

others are aboard, rather than when the boat is locked up. This is a solid blue rectangular flag. A similar blue flag bearing a white diagonal stripe is the guest flag, and an all-white rectangular flag is the meal flag. All are carried at the starboard spreader or yardarm.

Sailboats do not carry the ensign aft under sail. In an earlier day, the ensign was often sewed to the leech of the mainsail about two-thirds of the way up, which is a correct usage but seldom seen any more. Carrying the ensign at the stern under way is incorrect and marks a beginner.

One rule that does not appear in Rules of the Road but could well head up the list is the Golden Rule. If you have ever been below decks in a harbor taking dinner off the stove when some hot-rodder, with more exuberance than intelligence, goes crashing past at ten knots and sends his wake tumbling into your boat, or if you have ever been in a sailboat race at a tense moment with the crew moving on cat feet and the skipper barely whispering so as not to upset the trim, and had a speedboat go blustering across your bow apparently with a juvenile delinquent at the helm, you will know that loving one's fellow boatmen is not always easy.

FLAG ETIQUETTE FOR POWER VESSELS

ADAPTED FROM USCG AUXILIARY FLAG CODE

FLAG	WHERE FLOWN	HOW FLOWN
Nat'l. Ensign	Stern Staff, or Gaff—NOTE #1	0800 to Sunset
Yacht Ensign	Documented Yacht Only—NOTE #4	0800 to Sunset—NOTE #4
Auxiliary Ensign	Truck, Bow, Staff—NOTE #2, NOTE #13	Day and Night—NOTE #9
Auxiliary Officer Pennant or Burgee	STBD Yard, Bow Staff—NOTE #3, NOTE #6	Officer Aboard Day and Night
USPS Ensign	STBD Yard Only—NOTE #5	0800 to Sunset—NOTE #5
USPS Officer Flag	NOTE #6	Day and Night—NOTE #6
Yacht Club Pennant or Unit	Bow Staff—NOTE #10	0800 to Sunset—NOTE #11
Yacht Club Officer Flag	STBD Yard—NOTE #6	Day and Night—NOTE #12
House Flag	No—NOTE #7	NOTE #7
Gag Flags, Meals, etc.	NOTE #8	

NOTE #1—The National Ensign shall be flown from the stern staff on a power boat except when the vessel is equipped with a gaff, in which case, the Ensign is flown from the stern staff at anchor, and the gaff when underway.

NOTE #2—Auxiliary Ensign—(a) Shall be flown from the main truck when the vessel is equipped with a mast(s). (b) Without a mast from the Bow Staff.

NOTE #3 — Auxiliary Officer — Pennant or Burgee shall be flown from the starboard yardarm when the vessel is equipped with a signal mast. If the vessel has no mast, it may be flown in lieu of the Auxiliary Ensign from the Bow Staff. The Pennant of a current Officer shall take precedence over his own higher ranking past Officer's Burgee. However, as a matter of courtesy to a visiting officer, display the highest ranking officer flag (pennant or burgee).

NOTE #4—The Yacht Ensign—(a) Authorized by law to be flown from yachts Documented by the Bureau of Customs. However, the flying of this flag on a Documented Yacht **not** mandatory. (b) A Documented Yacht operating under official orders, becomes a Government vessel, and Government vessels **may not** fly the "Yacht Ensign." (c) All Facilities **not Documented** shall fly the U.S. Ensign, whenever the "Auxiliary Ensign" is flown.

NOTE #5—USPS Ensign—This is the only "service" organization recognized by this Code. The USPS Ensign may be flown only from the starboard yardarm of a signal mast, **never** from the stern staff or gaff. On Facilities flying the "Auxiliary Ensign," this position of honor is **reserved** for the "National Ensign."

NOTE #6—Officer Flags—Auxiliary, USPS, Yacht or Boat Club, either pennants or burgees, are flown from the starboard yardarm, except as noted in #3. Only **one** of these Flags may be flown at a time.

NOTE #7—House Flag—The Owner's private signal known as a "House Flag" is correctly flown at the truck between morning and evening colors; therefore, it **cannot** be flown at the same time as the Auxiliary Ensign.

NOTE #8—Gag Flags—Because of the quasi-official status of an Auxiliary Facility, cocktail flags, ball and chain, or other humorous flags **shall not** be flown when the "Auxiliary Ensign" is flown. Other flags, such as Crew's Pennant, Owner's Meal Flag, Guest Flag, Absent Flag, also **shall not** be flown with the Auxiliary Ensign.

NOTE #9—The Auxiliary Ensign—may be flown **day** and **night** on currently inspected facilities displaying decal.

NOTE #10—The Yacht Club Pennant—can be flown from the Bow Staff, except Facility Status (2) and (3).

NOTE #11—The Yacht Club Pennant, Flotilla, or Division—shall be flown from 0800 to sunset.

NOTE #12—Yacht Club Officer Flags—shall be displayed day and night.

NOTE #13 — No Signal Mast — When a boat is equipped with a Bow and Stern Staff, and does not have a signal mast, but has a radio antenna, the Auxiliary Ensign may be properly displayed by substituting the antenna for a signal mast. The height of the uppermost portion of the hoist of the Auxiliary Ensign should be affixed at a point approximately ⅔ the height of the antenna. **No additional** antennas or outriggers may be utilized.

GUESTS ABOARD ■ SECTION 31

The best assurance for a pleasant day afloat with guests enjoying themselves and skipper not driven to distraction is to explain in advance what clothing guests should wear, what kind of day they may expect, and about what time you may be back.

Footwear—Ladies, please do not wear high heels aboard. Gentlemen, please do not wear leather-soled shoes. Yachting shoes are best and rubber-soled shoes without heels are next best.

Clothing—Wear things that are loose and comfortable—preferably old clothes. If it's warm, be sure to bring a bathing suit and a towel to wrap it in after you change. If you plan to be out after sundown, bring a sweater and jacket.

Sunburn—If you are susceptible to sunburn, bring a hat and a long-sleeved shirt or blouse. If you have a special kind of lotion, bring that.

Food—If guests plan to bring food, have them check it out with you in advance so that there is neither excessive duplication nor unreasonable demands upon your galley.

Liquor—Let guests bring liquor if they wish or let them depend upon the ship's supply. But don't start drinking until the sun is over the yardarm—until you're moored or docked.

Seasickness—Seasickness is not a disgrace. Some of the best sailors who ever lived (including Lord Nelson) were subject to seasickness. The good skipper should keep some brand of dramamine or other motion-sickness remedy on board.

The guests have now come aboard, and are prepared to set out on a pleasant cruise. The fun and safety of all aboard can be greatly increased if the skipper will observe the following suggestions:

• Show your guests about the ship, above decks and below, and teach them the basic terminology of sailing such as starboard and port.
• Explain to them frankly about the head or have a direction card posted near it, describing both the operation and limitations of a sea-going toilet.
• Teach at least one other person on board how to operate the vessel in case of accident to the skipper.
• Give each of your guests a job to do or a post to man when getting under way or docking. This will keep them interested and also out of the way.
• Show them where the life jackets are and how to don them. Also show them the location and operation of the fire extinguishers.
• Show them where the binoculars are kept but ask them not to take them without the skipper's permission and to return them promptly when finished. Also urge them to put the straps around their necks, since a sudden roll or pitch may result in glasses being dropped overboard.
• Don't let guests dive overboard unless the boat is anchored. A boat will often drift faster than the average guest can swim. Set the swimming ladder out before any guest dives in.
• Keep a supply of inexpensive plastic raincoats, if you don't have enough foul-weather gear aboard for all guests. Nothing spoils a day's sailing more than the rainstorm that drives all the guests below and frequently ends in group seasickness. (Any old-timer knows very well that seasickness can be catching.) Guests will often find sitting in the rain exhilarating if they can keep reasonably dry, and there is no question that those who stay above decks are less subject to *mal de mer*.
• Counteract seasickness the scientific way with one

of the familiar motion-sickness preventives. If you run out or if the individual doesn't respond, pay no attention to the amateur MD's who recommend orange juice or whiskey or hot coffee or any other fluid food. It will only slosh around inside on a temporary basis. No sure cure works with everyone but, in general, salt crackers, salt beef, salty bread or pop corn tend to counteract the stomach acids and absorb the excessive liquid secretions generated in the gastro-intestinal tract.

• Explain to the guests about windward and leeward, especially if there is a good breeze. Throwing anything—from garbage to a cigarette butt—over the side to windward can be dangerous.

• If guests are helping with any of the shipboard chores in a seaway, teach them the maxim that every good racing skipper instills into his crew: "One hand for yourself and one hand for the ship."

• Never, never let anyone, guest or crew, hold a cup and saucer in his hand while someone pours hot coffee into it. Any pitch or roll will almost certainly result in a bad burn.

There are responsibilities which the skipper must never shirk, whether he has guests or family or simply his crew on board: he must be constantly aware of the state of the weather, the position of other boats, the functioning of his own craft, and the movements of anybody on his vessel. This will mean not looking at the people he talks to nor letting their talk distract him. It will mean listening and feeling and watching with deep awareness the relationships of all things and people about him. It will mean a dedication to the job of being skipper and, through that dedication, it will mean the security of his ship and those who ride aboard it.

SAFETY TIPS

• Don't use a portable stove or any type of stove employing gasoline on your boat. The greatest cause of accidents on boats is fire. Buy a good marine stove, preferably on gimbals. Have the galley area sheathed with fireproof material. Study the directions for lighting the stove carefully.

• Do as much cooking in advance at home as you can. Use deep dishes and deep cups with broad bottoms. In general, plastic dishes are a good choice. Plastic glasses of the thermal type are desirable — ice is always at a premium.

• If the ice compartment of your refrigerator (or "reefer") opens at the side, it is advisable to have a removable bar across the opening to keep a large block of ice from sliding out and smashing toes in a seaway.

• If you have a stove that burns gas from a tank, you will want to install the tank on deck, since cooking gases are heavier than air and sink into the bilge. If you suspect a leak in the line, don't look for it with a match. Make soap suds and rub along the line, to see where bubbles form.

• Ask your guests not to bring rigid suitcases on board. Soft bags stow more easily and don't fly about in a blow.

• Ask your guests not to wear their patent-sole yachting shoes ashore, since they tend to pick up pebbles and gravel which will not only scratch your paint and varnish work but will make slipping more likely.

• If you have children aboard, it is a good idea to keep them in life jackets constantly.

• If anyone falls overboard, the skipper should not be the one to jump after him; it is his duty to see that life jackets and buoys are thrown and then to maneuver the boat back to the person in the water as rapidly as possible. If anyone else on board elects to jump in, he *must* wear a life jacket.

• On any trips you make, keep a log recording your position, progress, time, and the state of the weather. Not only is this a helpful safety habit, but you will find your logbooks a fine source of happy nostalgia during the winters ahead.

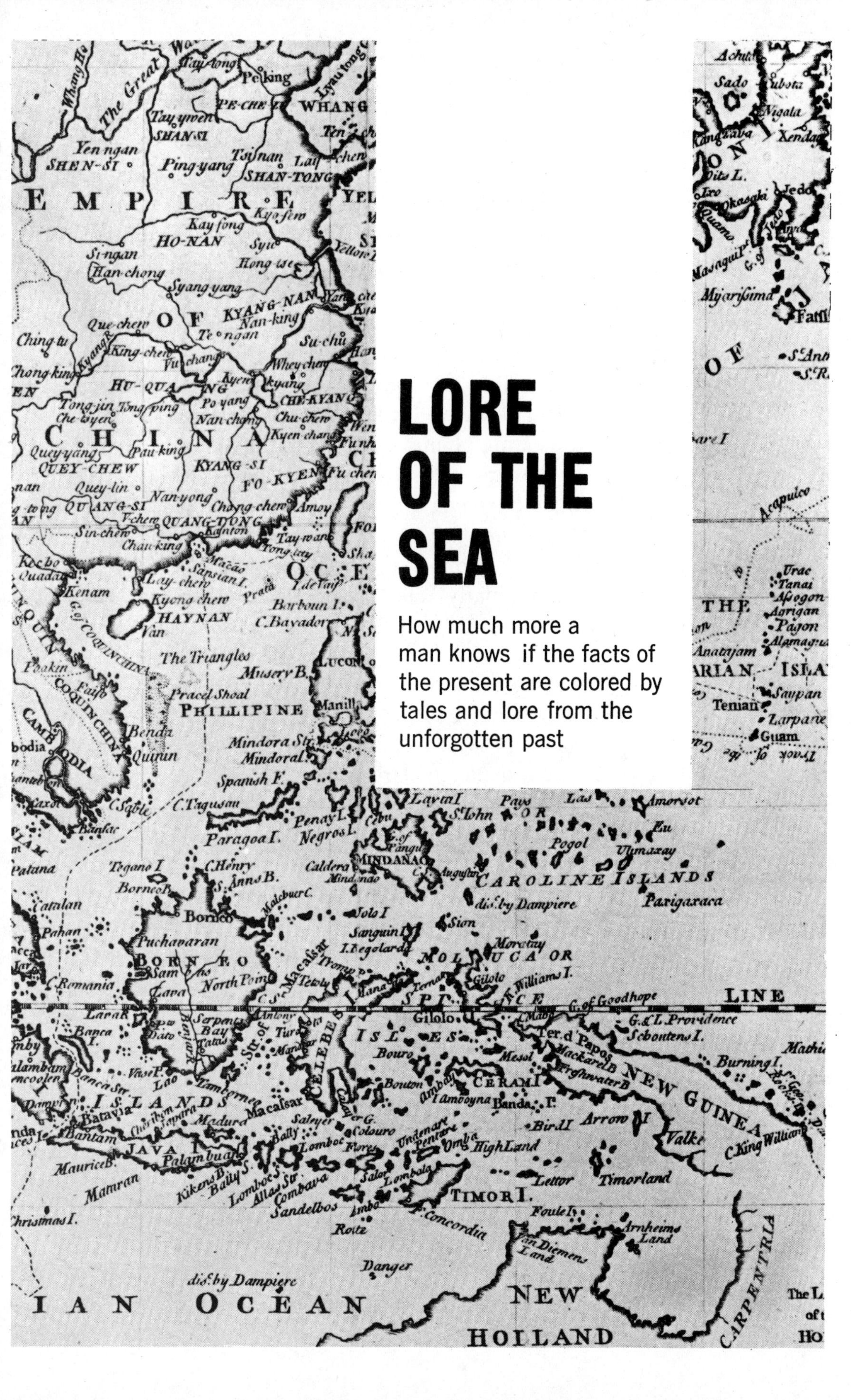

LORE OF THE SEA

How much more a man knows if the facts of the present are colored by tales and lore from the unforgotten past

In much the same way that a nation is proudly interested in its history, a college in its traditions, or a family in its genealogy, so the yachtsman searches eagerly into the mists of the past for the lore associated with the terms he uses on his boat.

The whole history of men and boats might well be revealed if we knew the origins of all boating terms. Some are irretrievably lost, but there are fascinating glimpses into the sailing past in others.

The terms "starboard" and "port" date back to Anglo-Saxon days. "Board" or "bord" was the side of a ship. Our modern word *board,* meaning a plank of wood, comes from this origin. Starboard was originally "steerbord," since the steering oar was on the right side. When the ship came to a dock, it naturally tied up on the side opposite the steering oar and was loaded from the left side. The loading side was the "ladderbord" (the same root from which our *bills of lading* come). In time, this was shortened to "larboard."

Then in 1844, since naval vessels had become larger and communication more difficult, it was agreed by the British Admiralty to change the name from "larboard" to "port," which was easier to distinguish from "starboard." The U.S. followed suit in 1896. Yet "port" too had its historical precedent, since the loading side was indeed the side that lay against the port or quay.

A term with an interesting boating history is "spinning yarns." In bygone days, after long ocean passages, sailors occupied time in port with recaulking the decks. Part of the process of caulking consisted of twisting strands of rope into the spaces between the deck planks and then tarring them. This twisting of the yarns was a tedious process and usually lightened by the recounting of tales of past voyages. The telling of the tales became so associated with the twisting of the strands that the process came to be known as "spinning yarns."

Why is the dial that fastens to the taffrail and (with the aid of the spinner and line) measures progress through the water known as a "log" rather than a speedometer? Here again, the knowledge and use of the device so far antedates the speedometer that the latter term was virtually unknown at the time that the log was already changing form. The log was originally a "chip-log" or chip of wood so weighted as to sit virtually motionless (or "like a log") in the sea until retrieved. It was dropped from the stern, and the time it took for a measured piece of well-shrunk line to be reeled out by the pull of the log gauged the speed of the vessel through the water. Nowadays, speedometers on boats are activated by pressure on a fin, by pressure on an open tube, or by the turning of a spinner. But the term "log" is still accepted.

Moreover, far beyond its own particular use, the little speed-measuring device has given us another nautical term that may well outlive its parent. That is the word "knot." Elsewhere in this book, we have defined a knot as "a nautical mile per hour." A nautical mile is longer than a land mile because it is a functional measure, equivalent to one minute of latitude, i.e. 6,080 feet. The knots on the log line were placed exactly 47′3″ apart and with them was used a sandglass that ran for 28 seconds. If a ship ran the distance between two knots or 47′3″ in 28 seconds, it was proceeding at one mile per hour. If the log line ran out 473 feet or ten knots in 28 seconds, the ship had to be moving at ten sea miles an hour. It was a simple matter to set the sandglass and then count the number of knots that ran out during 28 seconds.

What does a "bowline" have to do with a "bow line?" Today, nothing, but once quite a bit. The bowline was the knot that was used to fasten the line that ran from the leading edge of a squaresail to the bow to keep it hard on the wind. Later, the same knot was used with any sheet, even when it no longer ran to the bow. Now the term merely describes the knot itself and has won a separate pronounciation to keep it from being confused with a bow line.

"Why do they call it 'the head'?" How often skippers hear this question from first-time guests on board. And it's a fair query, since the term is certainly an unlikely way of describing a toilet. The answer goes back, of course, to the days before inside plumbing. In ancient days, vessels had tutelary deities, and effigies were carried at the bow. Later, these effigies simply became "figureheads" fastened to the stem at the bow. Under the long bowsprit of multi-masted vessels, a basket of ropes was usually rigged in which the crew stood while taking in the jibs. This basket of ropes became a convenient spot for performing the natural functions and, when a sailor expressed his intention of so doing, he usually stated that he was going up to the figurehead. Obviously it was a short step from there to saying simply that he was "going to the head." The facility changed over the years but, like much of sailing tradition, the expression did not.

A modern yacht would be about the last place in the world where you'd expect to find a cockfight.

Yet the comfortable, protected area in the rear of the ship carries the name "cockpit" and there is no question but that it derives from the old English ring where the roosters fought. Its history is interesting. On British men-of-war during the years when English seamanship was the standard for the world, junior officers had a cabin in which they gathered when off watch.

It's perfectly possible that these cocky young officers, occasionally victims of cabin fever on long trips, may have emulated the feathered species and thus gained for their quarters the name of "cockpit." However, it's more likely that since this was the room to which the wounded were brought during a battle, the tiers about the sides of the room may have suggested the shape of a cock pit.

Because of its protected situation, the cockpit becomes the helmsman's area on a modern sailboat and there with him is the compass. Young navigators are often puzzled by the fact that the north-seeking needle bears the same name as the two-legged divider which measures distance on a chart. The two instruments bear the same name for a very real reason: the word "compass" derives from the Latin ***cum,*** meaning "with" and ***passus,*** "step."

In ancient days, distance was measured by stepping it off, in the manner of the modern football referee. The nautical divider, with its two legs, actually seems to do this. Likewise the compass, with its 360 degrees, measures the directions around a circle—or around the horizon.

Merely studying the compass card offers some clues to its history. But first, let it be noted that the use of a lodestone to stroke a piece of iron and cause it to point north was known to the ancients.

Historians disagree as to whether the first use of the compass at sea is traceable to the Chinese, the Arabs or the southern Europeans, but the instrument was in use at the time of the Crusades.

At this time, the compass consisted simply of an iron needle, floated on water by means of a reed or splinter of wood, and free to turn. The compass rose, or wind-rose as it was first called, is far older than the compass, there having been such a circle in the Temple of the Winds in ancient Athens with the eight principal winds indicated. In early days, the north wind was marked with an arrow or spear crossed by a T for ***tramontano,*** the wind that came "across the mountains" from the north. The combination of the T and arrow became the fleur-de-lis which is still used.

The naming of ships has always been a subject of almost superstitious ritual. There are "good luck" names and "bad luck" names, and foolhardy indeed is the boat-owner who will name his vessel after any damned soul from Lucifer on down.

One formula whose origin seems lost in the fog of ages prescribes that the ideal name for a yacht should have seven letters. If possible, two of these should be a double vowel. Thus a name like "Fortune" or "Sea Song" is lucky, but doubly blessed are names like "Monsoon," "Typhoon," "Colleen."

The few little word histories cited here are a long way from being a definitive description of the origins of sea-going terms. But if they offer the yachtsman an insight into the rich tradition of his recreation and encourage him to turn to his own dictionary from time to time, they may, like the "long glass" at sea, give him a close look at a broad subject which may be worth exploring in detail.

GLOSSARY OF NAUTICAL TERMS

Words, like tools, give a man skills he did not know he had. Here is the common language of the world of boats

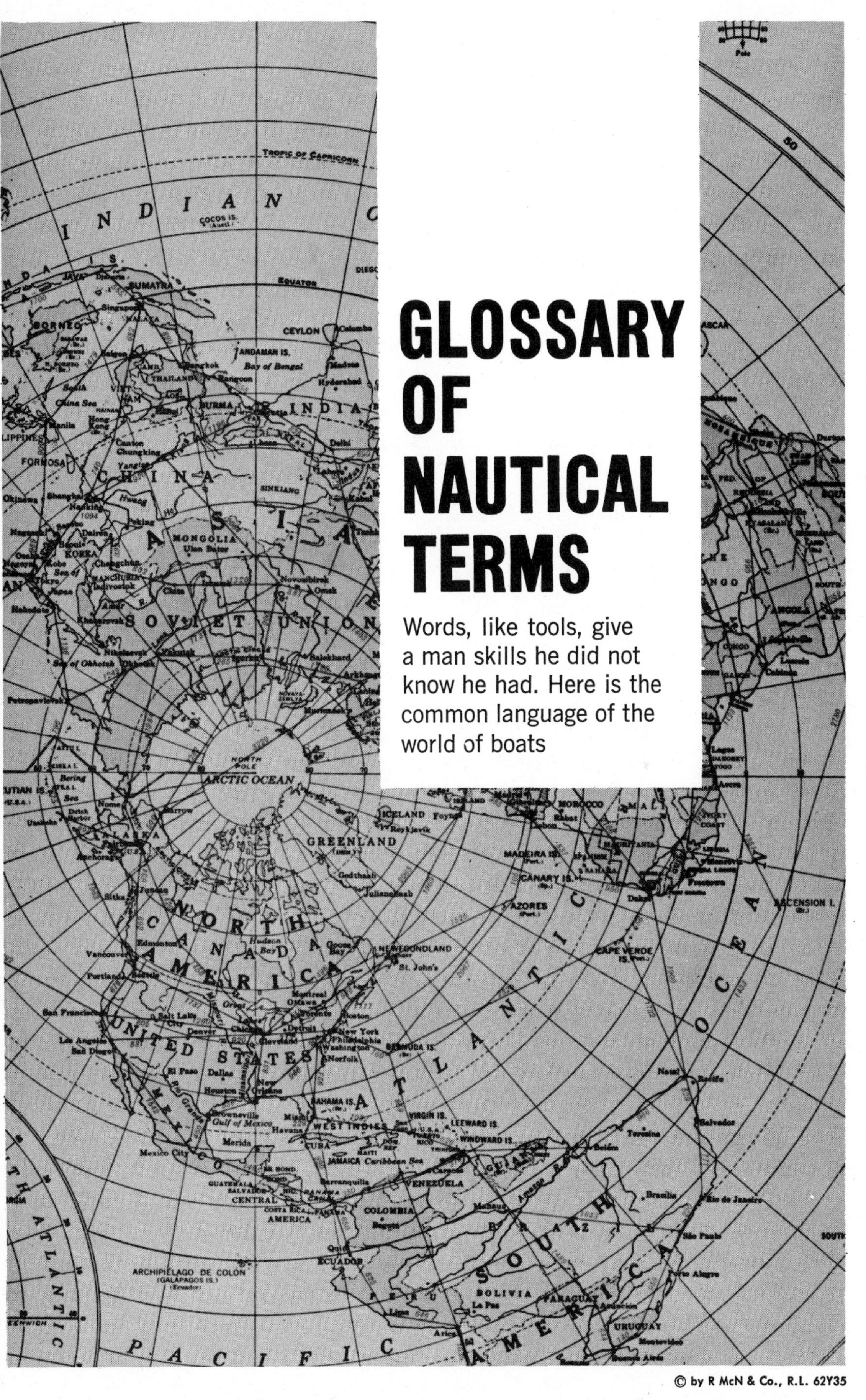

Abaft: Farther back than...farther from the bow than...
Abeam: At right angles to the fore and aft line and off the boat.
Aboard: On or in the boat.
Above: In a cabin vessel, the part of the boat which is above the interior.
Aft, After: Aft is the part of the boat toward the stern. After also refers to parts of the boat which are toward the stern, as the "after cabin," the "afterdeck."
Alee: Toward the side away from the wind.
Aloft: High up the mast or rigging.
Amidships: Toward the center from side to side or front to rear.
Anchor: A powerful hooked piece of iron for gripping the bottom.
Anchor Chain: A heavy chain connecting boat and anchor.
Anchor Light (also Riding light): A 32-point white light shown by a ship at anchor.
Anchorage: An area set apart for boats to anchor in.
Anchor's Aweigh: When the anchor has broken free of the bottom.
Anemometer: An instrument to measure wind speed.

Aneroid Barometer: An instrument to measure air pressure. A hand moves across a graduated dial, activated by the rise and fall of one surface of a partially-evacuated, sealed metal chamber.
Anti-corrosive Paint: Paint applied directly to metal to inhibit corrosion, usually bright orange or yellow.
Anti-fouling Paint: Paint applied to a boat's bottom, containing oxide of mercury or other poison to keep weeds and barnacles from clinging to the bottom.
Aport: Toward the left or port side.
Ashore: On shore.
Astern: Behind the ship; Go Astern: to move backwards.
Athwartships: Across the ship from side to side.
Auxiliary: An engine used to power a sailboat; also, a sailboat equipped with such an engine.
Avast: An order to stop or halt, as in "Avast there, ye lubbers!"
Awash: With seas washing over, as when decks are awash, or partly-submerged rocks are awash.
Azimuth: The bearing or direction of a celestial body.
Back: To reverse the direction of, as to back water with oars or to back a jib by holding it toward the wind.
Back Splice: A method of keeping the end of a line from unlaying by tucking the ends back in and under.
Back Wash: Water forced astern by the action of the propeller; also the receding of waves.
Backstays: Supporting lines on a sailboat usually running from a point about two-thirds up a mast to the deck on the windward side. Each time the vessel comes about on a new tack and the boom swings over, the backstay is set up on the side

opposite the boom and cast off on the leeward side.

Bail: To scoop water from the bottom of a boat with a bucket or container.

Ballast: Material of heavy weight placed in the bottom of a ship to give it stability.

Ballooner, Balloon Jib: A large, full-cut sail used for sailing off the wind.

Bare Poles: Sailing without any canvas raised, usually in a strong wind.

Barnacles: Small, hard-shelled marine animals which are found attached to pilings, docks and the bottoms of ships.

Barometer: An instrument for measuring the pressure of the air, used in weather forecasting.

Batten: To secure firmly, as to batten down a hatch.

Battens: Narrow flat strips of wood, usually ash, fitted into pockets to preserve the shape of a sail and keep the after end from curling.

Beach: The shore. To beach a vessel is to run her ashore, particularly by intention.

Beacon: An aid to navigation, usually of a conspicuous and easily recognized shape, normally unlighted. A Radio Beacon is a directional signal which is used for navigating.

Beam: The width of a ship at its widest point. Also a timber, running athwartships and supporting the deck.

Beam Ends: A vessel is said to be on her beam ends when she lies over on her side.

Bearing: The direction of an object from the ship, either relative to the ship's direction or to compass degrees.

Beat: To tack back and forth to windward in a sailboat.

Beaufort Scale: A table of wind velocities ranging from flat calm to hurricane, numbered from 0 to 12.

Becalmed: A sailboat is becalmed when there is no wind.

Becket: A short piece of line usually spliced into a circle or with an eye in either end.

Bed: Structural supports to which the engine is bolted in an inboard installation.

Belay: To make fast. To cease performing an action.

Belaying Pin: A stout pin of wood or metal set in the pin or fife rail near the foot of the mast and used to secure halyards and other lines on the mast. When removed from the rail, the belaying pin has been known to make a small, handy weapon.

Bell Rope: A short length of line made fast to the clapper of the ship's bell. Often referred to in the navy as the only "rope" on board a ship.

Below: Under the deck or decks of a ship.

Bend: A type of knot used for securing one line to another or to a spar.

Bend On: To attach; to make a sail fast to a spar or a chain to an anchor.

Berth: A bunk or bed on board a ship. An assigned mooring or docking position.

Bight: A loop or bend in a line

anywhere between the ends.

Bilge: The bottom of a ship below the flooring. Also the curve of the hull below the waterline. A vessel with a sharp curve is said to have hard bilges; a vessel with a gradual curve is said to have easy bilges.

Binnacle: A case, usually of metal and glass and usually mounted on a pedestal, protecting the compass and permitting ready reference to it by the helmsman.

Bitter End: The end of a line. Also the inboard end of the anchor chain, made fast in the chain locker.

Bitts: Short, stout wooden or metal columns on a deck or dock used to secure lines or hawsers.

Blinker: A searchlight used for signalling by code, usually fitted with spring-controlled shutter. Some are operated by pushbutton contact.

Block: A metal wheel enclosed in a wood or metal frame (the device which is known ashore as a "pulley") for the purpose of changing the direction of effort of a line. When used in a double or triple system, the purchase at the pulling end of the line is much increased. The wheel at the center of the block is called a Sheave, which is pronounced *shiv.*

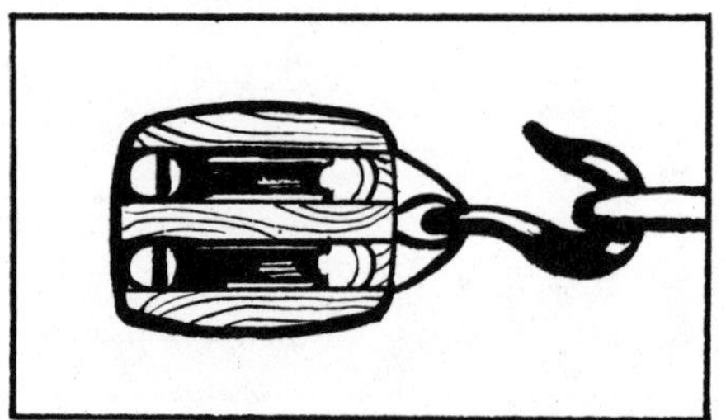

Block, Cheek: A block with shell on only one side, the other side being bolted to a spar or deck.

Block, Fiddle: A double block with two sheaves in the same plane, one being smaller than the other, giving the block a somewhat violin-shaped appearance.

Block, Snatch: A single-sheave block with one end of the frame hinged and able to be opened so as to admit a line other than by forcing the end through the opening.

Blower: A fan device in an air duct to ventilate the interior of the vessel. Blowers usually exhaust air and fumes from below decks, particularly from the engine compartment.

Boarding: Entering upon or climbing onto a ship.

Boat: Formerly a vessel carried aboard a larger vessel; now loosely used for any pleasure craft.

Bobstay: The wire or chain attached from the forward end of the bowsprit of a sailing vessel to the stem to balance from beneath the upward pull of the headstay.

Bollard: An upright wood or metal post on a dock for making lines fast; usually used interchangeably with bitt.

Booby Hatch: A hatch or access from a weather deck covered by a hood, often with a vertical door or doors.

Boom: The spar to which the foot of a sail is affixed.

Boom, Cargo: On cargo-carrying ships, a crane-like arrangement for moving merchandise between the dock and the ship's hold.

Boot-top: The area on the ship's hull along the waterline, usually painted a contrasting color.

Boot-topping: Special anti-fouling, grease-resistant paint applied for extra protection at the waterline or "between wind and wave."

Bottom: The part of a ship between the keel and the turn of the bilge. More loosely, all of the ship below the waterline.

Bow: The forward part of the vessel's hull.

Bow Line: A mooring line or dock line passing through the bow chock.

Bowline (Pronounced *bo-lin*): A knot providing an easily opened bight in the end of a line.

Bowsprit: A round or flat timber extending forward from the bow of a boat and carrying headstay and forestay to a point forward of the deck, thus providing extra sail area.

Box the Compass: To name the points of the compass in order, beginning with North.

Brace: On square-rigged ships, a line attached to the yard to turn it in trimming the sail.

Brail: A line secured to the after end of a sail and used to gather it up against a spar or stay.

Bridge: The navigating deck of a ship, usually with enclosed pilot house in the center and open wings on either side for observations.

Bridge, Flying: An open deck above the bridge, usually with a duplicate set of engine controls and navigating facilities.

Broach, Broach-to: To turn sideways to the seas when running before them, usually as a result of losing control.

Brow: A gangplank extending onto a dock, usually with rollers on the dock end to allow for movement of the vessel.

Bulkhead: Any vertical partition (wall) on a ship.

Bulwarks: Extensions of the sides above deck level.

Bumpkin: On sailing vessels, a single spar or V-shaped frame at the stern to carry the permanent backstay outboard of the deck, allowing free cross-over of the boom.

Bunk: A built-in bed on board ship.

Buoy: A floating marker used as an aid to navigation. Also any float which indicates on the surface the position of some object under the water.

Burdened Vessel: Now known as the "give-way vessel." Of two ships meeting, the one having to keep clear. (See "give-way vessel.")

Burgee: A swallow-tailed signal pennant.

Butt: The end of a plank where it meets the end of another plank.

By the: At or near—as "down by the head" meaning that the head of a ship is lower in the water. Also, "By the Mark" and "By the Deep" are calls used by the leadsman when taking soundings to indicate the depth of the water. "By the mark five!" indicates five fathoms of water. "By the deep six!" indicates the spot between markings on the lead line equal to six fathoms.

Cabin: Living quarters on a vessel. On a naval vessel, "The Cabin" refers only to the Captain's quarters.

Calking (also Caulking): Filling the seams to prevent leakage.

Camber: Athwartships curvature. The camber of a deck is usually the arching which drains the water off into the scuppers. Camber may be reversed.

Can Buoy: A red or red-striped buoy of round shape.

Capping, Cap-rail: The fore and aft finishing piece above the sheer strake in a boat.

Capsize: To turn over. This refers not alone to vessels, but a coil of line may be "capsized" or turned over.

Capstan: A mechanically or hand-driven machine with vertical axis used on deck for heavy heaving, as in hauling in the anchor.

Carlings: Short beams supporting the deck between beams.

Carvel: The mode of boat-building whereby the planks are laid side by side smoothly, as distinguished from lapstrake construction.

Cast Off: To let go.

Cat Boat: A sailing craft with one mast well forward and only one sail, the mainsail.

Cat's Paws: On a calm day, fingers of rippling water produced by light breezes.

Centerboard: A flat wood or metal plate used in a shallow-draft sail-boat to provide auxiliary keel area to reduce leeway. It is raised or lowered on a pivot from a box inside the hull.

Chafe: To wear by steady rubbing.

Chafing-gear: Protective coatings of canvas, rubber or plastic so rigged as to absorb the rubbing.

Chain: The anchor chain usually stores forward in the chain locker and runs up on deck through a hawse pipe.

Chain-plates: Strips of metal, well secured in the hull of a sailboat and rising above the rail. It is to the chain plates that the shrouds staying the mast are attached.

Charlie Noble: The stove pipe for the galley.

Check: To hold back or stop a line gradually. To Check: Paint is said to check when it cracks without peeling.

Chine: In flat-bottom or V-bottom boats, the chine is the line fore and aft formed by the intersection of side and bottom.

Chocks: Oval-shaped castings fore and aft through which the anchor line and dock lines may pass. Also the wedges which are used to secure the anchor or other bulky objects in place.

Chock-a-block: A halyard is said to be chock-a-block when the two blocks used for purchase are so tight that no further hauling is possible.

Clamp: The longitudinal plank connecting the beams on the inside of the hull, just under the deck.

Clear: To leave, as port. To pass safely, as an obstacle.

Cleat: A piece of wood or metal with projecting arms or horns, used for securing lines.

Clew: The reinforced after-corner eye of a sail used to secure the sail to the spar or to a sheet.

Clinker: A mode of boat-building in which planks overlap.

Close-hauled: A sailboat is said to be close-hauled when her canvas is trimmed flat and she is sailing as high into the wind as she can.

Clove Hitch: Hitch frequently used for securing dock lines to bitts or bollards.

Club: A spar or boom used in obtaining a flat trim on a headsail.

Coaming: Vertical wood railing around the cockpit or hatches to keep water from getting in.

Cockpit: The sunken seating-space on a vessel used to accommodate passengers, usually above decks, aft.

Companion Ladder: The stairs leading down into the cabin.

Compass: Device used to determine directions on shipboard. There are three main types in use: Magnetic Compass, employing magnetized metal needle which points to Magnetic North; Gyro or Gyroscopic Compass, which points True North through use of an electrically driven gyroscope; Radio Compass, which is a highly directional radio receiver capable of determining the direction of origin of a known radio signal.

Composite: Combination construction, usually metal frames and wooden planking.

Counter: The part of a ship's after end which overhangs the stern post above the water line.

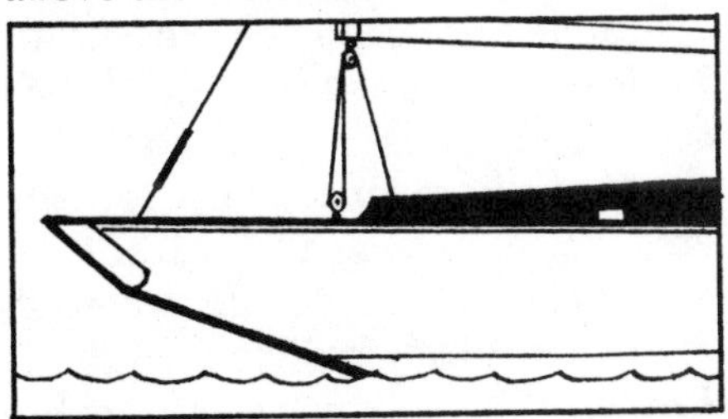

Cradle: A heavy wood or metal structure fitted to the boat's hull to support her out of water.

Cringle: A metal ring or thimble lashed into the bolt-rope of a sail which serves as tack or clew when a sail is reefed.

Crown: The crown of an anchor is the juncture of arms and shank.

Crow's Nest: A look-out station high up on the mast.

Crutch: A support which keeps the boom off the deck when it is not in use.

Cuddy: A small cabin in the fore part of an open boat.

Cutwater: The forward edge of the stem at or near the waterline.

Cutter: A single-masted sailboat with the mast stepped nearer the center than that of a sloop.

Davit: A curved spar or pair of spars with sheaves in their ends and which can be rotated out over the side to hoist a boat or an anchor easily from the sea onto the deck.

Dead Ahead, Dead Astern: Directly ahead, directly aft.

Deadhead: A partly-submerged timber.

Deadlight: Formerly a heavy metal cover to protect the glass of a ship's portholes. Now, more frequently, a thick glass permanently set in the deck or hull.

Deadwood: The flat, vertical hull material where the hull is too narrow to permit framing. The deadwood is usually in the after end of the hull but may also be found at the forefoot.

Deck: In large vessels, any flooring is known as a deck. Among pleasure craft, deck usually refers to the open surface on which the crew

and the passengers walk.
Deep Six: Nautical slang for discarding something overboard.
Dinghy: Small boat used as a tender by a yacht.
Displacement: The volume of water displaced by the hull of a vessel. The displacement weight is the weight of this volume of water.
Dodger: A folding hood, like a top on a convertible car, protecting the entry to the main companionway of sailboats.
Dog: A metal latch used to clamp water-tight doors or ports shut.
Doghouse: The raised after-portion of the deckhouse or cabin trunk of a sailing vessel to afford added protection and even living space at the forward end of the cockpit.
Dog-watches: Half the normal four-hour watch; namely, two two-hour watches between 4 and 6 P.M. and 6 and 8 P.M., to permit the entire crew to have supper.
Dolphin: Several pilings bound together and used by vessels for docking or mooring lines. Sometimes applied to single piles or bollards on piers.
Dolphin-striker: A metal strut extending down from the bowsprit to the bobstay to provide extra downward thrust.

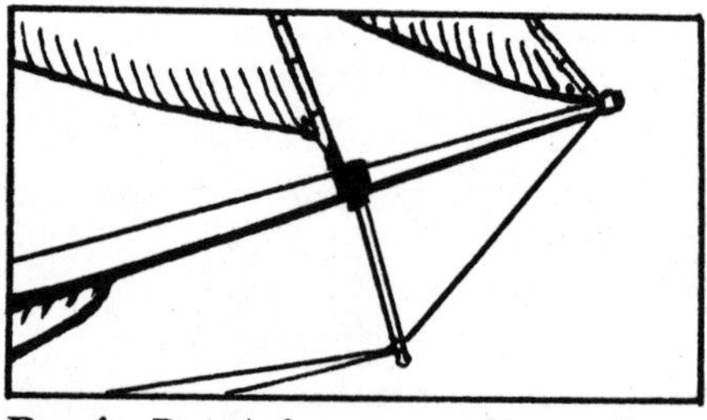

 Draft: Depth from waterline to lowest part of the hull or motor.
Drogue: A sea anchor—usually a conically-shaped canvas bag with a line from its wide end to the ship, to keep her bow into the seas when hove to or her stern to the seas when running before the wind.
Ebb: The falling tide.
Ensign: The national flag of a vessel.
Eyes: The very forward part of the deck of a vessel.
Fair Lead or ***Fairleader:*** A permanent fitting through which a line is guided so that it runs straight to a block or winch.
Fairway: The open water in a channel or harbor through which traffic normally passes.
Fair (Wind or ***Tide):*** Favorable.
Fake (or ***Flake) Down a Line:*** To coil it with each loop overlapping the next so that it is free for running.
Fall: The end line in a tackle on which the hauling is done.
Fall Off: A sailboat falls off when she sails less close to the wind than she has been sailing.
Falls: The lines at the davits used to raise and lower the boat.
False Keel: An extra keel secured to the bottom of the main keel to give added protection or extra draft.
Fathom: A measure of depth: six feet.
Feather: In rowing, an oar is feathered when it is turned parallel to the surface on breaking water to eliminate splash and spray.
Fender: A cushion, usually cylindrical in shape, to protect the sides of a vessel from rubbing against

docks or against other vessels.

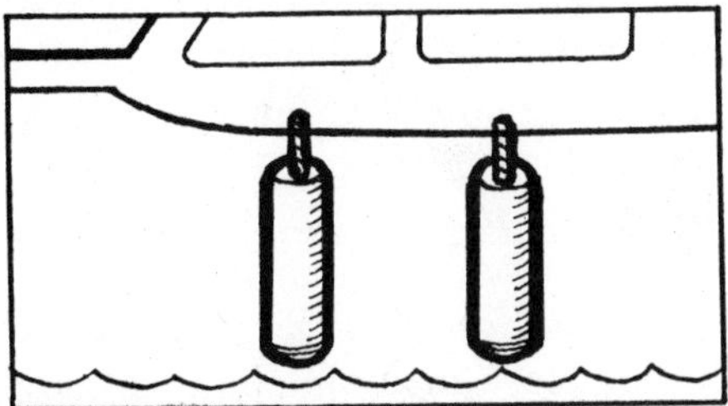

Fend Off: To push off with boat hook or by hand to avoid sharp contact with a dock or other vessel.
Flare: The outward curve of the topsides as they rise toward the rail. Opposite of Tumble-Home.
Flaw: A sudden gust of wind, often from a slightly different direction.
Flemish: To flemish a line on deck is to coil it in a tight, flat spiral.
Flood: The rising tide.
Flukes: The palms or broad portions of an anchor which hold it in the ground.
Fore: Term applied to portions of a vessel near the bow.
Fore and Aft: In the lengthwise line of a vessel.
Forecastle (Pronounced *fo'c's'l*): The forward part of a vessel below decks.
Forefoot: The point of juncture between the lower end of the stem and the forward end of the keel.
Foremast: In a schooner, the forward and shorter of the masts.
Foul: Said of the bottom when it is covered with marine growth. Said of a line or chain when it is tangled.
Found: A ship is well found when it is fully equipped or fitted out.
Founder: To fill and sink.
Free: A sailboat is running free when she is sailing before the wind.
Freeboard: The shortest distance from the waterline to the lowest part of the deck.
Full and By: Sailing close to the wind but with all sails filled and drawing.
Furl: To roll up a sail or an awning.
Gaff: A kind of rig employing quadrilateral rather than triangular sails on the mast. Also, the spar at the top of the sail, set at an angle to the mast.
Galley: The cooking area of a boat.
Gangplank: The structure running from ship to dock allowing passengers to board and debark.
Gangway: The opening in the side of a large vessel to which a gangplank may lead.
Garboards: The planking on either side next to the keel.
Gear: A broad term applying to rigging or to the personal effects of people on board.
Gimbals: A device in which the ship's compass or galley stove is set to keep it level when the ship heels.
Give-Way Vessel: Of two craft meeting, the one which does not have right of way and is obligated to keep clear. (Formerly "burdened vessel.")
Gooseneck: A swivel fitting at the end of a boom connecting it to the mast.
Granny: A false reef knot. The kind of square knot the average landlubber ties on a package. Hard to unfasten.
Grapnel: An anchor for small boats, having six prongs or hooks at one end instead of flukes. Also used

in dragging for objects on bottom.
Grommet: An eye in a piece of canvas, bound to prevent tearing and used to pass a line through. Also a rope ring.
Ground Swell: The general heaving of the sea in the absence of waves.
Ground Tackle: A group term for all gear used in anchoring a ship.
Gudgeons: Metal fittings on the stern post with cast or bored eyes to receive the pintles on which the rudder hangs.
Gunwale (Pronounced *gun'l*): The rail or upper edge of a ship's side.
Guy: A steadying rope or wire.
Halyard: A line used to raise a sail or signal flag.
Hand: A member of the crew, as in the expression, "All hands on deck!" A paid hand is a professional sailor. To hand a sail is to take it in or furl it.
Handsomely: Carefully.
Handy Billy: A pair of blocks and tackle of general utility purpose on deck where extra purchase is needed.
Hatch: Formerly a hatch was the cover for a hatchway but now it usually refers to an opening from the deck to the interior of the vessel. The forward hatch opens into the forecastle of a yacht, for instance.
Haul: When the wind shifts in a clockwise direction, it is said to haul. When it shifts counter-clockwise, it veers.
Hauling Part: That part of the line in a tackle to which power is applied in order to move an object.
Hawsehole: A hole in the bow through which the chain or cable passes.
Hawse-pipe: portion of area from hawsehole up through ship or boat.
Hawser: A heavy rope or cable used in mooring or towing.
Head: A ship's toilet.
Head Up: To point a sailboat higher into the wind.
Head-sails: Sails carried forward of the mast, including jibs, staysails, yankees, genoas.
Heave: To throw, as to heave a line.
Heave To: A vessel is said to be hove to in a storm when she is without forward progress, but carrying a sea anchor or just enough power or canvas to hold her position in the seas.
Heel: To lean over, normally away from the wind. Also, the after part of the keel is known as the heel of a ship.
Horns: The arms of a cleat are known as horns.
Hogging: When, through age and strain, the center of a vessel rises and the ends droop, she is said to be hogged.
Hold: Space below decks for stowage of cargo.
Hounds: Shoulders at the mast head and at the spreaders over which the upper ends of shrouds pass.
Hull: That part of a vessel from the deck down.
Inboard: Toward the center of a vessel.
Inshore: Toward land; in toward, near, or along the shore line.
Inboard-Outboard: Also known as outdrive and I/O, a motor installation with inboard engine directly

geared to an outboard drive.

Irish Pennant: A loose end of line, especially one dangling over the side.

Irons: A sailboat is said to be "up in irons" when she comes up into the wind and loses way, unable to fall off on either tack.

Jack: A small flag used as a signal or to designate nationality.

Jack Staff: The forward flag staff or bow staff which carries the jack when flown.

Jacob's Ladder: A rope ladder with wood rungs.

Jetty: A pier or wharf extending seaward.

Jib: A triangular headsail usually carried on the forestay.

Jibe: To bring the wind from one side of a sailboat to the other from astern. The opposite of tacking.

Jigger: The mizzen or small after-sail on a yawl or ketch.

Jury Rig: An emergency rig usually set up when a mast or rudder has been carried away.

Kedge: An auxiliary anchor of lesser holding power than the main anchor. Often carried out by a small boat and used for warping a vessel ahead. Also, a grounded vessel may "Kedge Off" when she pulls herself seaward by using an anchor carried out to deeper water.

Keel: The principal fore and aft timber at the bottom of a ship. It is the backbone of the vessel.

Keelson (Pronounced *kel-son*): An additional strengthening timber bolted to the top of the keel above the floor timbers.

King Plank: The center plank of the deck.

King Spoke: When the rudder is exactly amidship, the upper spoke of the wheel, usually scored or wrapped with serving to make it readily identifiable for steering in the dark.

Knee: Timber with a right-angled grain, used to connect the hull frames with the deck beams.

Knots: A measure of speed indicating nautical miles per hour. (A nautical mile is equal to 6080 feet.)

Labor: A vessel labors in high seas when her headway is slow and she pitches and rolls excessively.

Ladder: Any stairway aboard ship. A sea ladder or swimming ladder extends over the ship's side to allow boarding from the water. An accommodation ladder extends from the deck to the water with a small platform allowing easy access to and from small boats alongside.

Landfall: Sighting land after a crossing.

Lanyard: A piece of line attached to an object on board ship for the purpose of making it fast or controlling it without touching it.

Lapstrake: A mode of boat construction in which the strakes or planks overlap. Also called "clinker" built.

Larboard: Term formerly used instead of "port" as the opposite of starboard.

Latitude: A measure of distance north or south of the equator.

Launching: The process of putting a boat into the water.

Lay: To move or go, as "Lay Below" or "Lay Forward." On a sailboat, to "Lay Off" is to sail a little farther off the wind.

Lazaret: Below-deck storage space in the stern.

Leach: The after edge of a sail. A leach-line is the line that tightens the leach.

Lead, Lead Line: A sounding device consisting of a lead weight with a marked line affixed to the top and a hollowed base which may be filled with grease or wax to determine the character of the bottom.

Lee: The side opposite to that from which the wind is coming. When a sailboat is on the starboard tack, the wind is coming from the starboard side which is the weather side. The port side is the lee side. A lee shore is one onto which the wind is blowing. A sailboat is said to be sailing by the lee when the wind is astern and is from the same quarter as the main boom is on. This is a difficult point of sailing since the ship is in danger of jibing.

Leeward (Pronounced *lu-ard*): The direction toward which the wind is blowing.

Leeway: Sidewise motion through the water to leeward, caused by the pressure of wind and waves.

Life Lines, Life Rail: Lines along the rail of a ship, usually supported by stanchions, to provide safety for the crew when moving about the deck.

Life Preservers: Cloth jackets made with pads of buoyant material to sustain person in water.

Limber Hole: A hole or slot in the floor timbers or frames at the bottom of a ship to permit water to drain to the lowest part of the bilge.

List: The lean of a vessel to one side or another due to weight on board rather than to pressure of wind or wave.

Locker: A storage compartment on shipboard.

Log: An instrument carried over the stern for determining a vessel's speed. (See Taffrail Log.)

Logbook: A record of all matters pertaining to a ship's position or operation.

Longitude: Distance east or west of the prime meridian at Greenwich, England.

Loom: The loom of a light is the glare seen above the horizon when the light itself is not yet visible. The loom of an oar in a rowboat is the inboard portion.

Loran: A navigational device which affords lines of positions derived from signals emitted from pairs of transmitting stations.

Lubber Line or ***Lubber's Line:*** A mark on the compass indicating the fore and aft line of the ship.

Luff: To come up into the wind and allow the sails to flutter.

Main: As mainmast and mainsail, the principal mast or sail on the ship.

Man-rail: Same as Life Line.

Marconi Rig: Rig with a triangular sail on a tall mast as distinguished from the gaff rig with its four-sided sail on a shorter mast.

Marlin: Tarred cord about ⅛″ in diameter, made of hemp.

Marlinspike: A pointed metal tool used in splicing.

Mast Collar: A piece of canvas lashed to the mast and fastened to the deck to keep water from entering.

Mast Step: The fitting on the ship into which the bottom of the mast is set when it is installed or stepped.

Messenger: A light line used for heaving and affixed to a heavier hawser or cable.

Midships: Same as amidships, indicating the center of the vessel.

Mizzen: The after-mast on a ketch or yawl. Also the sail affixed to that mast.

Monkey-fist: A round knot at the end of a heaving line to make it heavier for more accurate throwing.

Mooring: Among pleasure craft, the mooring consists of an anchor embedded in the bottom, a chain from it to a buoy, and a heavy pendant from the buoy to the vessel, usually with a pick-up can or buoy to facilitate getting the pennant on board.

Motor Sailer: A combination of power-boat and sailboat, usually roomier and with more power than a sailboat, but with a mast or masts and complement of sails.

Mousing: Winding small stuff around a hook between its end and its shank to keep whatever is hanging from the hook from slipping or flying out.

Mushroom: A kind of anchor, like an inverted mushroom, used for permanent moorings. The wide, rounded base sinks into mud or sand and has great holding power.

Nautical Almanac: A publication used in celestial navigation, containing information about the sun, moon and stars for each day of the year.

Navigation: The art of conducting a vessel safely from a known position to a known destination.

Neap Tide: A tide that occurs when the sun and moon are in opposition so that high tides are not so high and low tides are not so low as ordinarily. The opposite of spring tide.

Nun Buoy: A red or red-striped buoy of conical shape.

Oakum: Rope fibers, sometimes tarred, used for calking, stuffing.

Off the Wind: A sailboat reaching or running; with sheets eased.

Offing: A ship's distance off shore.

Outboard: Away from the center of the boat; part of a rig projecting over the sides or stern; a boat equipped with a detachable motor fixed to the stern, or the motor itself.

Outhaul: On a sailboat, the rig used for pulling the clew aft toward the end of the boom.

Over All: The measurement from the extreme forward end to the extreme after end of the deck.

Overhang: Parts of the bow and stern extending beyond the waterline.

Overhaul: A tackle is overhauled when the blocks are pulled farther apart. A line is overhauled when it is freed up.

Pad Eye: A fitting consisting of a plate with a metal eye, permanently secured to a part of the ship.

Painter: A piece of line secured to the bow of a small boat for making it fast.

Palm: The flat inner surface of the fluke of an anchor. A device used in sewing canvas, consisting of a leather strap fitting around the hand and containing an indented piece of metal for pressure against the needle.

Parcelling: Winding strips of canvas with the lay around a rope, preparatory to serving.

Part: To break.

Partners: Wood timbers supporting the mast where it passes through the hole in the deck.

Pawl: A metal cog used inside winches and capstans to prevent the teeth from slipping back.

Pay: To cover a seam with tar, pitch or glue. Also to slack away a rope or chain.

Pay Off: To let a vessel's bow fall off the wind.

Peak: The top after corner of a gaff sail. Also, the fore peak and after peak are the extreme ends inside a vessel.

Pelican Hook: A ready releasing hook with a metal securing ring now chiefly used to break the life rail for boarding or leaving ship.

Pelorus: A navigational instrument similar to a compass but without a needle, used for taking bearings relative to the ship's heading. Taking a bearing with pelorus is a two-man job, since 0° on the pelorus is always in line with the vessel's bow. The man who takes the pelorus bearing on a distant object calls "mark" and the helmsman notes the ship's compass heading at that instant. From these two figures, the true bearing of the object is calculated.

Pennant: A three-sided flag. (A mooring "pendant" is pronounced "pennant.")

Pile* or *Pilings: Spars driven into the bottom with tops projecting above the water.

Pinching: Sailing too close to the wind so that a sailboat's progress is slowed below maximum efficiency.

Pintles: The male fittings on a rudder that slip into the gudgeons, hinging and hanging the rudder.

Pitch: The measure of angle of a propeller blade; the distance the propeller would travel forward in one revolution if there were no slip.

Pitching: The vertical rise and fall of a boat's bow in a seaway.

Planking: The boards used on the sides and decks of a wooden ship.

Plimsoll Mark: A symbol painted on the sides of merchant vessels indicating the maximum depth to which the vessel may be loaded in various waters at different seasons.

Port: The left side, looking forward. Also, an opening. Porthole.

Preventer: A wire or rope line

used as a stay or support for extra safety.

Propeller: A group of two or three helical blades which drive a boat through the water. A Feathering Propeller is one whose blades are so hinged as to line up fore and aft with little drag when a boat is under sail.

Prow: An archaic term for bow, no longer used.

Purchase: A mechanical advantage such as offered by a tackle for increasing the power applied.

Quadrant: A fitting to the rudder, shaped like a sector of a circle. The steering cable is affixed to this and controls the rudder through it.

Quarter: The sector of a ship from amidships aft to dead astern. A Quartering or Quartering Sea is one approaching the ship over the quarter.

Quarterdeck: The after part of the main deck from which pleasure craft are usually commanded.

Rabbet: A groove or slot in one section to receive a complementary fitting or tongue of another section and afford a smooth, well-mated juncture.

Rail: The upper edge of the ship's sides.

Rake: The angle of a mast, fore and aft.

Range: To lay out anchor chain evenly, as in preparation for running or painting. Also, a range consists of two lights or beacons affording a bearing to be used in piloting.

Reef: To furl part of the sail; to shorten canvas in a blow.

Reeve: To pass the end of a rope or chain through an opening.

Ride: To ride at anchor is to lie smoothly at anchor.

Riding Light: An anchor light. A 32-point white light shown at anchor after dark.

Rig: The arrangement of sails and masts. Also, to set up the rigging.

Rigging: A collective term for the various lines and stays used in supporting and operating masts and booms. Standing Rigging is rigging which is not readily movable. Running Rigging is rigging which is adjusted while sailing.

Ring Bolt: An eye bolt with a ring through it.

Riptide: Troubled waters where conflicting currents meet.

Roach: The outward curve in the after end of a sail, giving it extra area.

Risers: In a ladder, the vertical parts, the sides being the stringers and the horizontal parts the treads.

Roads, Roadstead: A protected anchorage, usually offshore.

Rode: The anchor line of a pleasure craft.

Roll: Sidewise motion of a vessel caused by wind and wave.

Rowlocks (Often pronounced *rul-liks*): Oarlocks.

Rub Rail: A strip of molding extending outward from the boat's sides to protect the topsides.

Rudder: The flat, hinged surface aft by which the vessel is steered.

Rudder Post: Same as stern post.

Rudder Stock: A vertical shaft having the rudder attached to its lower end and turned near its upper end by a quadrant or tiller.

Running: Sailing before the wind.
Sailing Directions: Book issued by the Hydrographic Office containing navigational information for all seas and continental coasts.
Samson Post: A single bitt on the foredeck of small vessels.
Scarf: The joining of planks at their ends by tapering them so that they will overlap without increase in thickness at the joint.
Schooner: A sailing vessel of two or more masts, the foremast being shorter than the mainmast.
Scope: The length of anchor chain out.
Scud: To be driven swiftly before a gale. Also, ragged fragments of rain cloud.
Scuppers: Openings in the rail to allow water to drain off.
Scuttle: To sink a boat intentionally. Also, a small hatch.
Scuttle Butt: The ship's drinking fountain. By extension, gossip or rumors often passed at the fountain.
Sea Anchor: A drogue, or drag.
Sea Cock: A valve opening or shutting a pipe connection through the hull.
Seaway: A place where moderate seas are running.
Seams: Spaces between planks in a ship's hull.
Seize: To wrap, bind or secure with small stuff.
Serve: To wrap the ends of ropes with small stuff so that they do not unlay.
Set: The direction of a tide or current.
Set Up: To tighten.
Sextant: Used in celestial navigation to determine the altitudes of sun, moon and stars.
Shackle: A U-shaped piece of metal with eyes in the ends into which a pin is fitted and screwed fast.
Shank: The main body of an anchor.
Sheave (Pronounced *shiv*): The wheel of a block which revolves as the rope runs over it.
Sheer: The curve of a ship's deck from fore to aft when seen from the side.
Sheer Strake: The topmost plank of the topsides.
Sheets: The lines used in trimming a sail.
Shell: The case of a block.
Shoal: Shallow.
Shore, Shoring: Timbers propping up a ship in dry dock.
Shorten Sail: To reduce the amount of canvas; to take in sail.
Shrouds: Main parts of the standing rigging of a sailboat, usually stainless or galvanized wire, staying the mast.
Skeg: Extension of the keel aft, supporting the rudder and protecting the propeller.
Slip: A vessel's berth between two piers.
Slack: To ease off, as to slack a sheet or slack a dock line.
Snub: To check quickly around a winch or cleat.
Soundings: To take soundings is to test the depth of the water with a lead line or fathometer. Off Soundings, in deep water.
Spar: A general term for masts, booms, clubs, gaffs, poles and other

slender pieces of wood, including spar buoys.
Spinnaker: A very light sail of great area used by sailboats when going downwind.
Spreaders: Horizontal members of wood or metal, attached to the mast and used to give added tension to the shrouds.
Spring Line: A line from the bow aft or quarter forward to prevent fore and aft motion at a dock and to help hold the vessel off the dock.
Spring Tides: Higher high tides and lower low tides due to conjunction or opposition of sun and moon.
Squatting: The tendency of the stern to sink low in the water at high speed.
Stanchions: Supporting upright columns of wood or metal. Most frequently on yachts, the metal supports for the life lines.
Stand By: An order to get ready, as, "Stand by to drop anchor!"
Stand-On Vessel: Of two craft meeting, the one which has right of way and is obliged to keep her course and speed except where necessary to maneuver to avoid collision. (Formerly "privileged vessel.")
Standing Part: The section of a line or fall which is made fast.
Starboard: The right side of the vessel, looking forward.
Start: To start a sheet is to ease it or loosen it.
Stays: The fore and aft supports for a mast, as, headstays, forestays and backstays.
Staysail: A headsail set between the jib and the mast.
"Steady As You Go!" A command to maintain course and speed.
Steerageway: Sufficient speed to keep the vessel responding to her rudder.
Stem: The foremost frame on the vessel, reaching from the keel to the meeting of port and starboard rails.
Step: A shaped and usually keyed receptacle affixed to the keel to receive the heel of the mast. On some modern, light sailboats, the mast may be stepped to the cabin top.
Stern: The after end of the boat.
Stern Post: The aftermost frame of a vessel, reaching from keel to deck.
Stiff: Said of a sailboat which does not heel readily in a breeze.
Stock: The crosspiece of an anchor which fits through the shank. In yacht anchors, this piece unships for stowage; then, when positioned, is held in place with a flat key.
Stopper: A piece of heavy rope or chain which may be secured to the anchor chain or rode to keep it from running.
Stops: Bands of canvas wrapped around a furled sail to keep it snug.
Stove In: When the shell of a boat is smashed in by impact, the craft is said to be stove in.
Stow: To pack away neatly.
Strand: A number of yarns twisted together. When strands are twisted together they form rope. Also, a vessel is stranded when she is grounded.
Stringer: A fore and aft strengthening member; particularly, the

sidepieces of a ladder into which the treads and risers are made fast.
Strut: The supporting piece which holds the propeller shaft in place between the propeller and the hull.
Stuffing Box: The hull fitting through which the propeller shaft passes, allowing the shaft to turn freely without leaking water.
Swab: Nautical term for a mop.
Swamp: To sink by taking water over the rail.
Swivel: A metal juncture permitting both ends to turn freely.
Swing Ship: To turn a vessel through all points of the compass while checking compass error for the preparation of a deviation table.
Tack: To bring a sailboat's head into the wind and about so that the sails fill on the opposite side. Also, the corner of the sail at the forward base.
Tackle (Pronounced *taykl*): A purchase formed by a rope running through one or more blocks.
Tachometer: A measuring device which indicates the number of revolutions per minute.
Taffrail: The rail around the stern.
Taffrail Log: Also referred to as "Patent Log," a device consisting of a counter, a line and a spinner, or "fish," which measures distance through the water.

Tend: The direction of the anchor chain or rode toward the anchor.
Tender: Said of a sailboat which heels quickly in a breeze. Also, a club or marina launch. The signal requesting the tender to come alongside is to raise the code flag, T.
Thimble: A piece of shaped metal placed inside an eye-splice in a line to protect the rope or wire from chafing.
Thwarts: The seats in a rowboat running from side to side.
Tideway: The part of a channel in which the strong tidal currents run.
Tiller: A fore and aft handle made fast to the head of the rudder for steering the boat.
Top Off: To fill up a tank.
Topping Lift: A line or lines from the mast supporting the boom when the sail is lowered.
Topsides: The sides of a ship between the waterline and the rail.
Transom: A flat stern at right angles to the keel, often varnished and bearing the yacht's name and home port.
Triatic: A supporting stay between main and mizzen or main and foremast of a two-masted vessel.
Trim: A vessel's balance when properly loaded. Also, used as a verb, to flatten a sail, as, "Trim the jib!"
Trough: The hollow between two wave crests.
Truck: A round, wooden cap at the head of a mast or flagstaff, usually containing sheaves for reaving flag halyards.
Trysail: Nowadays, a sail set in place of a mainsail, usually smaller

and heavier; generally called a "Storm Trysail."

Tumble-Home: The inward curve of topsides, rising toward the deck. Opposite of flare.

Under Way: A vessel is under way when she is not secured to shore or bottom.

Union Jack: A blue field with 50 stars, carried on the bow staff or jack staff.

Unwatched Light: A lighthouse or beacon that is unmanned and automatically or remotely controlled.

Veer: When the wind shifts in a counterclockwise direction. Opposite of haul. Also, to allow the anchor chain or rode to run.

Waist: The middle portion of the ship.

Wake: the path of a vessel left astern in the water.

Warp: To move a vessel by means of lines ashore or to an anchor.

Watch: A four-hour stretch of duty for crew members. The watches are reckoned from midnight, each watch having eight bells sounded successively each half hour. The dog watches are of two hours' duration only, between 1600 and 1800 and between 1800 and 2000 hours (4-6 P.M. and 6-8 P.M.).

Watch tackle: Utility block and tackle. Same as handy billy.

Waterways: The outside planks of the deck, adjacent to the rail.

Way: Controlled motion through the water. Legally, a vessel may be under way although motionless in the water, but she is said to "have way on" when she is moving.

Wear, Wear About: When a ship shifts from one tack to the other by turning her stern into the wind.

Weather: To windward.

Weigh: To lift or raise, as in weighing anchor.

Wheel: The alternative to a tiller in steering.

Whipping: Light twine wrapped about the end of a rope to keep it from unlaying.

Whisker Pole: A light spar used on small sailboats to wing out the jib when running.

Winch: Device for hauling on a sheet, halyard or cable by means of turning a handle which revolves the barrel of the winch with a mechanical advantage.

Windlass: A kind of winch used to raise the anchor. May be electric.

Windward: The direction from which the wind blows. Opposite of leeward.

Wing and Wing: Said of a sailboat when she is running before the wind with main on one side and jib on the other.

Yare (Pronounced *yar*): An archaic term meaning ready and manageable.

Yaw: The motion of a vessel when thrown off course by a heavy sea.

Yawl: A two-masted vessel with the taller mast forward and the shorter stepped at or aft of the waterline.

COLD WATER SURVIVAL
And Hypothermia

Should you find yourself afloat in deep cold water, whether wearing a life preserver or clinging to an overturned boat or floating object, the greatest threat to your safety may be hypothermia. Hypothermia is marked by the cooling of skin and tissues and, eventually, a drop in temperature of the heart and brain. When these organs get down to 90°, unconsciousness may occur. At 85° heart failure occurs and is usually the cause of death. In cold water, swimming and treading water does not keep you warm. It increases cooling by 35%.

Observe these life-saving rules:

1. If danger threatens, wear a PFD. This is a must.
2. If your boat swamps or capsizes, get in or on it, as far out of water as possible. Water conducts heat far faster than air. Most boats float even when swamped.
3. Remain still if in the water. Assume fetal posture (huddle as tightly as possible). Keep head out of water since 50% of body heat is lost through the head. If others are with you, huddle together for warmth.
4. Don't try swimming for shore unless absolutely sure you can make it and there's no other chance of rescue. Even strong swimmers cannot swim as much as a mile in 50° water. Boats are spotted much faster than swimmers.

Treatment after rescue:

1. Move victim to shelter. Do not allow him to walk.
2. Remove wet clothing. Handle gently. Do not wrap in blanket without heat source near body.
3. Apply heat to body through warm bath, hot water bottles or heated blankets. Rescuer may strip and warm victim with his own body.
4. Give warm sugary drink—*not* alcohol.

INDEX

CREDITS

DIAGRAMATIC ART: Harry Rosenbaum

PHOTOGRAPHS:

Abercrombie & Fitch Co.—pp. 162-165
Bruno & Associates—p. 215 (left)
Harry Brocke—pp. 56, 178
Chris-Craft—p. 215
Crow's Nest—p. 162 (lower left)
Evinrude Motors—p. 148
Johnson Motors—pp. 8-9, 132, 144-5
Hunter—p. 12
Mercury Outboard Motors—p. 26 (top)
Mobil Oil Co.—p. 59
Monkmeyer—pp. 28, 86 (Flecknoe); 64 (Frink); 63, 65 (Henle); 97 (Sievers); 31, 36, 40, 115
Official U.S. Coast Guard Photos—pp. 115, 192, 199, 205 (right), 208, 209, 213, 254-5
Volvo Penta—p. 31 (right)
Blair Walliser—pp. 6-7, 26 (lower left), 64-5 (top)
Wheeler Yacht Co.—p. 26 (lower right)

CHARTS & MAPS:

Mobil Oil Co. Marine Department—p. 75
New York Public Library—p. 223
Rand McNally International World Atlas—pp. 91, 229
U.S. Department of Commerce Coast & Geodetic Survey—pp. 98-101, 125

ENERGY SAVERS

Fuel conservation tips for boat operators.

1. Keep engine properly tuned. Check spark plugs, points, timing, carburetor, filters and belts often.
2. Keep your boat's hull clean. Obstructions and growth on hull can reduce performance 50%.
3. Measure and mix your fuel/oil mixture accurately.
4. Set outboard or lower unit in proper tilt angle for the most efficient trolling or cruising.
5. Avoid boating when weather does not permit cruising at an easy RPM. Rough seas can burn unnecessary fuel and can be dangerous.
6. Plan your cruises within a shorter radius of your home port and operate on a straight course as much as possible.
7. Buddy up on cruises. Form boat pools, but remember, don't overload.
8. Outboards are thermostatically controlled for instant warm-up. Do not idle engine for long periods before operating.
9. Get your boat up on plane quickly and once you're on plane throttle back until you are going as slow as you can and still staying on a plane. Only operate your boat at maximum RPM in an emergency.
10. Keep all fuel lines checked for leaks. Leaking fuel lines not only waste fuel but are very dangerous.
11. When possible, drift-fish with the wind instead of trolling.
12. Finally, re-check all maintenance tips in your owner's manual at various times during the boating season.

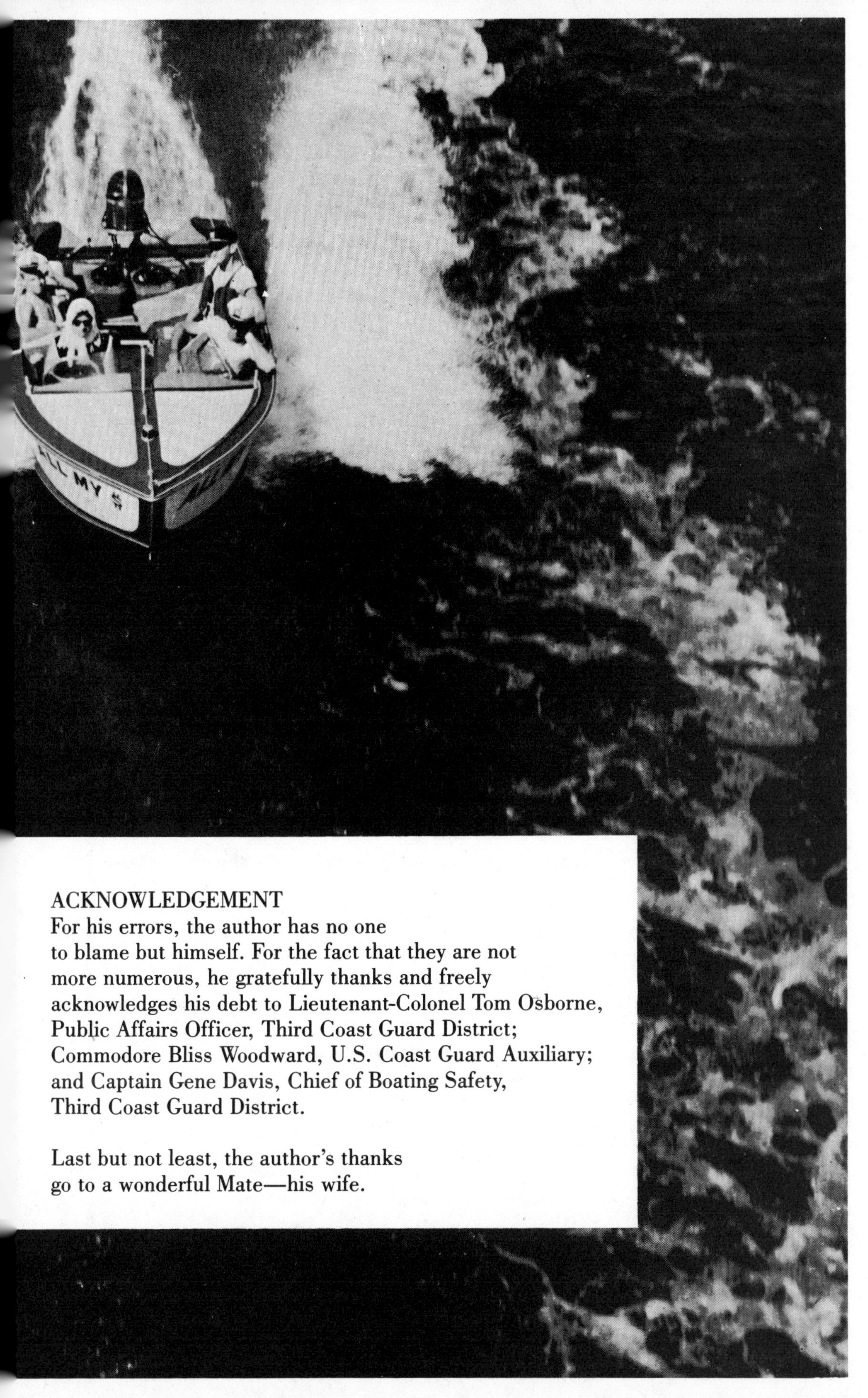

ACKNOWLEDGEMENT

For his errors, the author has no one to blame but himself. For the fact that they are not more numerous, he gratefully thanks and freely acknowledges his debt to Lieutenant-Colonel Tom Osborne, Public Affairs Officer, Third Coast Guard District; Commodore Bliss Woodward, U.S. Coast Guard Auxiliary; and Captain Gene Davis, Chief of Boating Safety, Third Coast Guard District.

Last but not least, the author's thanks go to a wonderful Mate—his wife.

Skipper's check list for
SECURING SHIP

	Inspect anchor line, mooring hawser and dock lines against danger of excessive chafing or coming unsecured in the event of a blow.
	Check bilges. Pump, if necessary.
	Close all sea cocks leading to hull openings.
	Shut off all fuel lines to engine.
	Close exhaust valve.
	Check ice box and sump tank. Pump, if necessary. Clear out any food likely to spoil.
	On sailboats:
	Carefully secure all sail covers and lash down both main boom and jib boom.
	See that all halyards are slightly slack to allow for tautening effect of moisture. To keep halyards from slapping mast, rig preventers from the shrouds.
	If sails are of cotton or natural fabric, take them ashore to dry out.
	Adjust ventilators to provide good interior ventilation.
	Open the engine compartment to assure through ventilation.
	Cover wheel, binnacle, winches, etc.
	Dog down, or close tightly, all ports. Secure hatches and lock companionway.